CHINATOWN

CHINATOWN

A Portrait of a Closed Society

GWEN KINKEAD

HarperCollins*Publishers*

FIRST EDITION

Designed by C. Linda Dingler

Library of Congress Cataloging-in-Publication Data

Kinkead, Gwen, 1951–

 Chinatown : a portrait of a closed society/Gwen Kinkead.—1st ed.

 p. cm

 Includes index.

 ISBN 0-06-016776-9

 1. Chinatown (New York, N.Y.)—Social conditions. 2. New York (N.Y.)—Social conditions. I. Title.

F128.68.C47K56 1991

974.7^{1}1—dc20   91-59931

92 93 94 95 96 ❖/RRD 10 9 8 7 6 5 4 3 2 1

For my father,
Eugene Kinkead,
with everlasting love

CONTENTS

THE SOCIAL STRUCTURE

PART ONE

THE CHINESE CONNECTION

PART TWO

GROUP PORTRAIT

PART THREE

Illustrations follow page 52.

PREFACE

When I began this book in 1989, I received a call from one of the Chinese-language newspapers in Chinatown, asking why I was writing about the community. Was it because of the "Asian invasion"?

Well, in part. I had become curious why I never heard or read anything about Chinatown. It was the proverbial puzzle—a booming community splitting at its seams in a giant metropolis, but completely unknown to its neighbors. It didn't seem possible for such an anomaly to exist. And why was it mute?

For reasons described in the first chapter, researching this book was like opening oysters without a knife. More than once, I felt like quitting. I didn't because it was also like reading a detective story. Behind every door was a clue to the mystery. I was hooked.

Asian-Americans are the fastest growing minority in the United States, and the least enfranchised. They are also the least understood. Few Americans know anything about the many Asian communities expanding around the country—the Koreans in Queens and Los Angeles (L.A. has more Koreans than any city except Seoul), the Cambodians in Phoenix and Milwaukee, the Vietnamese in San Jose and suburban Washington, D.C., for instance. Neither side makes the effort. As a result, violence and racism against Asian-Americans are increasing. Vincent Chin, a Chinese autoworker in Detroit, was beaten to death in 1982 in retaliation for Japanese auto imports into America; in 1988 a Chinese restaurant worker in North Carolina was murdered in an act of anti-Asian animus. In Chinatown one day, an older white couple and their friend, a white woman in her thirties, latched on to me as that rarity, a white face in Chinatown, and erupted. "Chinese are the worst," the wife said. "I've seen the Irish, the Italians, the Spanish, the Puerto Ricans, the blacks, and the Chinese come through here, and there's no comparison. Ninety-nine out of a hundred are the world's worst people! They don't help each other. I was walking with my grandson yesterday and an elderly woman fell. We ran across the street to help her. Five Chinese kept right on going! The father of a tenant in our building was beaten up in the foyer and the son wouldn't go down and help him. My husband had to chase his attackers.

"You're talking to the only white people left in the neighborhood. It's like we don't belong here."

The friend, who had been nodding her head in agreement with this diatribe, spoke up. "They put their garbage out in city garbage cans on the corners and the rats run in and out."

"Filthy!" chorused the older woman. "All their food comes from basements—aaaggh! You look down in there, the food's on the floor—aaaggh! They eat dogs and cats, you know. I'm not pulling your drumstick!"

"Walk through Chinatown," her husband advised me. "You're not in the United States. You're in Hong Kong."

Sadly, these white people assumed I thought the same as they did because I am white. More and more Asians will emigrate in the next decades, profoundly changing our society. They will bring their skills, capital, and culture, and we have to do better than we have done to remain one nation. Americans have things to learn from Chinese. Frugality, for instance. Respect for elders. Chinese can learn that they can't have it both ways—they cannot charge mistreatment and racism and, at the same time, refuse to talk to outsiders, or vote, or lend a cup of sugar to their neighbor.

ACKNOWLEDGMENTS

My foremost thanks are to Robert Gottlieb, editor of *The New Yorker*, for encouraging this research and for publishing much of it. I am deeply grateful to my father, Eugene Kinkead, a *New Yorker* editor and writer, for going before me and showing me the way.

Scores of people in Chinatown spent many hours assisting me over the course of two years of research. Many wished to remain anonymous. Their courage in breaking Chinatown's code of silence was moving and heroic. To my sources in the tongs and the gangs, many thanks as well. Sergeants Mike Collins and Mike Wagner of the New York Police Department taught me to read the streets. Former Jade Squad chief James McVeety shared his years of experience with me. Nancy Ryan, chief of the Trial Division in the Manhattan District Attorney's office, did likewise, then checked the manuscript for accuracy. I am indebted to Manhattan District Attorney Robert Morgenthau and to the prosecutors in the Eastern District of New York. Assistant U.S. Attorney Berryl Howell's voluminous court papers provided a vivid picture of Chinatown's underworld that was as intriguing as a novel. Catherine Palmer, the foremost prosecutor of Asian heroin cases in the country, was wonderfully helpful, as was Charles Rose of the Eastern District. Geoffrey Doyle, supervisory special agent in the Federal Bureau of Investigation in New York, provided invaluable assistance. So did Richard LaMagna and Al Gourley of the Drug Enforcement Administration.

Peter Lee, Paul Lee, and Paul's aunt suffered my many questions. Through their tales, Chinatown's past came alive. Peter Kwong, author of several fine books on Chinatown, provided useful suggestions and contacts. That infectiously funny man, Charlie Chin of the

Chinatown History Museum, gave me insight into the complexity of Asian culture.

I am particularly grateful to Robert Lee, the Chen family, Mr. Lin, the Kong family, and Leslie Lim. They agreed to stand out. As Leslie Lim said, finally deciding to tell me his name, "This is America, right?"

Connie Pang, my translator, was good company, day and night. My father-in-law and Harvey Smith labored to help me computerize this manuscript. My husband's kind and loving encouragement bolstered me always.

THE SOCIAL STRUCTURE

PART ONE

1

CHINATOWN

At the southern end of Manhattan is the largest Chinese community in the Western Hemisphere. The crooked streets of one of New York's oldest ghettos smell of salt and fish and orange peel. This booming, chaotic little piece of China, overflowing with new immigrants, is a remarkably self-contained neighborhood—virtually a nation unto itself. To a degree almost impossible for outsiders to comprehend, most of its inhabitants lead lives segregated from the rest of America.

The new arrivals overwhelming Chinatown are part of the biggest wave of Asian immigrants in American history, the consequence of a momentous change in immigration policy several decades ago. In 1965, Congress replaced laws that had for more than eighty years barred many Chinese—and, for half that time, almost all Asians—while admitting large numbers of Europeans, with a quota for the Eastern Hemisphere that is significantly larger than that for the Western Hemisphere. Since then, Asians have become the leading immigrants. Chinese, the second largest Asian group, after Filipinos, to immigrate under the new law, head straight to New York, their first choice among cities in the United States. With some fourteen hundred people arriving every month, Chinatown has burst out of its former confines below Canal Street, sprawled into SoHo, revitalized the Lower East Side, and spawned satellite communities in Brooklyn and Flushing, Queens. About a hundred and fifty thousand Chinese live in Chinatown, and another hundred and fifty thousand live in the outer boroughs. In addition to immigrants from Taiwan and the People's Republic of China, Chinese from Malaysia, Singapore, Laos, Indonesia, Burma, Thailand, Vietnam, Cambodia, Cuba, South America, and the Philippines have come, bringing their various dialects. Northern Chinese and Taiwanese speak Mandarin, while those from southern China speak Cantonese. Many of the new immigrants cannot understand one another. Cantonese, who were among the first settlers, complain of being strangers in an all-Asian stew. Still, the residents make their way around Chinatown's two square miles of tenements with little mutual rancor.

They have turned Chinatown into the city's clothing manufacturing center. Its nearly six hundred factories have an annual payroll well over $200 million. It is also an important jewelry district now, turning over $100 million in gold and diamonds a year. Its three hundred fifty restaurants draw tourists and conventioneers. And it has become the center of Chinese organized crime in the United States. The Justice Department ranks Chinese organized crime as the principal rival of the Cosa Nostra, and in some lines of business, it has supplanted the Cosa Nostra. The French Connection, the old heroin-smuggling route from Turkey to New York by way of Marseilles, has been replaced by the Chinese Connection, which begins at the Golden Triangle, the area where Laos, Thailand, and Burma meet, and continues, generally through Hong Kong, to Chinatown. Half of the heroin smuggled into this country is under the control of organized crime in Chinatown.

The portal to Chinatown is Mott Street. At the intersection of Mott and Canal is a concrete building with a pagoda roof and several of the painted balconies characteristic of Chinese architecture. This building houses the tong, or fraternal association, of the On Leong, the Chinese Merchants Association. Down the street and around the corner, on Pell Street, is a brick building with green fire escapes and a large green sign bearing gold calligraphy. (Green symbolizes growth; gold symbolizes prosperity.) This is the Hip Sing tong. A block east, on Division Street, is the Tung On. These three organizations, and another on East Broadway called the Fukien American Association, are referred to by both residents and law enforcement officials as the Chinese Mafia. Their members run social events and support community activities, and some sanction crimes that keep Chinatown in a stranglehold. Each tong is affiliated with a "standing army," a gang of between thirty and fifty members. Much of the activity that goes on around these streets no one ever hears about and no one ever reads about; most of it is not reported even in Chinatown's four Chinese-language daily newspapers. The crimes that take place here are often so serious and so bizarre that the area sometimes resembles Hong Kong at its wildest. In Chinatown, there is a social order so ruthless that its very existence seems to be against the law, but, because the area is so isolated from the rest of society, most of the people who live here accept it as normal.

For months, I roamed the streets, trying to find people who would talk to me. For a long time, no new immigrants would speak to me. I was a *low faan,* an object of fear, distrust, indifference. Any outsider in Chinatown is called a *low faan,* which is short for *guey low faan,* or "barbarian"—a term that has been in use since the community's beginnings in the 1870s. Chinatown's inhabitants are largely first-generation—eighty percent of them are foreign-born, half of these having been here fewer than five years—and they are as ethnocentric as the first Chinese who settled Mott Street. "Because you are a barbarian, we don't have to care too much about you," one resident candidly told me. "Because you are a barbarian, some of us may be scared of you—we don't know your language, why you are the way you are." Others assured me that *low faan* had lost its pejorative meaning and merely conveyed the superior exclusiveness with which Chinese have regarded all outsiders for centuries. "Did you understand when Chinese call white people *bot guey,* 'white devils,' or *guey low,* 'foreign devils'?" an elderly resident asked. "It's not meant to insult or dishonor. We say *low faan* so much, we refer to all whites as 'demons'—because we think it's the right term for them. Their noses are so huge and their eyes so blue. Chinese are unlike others—they think China is the center of the earth." Eva Tan, who was a special adviser on Asian affairs to New York's Mayor Edward Koch, says, "Don't forget, foreigners forced China to open up and be ruled by gunboat diplomacy. We have been living for years with foreigners looking down on us. You must have heard of the famous signs at foreigners' hotels in China: CHINESE AND DOGS NOT ALLOWED." Long-term Chinatown residents, remembering the racism that treated Chinese worse than dogs in this country, use *low faan* with the sting of bitterness. New immigrants, to whom Chinatown represents a chance to rise out of poverty, use it matter-of-factly, descriptively, to mean "non-Chinese." The universal use of *low faan* in Chinatown was my first sign of its closed and secret life.

I particularly wanted to talk to Chinatown's "invisible" people, the new immigrants working in its garment shops and restaurants, who speak no English. With the help of my translator, Connie Pang, a Columbia University graduate student from Hong Kong, who, like all educated Hong Kongese, speaks both Mandarin and Cantonese, I slowly found people whose confidence I was able to gain. Very slowly. One merchant talked to us because every Friday for a month I had passed her store and smiled and waved at her young niece, who was newly arrived from Canton, though the niece had said that she herself had no time to speak to me. The merchant, after getting used to the sight of me, decided that I must be interested in her business. I was the first white person she had spoken to in twelve years of living in Chinatown. Another resident agreed, after four or five invitations, to have dinner with Connie and me because I'd met his daughter and admired her cheerful spirit. He, too, had not had a conversation with a white person since arriving in Chinatown, six years earlier. China-town's professional class is large—the local business directory lists a hundred and forty-four lawyers, fifty dentists, and more than a hun-dred accountants—but many of its members wanted no part of a *low faan* with a notebook. One prominent lawyer ignored my phone calls for a year and a half before he said hello. I got used to having people hang up on me, walk away from me, give me "white eyes" (turn up their eyeballs and show me only the whites of their eyes, which is the Chinese way of ignoring strangers), and duck my questions with the handy excuse, in English, that they spoke no English. In one of Chi-natown's oldest stores, I asked a clerk when it was built and got a stony stare. I asked again. The same stare. I asked at another store, down the street, and got an explanation: "Oh, they think you're the tax lady or the government inspector." So few whites hang around China-town that any who do are assumed to be there on police or govern-ment business, and people shut off automatically at the sight of a white person—especially one asking questions.

Low faan have gotten this reception for years. My father, a reporter for *The New Yorker*, was sent by editor Harold Ross to report on Chinatown in the thirties. Residents passed him from one person to another. "Go see Tommy Lin, he'll speak to you," they advised. Tommy Lin had not the slightest interest in talking to my father about anything but benign matters like *mui kwe lu,* the potent Chinese liquor flavored with rose petals, and passed him to Peter Su. Peter Su referred him to Harry Leong. After weeks of this, my father gave up.

Until he retired recently, Emile Bocian was the editor of the Chinese-language daily the *United Journal,* and one of the few Caucasians living and working in Chinatown who are accepted by the community. Bocian made a little noise like a snort when I asked him why only two or three white people had studied the community in the last hundred and twenty years. "The reporters get lost," he said. "They get into quicksand and they disappear. Unless Chinese know the interviewers, they won't talk. That's why you have Chinese interviewing Chinese. The Chinese laugh at the stories that come out of Chinatown. Most are inaccurate." Of the many parts of the world in which I had done reporting, none surpassed Chinatown for its difficulty—neither South Africa, where phones are tapped and the government restricts the news, nor the Amazon, where at least people who have never seen a white reporter enjoy talking.

Teachers, social workers, police, census-takers, letter carriers in Chinatown all report similar difficulties. New immigrants have come from societies where terror taught them to keep their heads down and their mouths shut. The Chinese from Southeast Asia, for instance, were often the first to be kicked out of their countries in the political turmoil that arose in that region after the Second World War. In nearly every one of those countries, Chinese controlled the retail trade, and often the economy, but refused to assimilate, and they were widely resented. According to *Strangers From a Different Shore,* by Ronald Takaki, a historian at the University of California, Berkeley, Chinese in Vietnam constituted seven percent of the population but controlled eighty percent of the retail trade. They spoke Chinese, sent their children to Chinese schools, and lived in Chinatowns. They were always targets of discrimination in Vietnamese society, but they suffered disproportionately as the Communists nationalized the economy. Fifty thousand Chinese from Vietnam—boat people, mostly— are estimated to have settled in New York City since the late 1970s. Thriving again as small business owners, they don't want to risk more discrimination here by standing out. Other ethnic Chinese, including, recently, a great many from Malaysia, are undocumented and afraid to tell strangers their names. Still others, notably Fujianese, from China's Fujian Province, have been smuggled in and are terrified of any notice. "You have to be like a hunting dog," one weary Chinese census-taker told the *New York Times* in 1990 as she trudged about the tenements in Chinatown, finding everywhere illegal aliens living in unmarked apartments. Perhaps one of every five people in Chinatown is there illegally.

Far and away the largest number of new arrivals are from the People's Republic of China. Under the 1965 immigration law, each country in the Eastern Hemisphere has a quota of twenty thousand immigrants per year. In 1982, three years after the United States established full diplomatic relations with the People's Republic and broke off formal ties with Taiwan, the People's Republic was also given a quota. The mainland Chinese in Chinatown are mostly from farms, and they especially shrink from contact with other people— even from other Chinese. "They don't want people to know them," one Chinatown resident told me. "The government uses the people against each other in China. That's how it gains its information—even within families. I've been waiting for several years for some to return my friendship." Peter Lee, a reporter who has covered Chinatown for a decade, said, "This is a new and foreign thing for us, this freedom of expression and freedom of speech. The June 4th movement was fought for that. If one and a half billion people in China don't have those freedoms, then we don't have them here, either. It's not in our culture; it's not in our blood."

Scholars believe that at least eight hundred thousand people died in Mao Zedong's campaigns of the early 1950s to liquidate the landowning class, silence dissenters, and root out corruption, and that more than twenty million died in the famines of the late fifties and early sixties resulting from the disastrous Great Leap Forward. Half a million are thought to have been killed in the Cultural Revolution, and perhaps as many as a thousand in Beijing in the Tiananmen Square massacre and its aftermath, with several thousand more imprisoned in China's vast gulag system for supporting the pro-democracy movement. Four decades of political upheaval since the Communist Revolution of 1949 have given immigrants a horror of speaking their minds, taking a stand, or asserting an opinion—and, underneath the fear, a passionate admiration for those who died for doing so, like the students in Tiananmen Square. Sherman Eng, an immigrant from Hong Kong who is the head of an association of Chinatown garment factories, reminded me that China's authoritarian governments have always devoured the outspoken: "I have a right to exercise my right to free speech, but a lot of Chinese people don't think that, because they were controlled by emperors for four thousand years, and if they said the wrong thing, insulted the emperor, they would die. A lot of Chinese don't talk. Just afraid to say the wrong thing."

Chinese prize self-effacement. Even Chinese who grew up singing "I Am Mao's Little Soldier" in school hold to Confucian values: Communism has failed to shift the traditional Confucian loyalty from the family to the state. With the family the sacrosanct center of the culture, the individual is of no account. The proper Chinese says, "I am an ant." In a garment factory, I asked a seamstress her name. She blushed, hid her face, and began to sweat. I could not coax one word from her. Her neighbor, too, broke out in a sweat and shook her head. "Not the Chinese girls," said their boss, who was also a young Chinese woman—but she was from Hong Kong and not, like her workers, from the People's Republic. "They don't want to be in the newspaper. It's a tradition. Usually, they don't want to expose themselves. They are afraid someone will recognize them on the street."

Being interviewed or expressing one's individuality in any way is generally frowned upon because it means committing the cardinal sin in Asian cultures: losing face. It puts one in a position of prominence, which may cause jealousy in one's neighbors. Harold Ha, the first Chinese jeweler in Chinatown, is one of a handful of new millionaires to have risen from Chinatown since the immigration laws changed. But Ha no longer sells jewelry wholesale to Chinatown merchants, his former clients, because they are too resentful of his success—he has a $15-million business, a midtown factory, and factories in Shanghai, Nanjing, and Ireland—to buy from him. "In American culture, you successful, everybody follow you. In our culture, they try to destroy you," Ha says. "We don't like to stand out." Heo-Peh Lee, a developer and builder, says, "Americans like to show off. The Chinese don't. We think stay low-key so we will have the least obstacles to success. We have an expression. When you have a glass of water, if it's empty, you shake, it don't make no sound. When you have a full jar, you shake, it don't make any noise, either. When you are really poor, you don't say anything. When you are really rich, you don't say anything, either." Prominence also invites supernatural evil. In Chinese cosmology, *yein*, or evil spirits, constantly hover, ready to snatch good fortune from boasters. Chinese mothers curse their babies to save them from the *yein*.

Many new arrivals are unaware that the United States is governed differently from China, and that here they have a right to free speech. Seward Park High School is the largest high school in Chinatown; just over half of the students are Asian, primarily Chinese. Students enroll within a week or two of their arrival in New York, and for most of them classes are their introduction to America. Teachers in the bilingual instruction program say that their students arrive knowing little about this country. I met with some of the program's staff members one day, and they all spoke of the students' lack of understanding of life in the United States. "They come here blind," Katherine Sid, the program's director, told me. "They come because their relatives say this is a better life. They're thinking in economic terms. Democracy is not a pull. Democracy is very, very hard for them to grasp."

"I just think they know nothing," Yong Li, a staff member, said. "Only some in city know McDonald's and Kentucky Fried Chicken."

Helene Dunkelblau, another staff member, said, "They ask me, 'Is it true that everyone's divorced, everyone's rich, everybody has a car?' They have some very, very strange ideas."

Ms. Sid laughed. "They really haven't the faintest idea about America," she said. Looking embarrassed, Mr. Li added, "A lot don't even know that America is a democracy. They ask me, 'What does it mean, this democracy?'"

Ms. Dunkelblau pointed out that democracy is a dirty word in China.

"Chinese schools don't teach about America," Ms. Sid said. "Students learn Chinese history and the history of Communist thought. No music. No art. A little European history—maybe some would have heard of the Renaissance. Generally, they lack knowledge of other countries and other people. They take a foreign language—usually English—once or twice a week, and work on grammar. But they have very little idea of American society. You ask them, 'Who is the President of the United States?' 'Who was the first President of the United States?' 'What is the 4th of July?' The new ones can't answer that."

In addition to the historical and cultural reasons, people in Chinatown guard their lives with silence because crime is woven into the social fabric, into the institutions that keep Chinatown cohesive and isolated, and they fear reprisals. Chinese gangsters are methodical about wiping out protesters.

For most of its history, Chinatown has been silent. Unwanted in America for many years, Chinese lay low, encouraged by their leaders to distrust outsiders and the authorities that mistreated them. Chinatown now is divided between the old guard—the conservative Cantonese who run the family associations and district associations and tongs, and their umbrella group, the Chinese Consolidated Benevolent Association—and a new guard, consisting of younger, second- and third-generation Chinese-Americans and some of the new immigrants from other parts of China and Asia. The old guard still advises residents not to wash their dirty linen outside Chinatown and to remain more Chinese than American. The younger leaders, many of them formed by the civil rights movement and by the Asian-American movement—a 1960s awakening of Asian pride, similar to the Black Power movement—run most of Chinatown's social welfare programs. They urge the community to merge with America.

Breaking free of isolation and merging with America is not the uppermost concern in Chinatown, however. What is uppermost is work. Even losing minutes in conversation is painful. Chinatown is given over to making money as exclusively and intensively as Wall Street. Residents work any number of hours necessary to do business, without regard to fatigue or to their stomachs. Their extraordinary schedule has led some outsiders to think Chinese work backbreaking hours because they like to, but I met only one person who was smug about his long hours. In fact, Chinatown embarrasses a lot of its residents: Ashamed of its dirty streets, running with water from overflowing vegetable and fish stands, and of its chaos, its crime, and its street gangs, they work to leave it.

Many immigrants start out as street peddlers. In three or four years, they have saved enough—between $50,000 and $100,000—to start small businesses. I didn't see how that was possible until I met Mr. Lin.

Lin works for a Korean boss, selling fruit and vegetables at a busy corner in Chinatown. He arrived, broke, from the People's Republic six years ago, hustled firecrackers and toys by himself for two years, then hired on with the Korean, who was forced onto the street after a prostitute stole his savings. The Korean trucks in produce from the Hunts Point market, and Lin loads and unloads the truck and makes sales. The Korean needs Lin because all his customers are Chinese and he himself speaks only Korean. On Sundays and rainy days, Lin sells umbrellas on the same street corner.

In winter, Lin wears a hat with earflaps sticking out at right angles. In warmer weather, he wears a baseball cap. Lin is sixty-four years old. He's slightly bald, bowlegged, stout-necked, and very strong. His work clothes, always worn in several layers, are stained and dirt-encrusted. He often throws on a Federal Express jacket over his sweatshirts. Lin's face is open and lively, and he laughs a lot.

In six years, Lin has met only one white person—me. He has been out of Chinatown only a few times.

"No go outside," Lin said, puzzled, when I asked him if he had seen New York City. "Usually, I work. When I no work, I clean myself, wash clothes, and rest," he went on, in slow, clear English. Curious about whether Lin was at all interested in his new hometown, I asked him if there was any place in the city he wanted to visit. He thought a minute. "I hear about her, not too far from here," he said, cupping his hands above his head like a Thai dancer.

"The Statue of Liberty?"

"Sometime I go there," he affirmed. "That's one thing I do."

I offered to take Lin there, or to any other place he wished to see. Lin decided that the Statue of Liberty was too far, and picked my second suggestion—Central Park, which he'd never heard of. We rode uptown in a taxi. Lin was very uneasy. "No go far, right?" he asked several times. "Not too far."

In Central Park, Lin admired the ducks at the Fifty-ninth Street pond for a minute or two and glanced at the skyscrapers. "China cannot build so high," he said, and he seemed much relieved when, soon after arriving, we headed back downtown. Provided we met in

Chinatown, Lin was always open, expressive, eager for dialogue.

A graduate of a noted Chinese university, a civil engineer, and a well-known sprinter, Lin had been in the vanguard of Mao Zedong's first Five-Year Plan, from 1953 to 1957, helping to design a secret weapons plant in Inner Mongolia. When Russian advisers arrived, Lin worked with their general. "We talk where highway goes, where railroad goes, where buildings, how high, how far space in factory," he told me. "I am leader, because they think I am willing to join the Party." Lin and his boss traveled around China in a specially built railroad car guarded by armed soldiers, carrying the plant's secret blueprints. "Every city leader welcome us, making dancing, parties." Every day when he left work, Lin was strip-searched. In the plant, China was building its first atomic bomb, with plans from Russia. "Even tops of trees have guards and watch, you know."

Mao urged "a hundred flowers to bloom" and "a hundred schools of thought to contend." In 1957, Lin criticized the government, as Mao urged, and, like hundreds of thousands of intellectuals, was branded a "rightist" and a traitor to the state, and was imprisoned. In jail in Manchuria, he survived on corncobs. "No food there, all sent to Russia. Very hard life. Many dead." After prison, his punishment continued: for several years, he was forced to pull a heavy farm cart, a beast of burden. In 1964, China exploded the A-bomb.

During the Cultural Revolution, Lin's brother committed suicide. "Everyone had to become a cadre. They call him Guomindang"—Taiwan's ruling party—"beat him till his head no good." The brother threw himself off a building in Beijing. Their father, a customs officer, starved himself to death. Denounced as an anti-revolutionary, he had been forced to wear a dunce cap while being publicly criticized. He had refused to accuse his boss falsely of a "political crime," and had been jailed. He had refused a second time and had been jailed again. In prison, he had contracted pneumonia and had been denied medicine. "After, my father no eat."

In the seventies, Lin was allowed to design buildings again, but he was not restored to the status of engineer until Deng Xiaoping returned to prominence in early 1978 and brought about the rehabilitation of many former prisoners. Lin came to Chinatown in 1986 on a tourist visa, proud that he had never joined the Communist party. "Here, if a little bit of freedom, enough for me already," Lin told me.

"Only a little bit of freedom. I don't care what kind of car I have or what apartment or clothes. Somebody laugh at me. 'You so old, you work so hard, you make enough money for your living.' Many laugh at me. I say, 'I work hard. I do everything. Not too long time for me.' One day I die. Under Communism pressure, I work hard; now I work for freedom. I only desire to oppose Communism."

Lin lives in a *gong si fong,* a traditional "public room." This arrangement has enabled bachelors to gain a foothold in Chinatown ever since the beginning of the community. "I have only a bed. It's cheaper." One evening, Lin offered to show me the *gong si fong.* I was early for our meeting, so I walked about Chinatown. At seven P.M., the neighborhood was still toiling. The Vietnamese, darker than the Chinese, and nicked and pocked, were hawking $15 made-in-Taiwan watches in noisy open-air bazaars along Canal Street. At the corner of Canal and Mott, in old Chinatown, the Chemical Bank was bustling: couples talked to loan officers; long lines of workers deposited their pay. Chinese run quickly to the bank with any checks. They like only cash, and, besides, they worry that their factory will go out of business before they can cash their checks. Chinatown's cash economy enables them to avoid paying taxes. Banks in Chinatown stay open six days a week, so they have the longest banking hours in the city.

That night, in the turmoil of the crowds, I noticed many well-to-do Chinese in furs, women wearing makeup, and middle-class couples out on dates, kissing in the streets. Such display used to be unheard of. These people were "ABCs," or American-Born Chinese, and they stood out from the drab new immigrants, the "FOBs," or those Fresh Off the Boat, and from the old-timers, particularly the bent Cantonese women in knitted hats, layers of sweaters, and men's vests. The old-timers never call attention to themselves in any way—neither by clothing, manners, nothing.

In a few hours, buses taking gamblers to Atlantic City would line the block outside Chinatown's biggest restaurant, the Silver Palace, on the Bowery. For now, only peddlers lined the block, with mountains of batteries, plastic toys, and socks on trolleys like the old Jewish peddlers' pushcarts. Shoppers on Canal picked their way carefully between storefront produce stands and the curbside peddlers. Bumpy green durians, foul-smelling, deliciously sweet fruit from Indonesia, brought by the newest ethnic Chinese, were for sale among bitter melons. Fish flown in fresh daily from China—lionfish and belt fish (two feet long and stout enough to hold up one's pants)—flopped around in boxes. Ice water dripped from the profusion of produce, and among the gagging smells rising from the sidewalk and the gutters, where the food was cleaned, was a whiff of orange peel. The singsong of Indonesian and Burmese dialects drifted by.

Herbalists in tiny stalls doled out cures. Doses of ground antler, starfish, roots, and ginseng were measured and poured onto sheets of paper. Chinatown has many new herb stores run by pharmacists from the People's Republic, who know the secrets of combining the several hundred traditional ingredients of the Chinese pharmacopoeia.

Chinese and Vietnamese jewelry stores along Canal Street were jammed. Young black couples were trying on medallions and gold chains and chunky, gold-plated door-knocker earrings. Chinatown is a jewelry district for the working class. For wholesale, the trade goes uptown.

Number 11 Pell Street is a gang hangout—a tea shop where the Flying Dragons, one of five major gangs in Chinatown, congregate. It was full of thirteen-, fourteen-, fifteen-, and sixteen-year-olds with punk haircuts. The kids look like hoodlums from the fifties: tight black jeans, bare ankles, black leather jackets. Across the street, at Number 16, was their sponsor, the Hip Sing tong. The rule of the streets is to not hit *low faan,* because tourism is necessary, but the rule is often broken. I hurried by Number 15, where a club called Eng Suey Dong was marked by a red sign in English above a basement stoop. It is a mah-jongg parlor and, according to the police, one of Chinatown's many illegal basement gambling houses. Generally run by the tongs, the gambling houses are protected by steel doors, peepholes, video monitors, and gang members with submachine guns.

Rain was thinning the crowds on Mott Street. The oldest store in Chinatown, Quong Yuen Shing & Company, at Number 32, looked dead. In the window were a few stacks of rice bowls, some figurines, a birdcage. A single light was on in the back, picking out beautiful wooden scrollwork, made in China a hundred years ago.

In front of Confucius Plaza, a publicly funded housing project on Division Street, stands a ten-foot bronze statue of the sage. This was a present from the Chinese Consolidated Benevolent Association, which functions as Chinatown's unofficial governing body, and it caused a controversy when it was proposed in 1976. The leftists, who support the People's Republic, didn't want it, because all forms of feudalism were being wiped out in China. The rightists, who champion Taiwan, thought Confucius the best symbol of Chinese cultural heritage, and the statue went up. In a community bought lock, stock, and barrel by Taiwan's Nationalists, and forever fighting the 1945–49 civil war, it remains a symbol of division.

Down East Broadway, the lights of garment factories in six-story tenements were still shining. They turn off at nine P.M., the end of a twelve-hour day. Farther up East Broadway is the Wild West of Chinatown—the newest settlements, hotly disputed by the gangs.

Before I met Lin, I peeked into Triple Eight Palace, one of a number of new, Hong Kong–style restaurants, in a mall under the Manhattan Bridge. Hong Kong cooking is a more elegant version of Cantonese, and the Cantonese are epicures. Sea bass were swimming in saltwater tanks set into the walls above diners' heads. Neon sculptures blinked distractingly in the gigantic dining room. Among the crowd were a lot of elderly Chinese men in baseball caps and windbreakers.

Almost nothing is left of Little Italy—just one or two blocks of Grand and Mulberry streets. Chinese with suitcases of cash have been buying out Italians. Many buildings in Chinatown have been sold for more than a million dollars. Since the early eighties, when China began threatening to reclaim Hong Kong, flight capital from the world's third largest financial center has gilded Chinatowns worldwide. As 1997—when Hong Kong reverts to China—nears, the outflow has become a torrent. British Columbia is receiving $4 billion of investment a year from Hong Kong. San Francisco, Sydney, Toronto, and other cities that Hong Kongese consider classy have received similar infusions of money. Chinatown has received comparatively little—maybe a billion dollars. The money has brought the first condos; fancier restaurants, with midtown prices and sea bass swimming in the walls; *karaoke* nightclubs; and higher rents. Hong Kongese do not want to live in Chinatown; they buy a condo here as an investment. Until the Beijing massacre, People's Republic government officials bought condos, too, and planned a hotel. The money from the "other side" has not changed most of Chinatown. It is still a slum, with some of oldest housing in the city, a third of it built before 1900.

In the dim light of one bare bulb hanging from a rusted tin ceiling, the old Mee Heung Chow Main Corporation, on Mott Street, was quiet. The day's production of noodles lay boxed and stacked on the wooden floor. Off to the right, in a small office, a slight man in a white shirt and black pants—the colors of servitude in Chinatown—tallied the books. As I stared into that old-fashioned shop, unchanged since the 1930s—at a cigarette smoking in a cheap tin ashtray, at storage racks in back, at a colorful poster of a Chinese opera character—a giant rat ran across the floor to the storage racks. It paused there, sneaked ahead carefully until only its tail, slender and quivering, was visible, and then, in a flash, slid between the boxes.

Lin and I met on a street near the East River. He was eager to show me the *gong si fong,* but, he said, we must hurry. The other bachelors in the apartment were waiters, and were out working now. Lin was worried that one might return unexpectedly and find him with a *low faan* in the apartment. I agreed not to mention the location of the *gong si fong,* because it is in a city-subsidized housing project, and is illegal.

The place, originally a one-bedroom apartment, was dark and close-smelling. A twenty-foot-long corridor that ended in a grimy window ran along one side of it. The left wall of the corridor, made of rough, unpainted plywood, enclosed what used to be the living room. It had been subdivided by more thin plywood partitions into three bedrooms, for six people. The bedrooms had sliding plywood doors, each secured with a tiny padlock, like cabins on a ship. The landlady had come from China in 1981, gone into business, and made good. She had put up the partitions and then moved on, and she now charged her sublessees a total of $850 a month for a $317 rent-subsidized apartment.

Lin showed me his bedroom, the compartment nearest the windows. It was seven feet by six—smaller than many closets in New York City apartments. A bunk bed took up most of the space. The top bunk had a straw mat over bright sheets. The bottom bunk was Lin's. The distance from the bed to the windows was two steps. Two people could not pass in the space. Under the windows, on shelves, were some coffee mugs, a small TV, a telephone, and a few personal effects, such as a plastic bag containing Lin's private papers. A partly filled-out census form and a Chinese entertainment magazine were stuffed into the bag. A bare light bulb hung from a hook on the wall. About three feet of space between the ceiling and the upper bunk served as a closet; pants and shirts hung on nails in the partition.

The kitchen, about five feet by eight, had the same air of desolation. The faucet was broken and ran incessantly—a melancholy sound. There was a small four-burner gas stove, used mostly by Lin and his bunkmate, a clothes presser in a garment shop, who was about his age. The icebox worked. The one window was streaked with something that looked like soy sauce. No one had cleaned in here anytime recently. I asked Lin what was in the cupboards. He opened one, and ten roaches ran past a few bottles of cooking oil.

In the bathroom, the toilet had no seat. The base was brown with crud. In back of the bathroom was the original bedroom, where four more people, one of them a smuggler importing Chinese from Fujian Province, lived.

The *gong si fong* could accommodate ten people, but some of Lin's roommates had moved away recently, leaving seven. The man living alone in the cubicle next to Lin's paid $200 a month rent; Lin and his bunkmate paid $125 apiece; and the four occupants of the rear bedroom paid $100 each.

Lin forgoes any privacy or comfort not because he is poor but to save money. He earns $360 a week peddling vegetables and fruit. Selling umbrellas is more lucrative, bringing in from $80 to $100 a day. His monthly income, Lin says with utter frankness, and with a relish common to most Chinese when they discuss money, averages $1,800. He has saved some $18,000 of his annual $22,000 income in each of the last four years. He pays no taxes and, like a lot of illegal immigrants, keeps his money hidden from the Internal Revenue Service with the connivance of a Chinese bank. "They give me letter. If you work illegal in America, you must give government interest. If no work, you no pay. So I say, 'Let me sign I no work!' Bank officer know I work. He just open one eye and close one eye," Lin said, using a Chinese expression meaning "to blink at corruption." All told, Lin has $70,000 tucked away for a small business.

I asked Lin how it was possible for him to save eighty percent of his income.

He explained that he spends only $250 a month—the money for his rent, a few dollars on the telephone, and about $100 on food.

"Rice very cheap," he said, smiling. "And boss give me lunch."

Tens of thousands of Chinese live spartan, insular lives like Lin's, never mixing with outside society, renting beds in basements or in *gong si fong*, sharing a one-bedroom apartment with ten or fifteen people, or doubled up with other families in tiny apartments in lower Manhattan. Almost no one in Chinatown lives alone. Some sub-sublet their bunks to others and sleep in shifts. They work, work, work. Working six days a week, from sixty to eighty hours, is typical. In Chinatown there is no TGIF. Everyone wants, like Lin, to save a pile of money. The expressions I heard most often in Chinatown as I talked to its residents were "big money," "U.S. dollar," "easy money," and dozens of other variations on the theme of money.

2

WORK

Most people in Chinatown have endured so many hardships abroad that they are willing to accept many more to build up economic freedom for the first time in their lives. Some have swum the river from Canton to Hong Kong to escape from the People's Republic, or climbed over the mountains at night to reach the colony. Others have paid smugglers from $30,000 to $50,000 to slip them into the United States and live here virtually as indentured slaves until they repay their passage. Some are Chinese boat people from Vietnam, or Chinese-Vietnamese from the Orderly Departure Program—the product of a 1979 agreement between Vietnam and the United States that admits, in addition to refugees, twenty thousand Vietnamese a year who have family members here. Others wangle visas in order to have more than one child—the limit, by law, for Han people, the majority race in the People's Republic. Mail-order brides are common, as are arranged marriages. Couples work two jobs and are seldom home. A good many have no time to bring up their children and no money for babysitters, so they send their babies to relatives in Hong Kong or Taiwan to be brought up. Other couples split up: the wives live here with the children so they can attend American schools, and the husbands remain behind in the Far East to work.

Considering how little most Chinese earn, it is amazing that they can save at all for what they call the "eight bigs"—a color television, a refrigerator, a car, a VCR, a camera, a set of furniture, a telephone, and a washing machine—to say nothing of saving enough to start a small business. Chinatown exploits its workers. Most live in peonage, working long hours for less than $10,000 a year. Average salaries run about $9,500 for a union garment-shop worker or a dishwasher; nearly $20,000 for a waiter. Nonetheless, Chinese save. Lin's eighty percent savings rate was the highest I encountered, but I met many people whose ability to save was equally extraordinary. Leslie Lim, a native of Singapore, was one. He reminds me of the actor Joel Grey—he has the same nimble walk, white face, and a grin that takes up most of his small, neat head. A waiter in a Vietnamese-Chinese restaurant, he looks nineteen but is twenty-five years old. He picks up languages easily and, like many people from Singapore, is bilingual in Chinese and English.

He dreams of saving $20,000 so he can go home and open a timber company. The son of rubber tappers, he grew up in a mountain village near Johore Bahru—"so pretty, so clean, no garbage," he told me when I talked to him in Chinatown one evening. "The house is poor. No TV, no sofa, only chopsticks, two chairs, glass windows." His parents scraped to send him to Singapore's Chinese Methodist High School. "I try to work in salesmen, like Amway, but I lose money. Nobody would buy from me. I'm shy. I scared to try to talk to somebody," Lim said, a huge grin spreading across his face. "Here, I have to brave and try to talk every things. I like America. I'm glad I come. U.S. dollar—what I like about this country." Lim laughed merrily. "I have worked twelve hours a day without stop. Yeah, I look happy, but I have to worry for my house. Everything for the U.S. dollar."

Before Lim borrowed the air fare to New York, he bought his parents a house in Singapore: in Chinese culture, it is his duty as the number one son to provide for his parents after they retire. The house has a $15,000 mortgage, and from his monthly earnings of $1,500, Lim sends home $350 for the mortgage and for his brother's school fees, another of his responsibilities as firstborn. For himself, he rents a bed in a *gong si fong* for $200 a month. Lim devotes every waking hour to making money and saving it. The only thing he spends money on is newspapers.

"No movies, no drinking, no gambling," he told me. "It's too expensive for a movie—five dollars. In Singapore, only one dollar, and it's first-class. But here, five dollars—that's about ten dollars Singa-

pore money. Oh, my God! I don't know where is sports. I like baseball. Gambling is too expensive. Not interesting to me. Many my
friends on their day off go to Atlantic City, but nobody say they win.
They lose. They all lose. They crazy. I went once. Wow—too boring. I
don't know how to play. And to sit down alone? I don't like alones. No
way buy a house here! I have to go back and see my mom and stay
together with my mom. Because we are a family. I love my parents
very much."

Though Lim is halfway to his goal, having saved nearly $10,000 in
the ten months he has been in America, he is a little restless. "Chinatown is so cheap," he said. "You can't make much money here. Chinatown restaurants only pay three hundred dollars a month to waiters—
the rest is tips. For a waiter, seventeen hundred dollars a month
should be minimum. They don't earn it, they go away. Head chef
earns two thousand a month. Other cooks, one thousand and three
hundred to fifteen hundred dollars." Lim was quiet a minute. "Maybe
uptown is better. I don't like working here. You must work harder
than uptown, longer hours, low pay. At least eighteen hundred dollars
a month I want to make. Just to save it. When I get a day off, I deliver
menus. Fifty dollars a day."

Dreaming of his timber company, working from eleven A.M. to
eleven P.M., Lim is "so lonely," he told me. "Here, right, is so boring. I
never think how to make myself less lonely, just how to make more
money. I don't think it's a mistake. When I get the money, I go home.
That's all."

Lim plans to marry eventually. "First, I make the money here. My
own opinion, first the money. If I don't have the money, I don't have
everything that's necessary. If you don't have the money, nobody is
close to you. I tried this dating in Singapore. Just alone in the house,
nobody close to me." Lim closed his eyes, anguished.

"Why not use your day off to see friends, make life here more
agreeable for yourself, enjoy the pastimes you liked in Singapore—
stamp collecting, for instance, football, baseball, dancing?" I suggested.

"I don't want to waste time anymore," Lim said, and added that
Chinatown people have no time for friendships. The only outsiders he
knows are a policeman and me. "I made the right decision to come
here. Only want to go back to Singapore. Nobody talk to me when I

get a day off. Everybody go to work. When you talk together, time flies."

On the street, as we parted, Lim said, "I'm happy tonight." He grinned shyly, ear to ear. "Nobody talk to me for such a long time."

There are many people like Leslie Lim in Chinatown, enduring lonely, threadbare lives in crowded, unsanitary apartments, dreaming of a small business, and earning money to the exclusion of all else— learning about America included. I grew used to hearing about immigrants with more savings than many middle-class Caucasians I knew. Chinatown has twenty-seven banks—an enormous number for a community of a hundred and fifty thousand. Their combined deposits, according to 1990 figures, come to $3.5 billion. Probably half is flight capital. Some is laundered drug receipts. The rest is testimony to the fabled Chinese thrift. Actually, the community has accumulated far more capital than these figures show. Lots of Chinese bank with their family associations or keep their money in safe deposit boxes rather than in bank accounts. The National Westminster Bank, for instance, has more safe deposit boxes rented in its Chinatown branch than any other in the city, except the branch in the jewelry district. Bankers in the community say that two-income couples save between thirty and forty percent of their pay. "Give them three to four years," Dean Lui, a local real-estate broker, says. "They'll buy a two-family house in Flushing, the second Chinatown. They put down cash, thirty to forty percent of the price. Even fifty percent. Chinese don't like debt; they don't like paying interest. They'll rent out one half of the house and use the other, or rent out both halves. The average turnover of a new house is five to seven years. Chinese will sell it in two or three years and buy a one-family house. In ten or fifteen years, they'll move to the suburbs—Long Island or Connecticut."

Flushing has thirty-one banks, with $2.8 billion in deposits in 1990. Deposits are growing so rapidly that Flushing will surpass the money deposited in Chinatown shortly. The area was settled in the early 1970s by the first wave of immigrants after the change in the immigration laws, and is now Taiwanese turf, almost exclusively Mandarin-speaking. Encouraged by Taiwan's churning economy and the second largest foreign-exchange reserves in the world, more Taiwanese have invested in Flushing recently, often buying second homes and rental properties as hedges in case China reclaims its capitalist enemy. Albert Liu, the former president of Asia Bank in Flushing, told me, "There are about sixty-five thousand Chinese in Flushing, increasing at about two thousand to three thousand a year. We opened bank eight years ago. Eight years ago on this block, no Chinese stores." Liu smiled like the Cheshire cat. "We chose this block, and many Orientals moved to it, and it is now all Chinese. Look at the signs—no English!" He laughed heartily.

"Brooklyn on Eighth Avenue, the third Chinatown, mostly refugees or immigrants from mainland," Liu went on. "They don't have money to start. Lot of garment business go there. The community board asked us to come in—they have special interest in our bank. Ha-ha. We try to calculate whether they have enough business for us. Thirty million dollars in deposits is good enough, maybe, to make bank break even. They have ten million in deposits, I believe so. Thirty to forty thousand Chinese there, but different—not rich. Not same people we have here, who own homes and businesses. They are Chinese from Malaysia, Vietnam. Vietnamese have to buy their lives in gold—so when they come here, they have nothing. Malaysians—you know what happened. Before, Malaysia controlled by Chinese—seventy percent Chinese. They weren't smart enough. Then they should have gotten the political power. Chinese too conservative. Just enough money to control the economy, but not political power. They squeezed out."

In Chinatown, starting a small business is phenomenally expensive. To set foot in a new shop, a shopkeeper has to pay under-the-table "key money" to the landlord—$100,000 for a ten-year lease on a commercial site on Mott Street, or $50,000 for a five-year lease, for example. Rents, pushed up by Hong Kong investment, run about $7,500 a month for a twelve-hundred-square-foot store on Canal Street—higher than some rents in the World Trade Center. To recoup, many shopkeepers illegally sublet the three to five feet of sidewalk in front of their stores to peddlers and entrepreneurs for as much as $2,000 a month.

Mrs. Kong is one of Chinatown's lucky ones. She recently moved away from Chinatown, to Westchester County, and commutes daily to her business, one of the largest soybean retail outlets in the community. She arrived from Hong Kong in 1972 after escaping from the

People's Republic, and, at first, she peddled vegetables on the street. She earned enough to feed three babies and to open a soybean shop, which had been her business back in Canton. Now she and her husband own four shops, including one in Flushing. They have eighteen employees, all but five of them family. Business is good. Mrs. Kong's main shop is on Mulberry Street, but her busiest is on Canal Street, next to an East Side subway entrance. The shop spills out onto the sidewalk with vats of chrysanthemum tea and hot, sweet soybean curd, a custardy dessert; plastic bottles of jelly grass and soy milk; and *chow fun* and *ho fun*—big, slippery white-rice noodles, heavy and sleek.

Mrs. Kong's daughter Tina, a jovial young woman, pregnant with her first child, speaks some English. She told me, "This family business. My mother run around Chinatown, she always run around. So I'm helper here, twelve hours a day before I'm pregnant. My mother works seven A.M. to nine P.M. almost sixteen years. No day off in almost sixteen years. Only New Year's, only. Cousins never have a day off—they don't want it, because they're new immigrants, and also the financials not that well, maybe they need to save money for their own house or a store. My grandmothers work seven days a week—almost ten hours a day. They make bean curd and cook lunch for workers. Anything—they can handle it. Ages seventy-six and sixty-two. They like it. They strong, they never sick. No sit." Tina shook her hands vigorously in denial. "Only stand up, ten hours a day."

Tina's older grandmother, who is four feet tall and densely wrinkled, with short gray hair held back with bobby pins, sorts tofu in the "factory," a large white room at the back of the railroad-car-shaped store on Mulberry Street. Tina's other grandmother, wearing a black pants suit, bags the brown, rubbery fried curds in plastic. Tina's two cousins, who are also pregnant, cook the tofu on an industrial stove. Two young boys in boots shovel soybeans into machines that crush them in water. Tina explained that they boil the mixture and then separate the solid portion from the soy milk. To the milk they add white plaster, to help separate the curds from the whey. The whey drains off, and they let the curds solidify in molds cooled in tubs of water.

Speaking Cantonese, Mrs. Kong told Connie and me that she doesn't know English and that it's a big disadvantage. She wants her children to know English so they can get into the mainstream.

Tina interrupted to say, "My parents almost no education. Only one or two years in China, and only Chinese, no English. Is a problem."

"How can I learn English!" Mrs. Kong exclaimed. "No time! I raised three children." She laughed hard.

"My parents think in whole family no one has a very good education, including me," Tina said sorrowfully. "I went six months to high school and drop out. Being an immigrant, I didn't learn that much. I couldn't catch up that much. So make me a headache. Five years ago, they had limited bilingual program." She added, "We make good profit. We are not rich."

Mrs. Kong nodded. "No rich." She paused, then said, "I put great expectation on my children. For me, it's very difficult to merge into American society, and I expect my children will have a better time."

Mrs. Kong moved to Westchester so that her son could have a better education. She has memorized the drive into the city because she cannot read highway signs. She has no Caucasian friends in Westchester and doesn't participate in the weekend life there, for she works seven days a week.

Her daughter Tina is also too busy saving for her future to assimilate. "My husband and I cannot save that much money," Tina told me. "Of course, some, but not boss, like my mother. I feel my salary is a little low—sixteen hundred dollars a month take home. This is family business—no benefits, no vacation, no insurance. This is usual in Chinatown. Almost no business give benefits. We had two workers take a vacation. Were here two years, we gave them one week. But they eat here three times a day—lunch, dinner, tea. Anything to drink also.

"My husband is a driver for a limo service. Not very hard work—better money than restaurant work. Fourteen hours a day, but he is his own boss. Only at night we see each other. We live in my mother's old apartment on Mulberry Street. Five hundred dollars for one bedroom, with tub in kitchen, toilet in hall." Tina laughed, describing the typical tenement built before the 1901 building code requiring toilets in each apartment, and passed down through generations of German, Irish, Italian, and now Chinese immigrants. "No lease," Tina added. "Illegal tenant."

Many immigrants are caught in a vicious circle: working sixty or eighty hours a week to save money to get out of Chinatown, buy homes, fulfill Confucian duties to their parents, and open small businesses—the traditional way newcomers without means establish themselves—they have no time to learn English. They become prisoners of Chinatown. They are paid so little that it takes them decades to save enough to escape. When they do escape, they can't assimilate, because they can't speak English.

Garment factories, the economic backbone of Chinatown, perpetuate the vicious circle. Four hundred and seventy-five union shops provide the community's only health insurance and benefits such as maternity leave and paid vacations. "New immigrants choose the work just for the health benefits," I was told by May Chen, the assistant education director for Local 23–25 of the International Ladies' Garment Workers' Union, which covers Chinatown. "One of the shocks for newcomers is that we have no national health system. The People's Republic, Taiwan, Hong Kong, all have national health insurance." Garment workers' pay fluctuates with the market, and, besides, workers are often cheated. But they can't stop working because their job provides their family's health insurance and the margin that allows the family to save. By week's end, many workers told me, they have no energy to take evening English classes or search for better-paying jobs uptown.

Chinatown specializes in the "spot market"—small runs of trendy styles, sewn quickly, so that Seventh Avenue manufacturers who contract the orders to Chinatown can deliver the clothing to stores within a week. Garment workers routinely work Saturdays and, if a panic is on for a big order, Sundays as well.

The pressure is extreme. Workers are paid by the piece and do one task all day long. Merrow operators run the machines that sew seams, and are paid from 10 cents to 20 cents a seam, perhaps a dollar a garment. Seamstresses add collars, cuffs, zippers, pockets. Piecework that is easy and quick, and therefore lucrative, is called "soy sauce chicken." No one wants "pig's bones"—tricky garments that take time and pay little. The lowest-paid workers, who are mostly women in their sixties and seventies, are thread cutters; they snip threads from finished garments. Men or teenagers stitch buttonholes, and steam pressers, all of them men, lay garments on padded ironing boards and, with foot pedals, press the clothing into shape. One man puts stiffening on the shoulder seams of suits, to be heat-sealed against the fabric. All day long, he places stiffening on the same seam of thousands of suits. The last step is the work of finishers; they sort the garments by size and shape, put them on hangers, and trim off any excess threads that remain before bagging the garments in plastic. Chinatown doesn't design, cut, or market: it only sews, chiefly sportswear.

Recently, piece rates have been dropping as a result of tough competition. Koreans have muscled into the spot market in the last five years, and Korean factory owners are incorrigibly anti-union. The ILGWU says that Koreans run true sweatshops—worse than the ones in Chinatown. Only in Korean shops, which are mostly in the mid-town Garment District, do workers earn $200 for fifty-four hours, I was told by Jeff Hermanson, the director of organizing at the ILGWU. But in the four Chinatown shops I visited, everyone put in at least sixty hours a week, some for less than $200. A handful earned over $300. The majority made about $4 an hour, slightly less than burger flippers in McDonald's working nine to five at minimum wage—$4.25 an hour. John Lam, one of Chinatown's largest garment contractors, who runs a $60-million business, with fourteen factories, pays an average of $4.50 an hour.

When piece rates drop below union minimums, or minimum wage, workers silently knuckle under and try to recover the lost wages by working even longer hours. Wing Lam, a labor organizer in China-town, pointed out that piece rates are now so low that Hong Kong fac-tories, which compete with Chinatown factories, have moved into the community. For the same reason, some U.S. makers have withdrawn from Asia in favor of Chinatown in the last few years. "The union doesn't enforce the wage laws, because of, it claims, overseas and non-union competition," he told me. "There are fewer and fewer Seventh Avenue manufacturers, so when Chinatown contractors offer twenty cents a piece the manufacturers can insist on eighteen cents a piece. If the contractors don't take it, they don't work. You can imagine how low the prices go. Chinatown struck in 1982—twenty thousand women marched in support of the union contract that the owners had rejected. Since then, I've heard of no women sitting down at the machines to strike. A few try, but the contractors close and open under a different name."

One day in 1990, I accompanied Joseph Halik, Gene Lee, and Angelo Valdevitt, inspectors from the state Department of Labor's

Apparel Industry Task Force, which enforces state labor law in New York's six thousand garment factories. Hugh McDaid, the chief investigator of the task force, defines a sweatshop this way: "It violates as many laws as it possibly can—minimum wage laws, workers' compensation, child labor, unemployment, fire safety. The people who run the sweatshops are the most egregious and deliberate of violators."

Many sweatshops in the city take great care to hide their operations. They put up no signs. They shutter their windows, or they block their curtains with wood planks, so no one can peek around the edges of the curtains into a shop. They bolt and shutter fire doors. They roll down their outside metal gratings, so the shop looks abandoned. Only by putting an ear to the door and hearing the drone of machines can inspectors find such a shop. The sweatshops that honeycomb Chinatown, however, don't hide. They perpetually need workers and advertise jobs on squares of red paper or cloth pasted on the ground floor of tenements. On East Broadway, we found a tenement with a typical sign on the door: MERROW OPERATORS AND TWO THREAD CUTTERS NEEDED.

Seeing *low faan* in trench coats, badges displayed, coming up the narrow, stinking stairwell, a Chinese man descending the staircase asked, "What is this, a party?" and turned around and followed us back up to the second floor. There, we peered into a locked and empty factory. "They left overnight—without paying the rent, left only garbage!" the man complained wildly. "Disgusting! Happens all the time!"

On the third floor of the tenement was Waylon Sportswear, a new union shop. Thirty-eight middle-aged women, bent at forty-degree angles over their computerized Japanese sewing machines, lifted their eyes just briefly from their work as we entered. The high-speed machines shrieked like buzz saws. As we made our way down an aisle piled with boxes and clothing, a girl in a red and white diamond-patterned sweater and black jeans grabbed her schoolbag and ran for the door. Halik and Lee caught her. Her little brother waited by their mother, a seamstress. "I'm sure the boy was working, but I didn't see him," Halik said. The girl was slender and wore gold hoop earrings under her long hair. The boy was eight or nine. Mother and son watched fearfully as Lee asked the girl's name and address.

"Hui Quen Chen comes here about three-thirty P.M.," Lee translated. "She's sixteen years old, arrived from China about three months ago. Goes to school here from Brooklyn, where they live, so she and her mother can travel on the subway in the evening and morning together. She's paid by the piece and makes an average of thirty dollars a week. Slightly over minimum wage for about eight hours." Lee told the teenager that as a minor she could not do this work unless she had a certificate from the Board of Education.

"Everybody's upset about child labor," Halik interjected. "You ought to do a geriatric story—this Chinese woman we saw last week must have been a hundred years old! A thread cutter!"

Waylon was a mess: Scraps and boxes littered the room, which was about twenty-five feet by seventy. Its floor was cardboard nailed onto wood slats. The grilled windows were grimy, the fire escapes blocked and locked, without exit signs. The toilet was dirty, and there was no toilet paper. But the room was light and decorated with some Chinese calendars and New Year's greetings. In one corner, incense burned at a shrine to the warrior Gung Gong, a good-luck fixture in every Cantonese business. Steam pressers and thread cutters worked on mounds of orange and turquoise Hawaiian shirts at one end of the room. At the other end, seamstresses sewed at long tables, five or six to a table, or at individual work stations. They wore masks over their noses to protect themselves against lint, and aprons over their clothing. Their lunches hung in plastic bags above their heads, hooked onto their machines. On the window ledges were radios and jars of instant tea. One woman sewed a doll-sized pair of pants and held them up, making them dance on her fingers.

"These ladies are here for the duration," Halik said. "They've resigned themselves to that, and they make the most of it. It's piece rate, so it's more flexible. If a lady wants to leave for an hour and buy fish for dinner, she will, and the boss won't get on her."

Each woman was rushing through a stack of fabric. I watched one woman with a pile of yellow and brown patterned synthetic. She took a piece, fingered it to find the right side of the cloth, added a lining, turned the seam, and sewed the fabric and the lining together. She stopped to take a drink from a jar of water by her side for which she had made a bonnet of cloth. On the back of her chair, she had sewn a sort of knapsack. She got up, slipped her work apron into it, and walked out to pick up her daughter from Chinese school.

Meanwhile, Lee and Valdevitt were questioning another young woman. She earned $150 a week on the average, she said, or $2.80 an hour. She was twenty-one years old. She began work at eight-thirty A.M. and usually worked fifty-five hours a week, sometimes including Saturdays. Lee jotted a few figures on a pad, checking her wages: She should be paid the minimum wage (then $3.80 an hour) for forty hours, he noted, plus time and a half for fifteen hours of overtime, and a bonus, an extra hour's pay a day, for working more than ten hours continuously every day. He discovered that the woman was being cheated by over $100 a week. The woman betrayed no surprise. Lee promised to collect the back pay for her.

Other violations—the absence of exit signs, the blocked fire escape doors, aisles less than three feet wide, loose wires hanging from the ceiling—would be referred to the Fire Department. Lee asked the women if they had any complaints. The women said this shop was like any other—they were all the same.

Child labor and cheating workers of overtime are endemic in Chinatown, and Waylon is far from the worst offender, the inspectors said. "You see five or six minors in one place, working as thread trimmers, or standing by the machines, handing their mothers bundles of cloth," Halik said. "By saving that step, a mother might take home an extra three bucks a day. The boss doesn't care—it's all on the piece rate. It's either paying the kids or paying the mothers time and a half. That's how they survive."

"The worst are basement shops," Valdevitt said. "No exit doors. Child labor working fifty to sixty hours a week for three dollars and twenty-five cents an hour, under minimum wage. No records whatsoever. No overtime. No time cards. No ventilation. I've seen eight- and nine-year-olds working in these basements."

"Bosses let workers take sewing home—that's a very big violation," Halik said. "Especially in the Bronx, you'll see a lot of homework. Whole Vietnamese and Cambodian families stay home and make bows and hair bands—the ones sold at newsstands. We tagged a few big operations for industrial-homework violations—fifty to sixty people. It's cash all the way down the line: ten cents apiece, dollar a dozen, for cutting the ribbon, tying it up, gluing the clip into it. Asians don't go on welfare. If you have four or five family members making hair bands ten to twelve hours a day, seven days a week, you scrape by."

"In Hong Kong, they do skilled work," Lee said. "Here, they just throw the workers to a machine and see how many pieces they can turn out in a day."

"We've found some places giving people three rubber checks in a month and then calling Immigration to raid the place. The feds got wise to it finally," Halik said.

"The new immigrants are an intimidated labor pool," Hugh McDaid told me. "Chinese are not acculturated to their labor rights. They come from cultures where the government is the union is the employer, and they're not used to the government enforcing laws in their favor. They don't report violations themselves."

"The number of individual grievances taken to arbitration is probably lower than any other local in the country," May Chen of the ILGWU said. "Workers here are very frightened. Their employers blacklist them if they complain. It's a small community, it's easy to get ostracized, and then they don't work. A few years ago an employee took her case all the way to arbitration. Her employer published her picture in the paper and warned everyone not to hire her. A lot of people remember that case."

Factory owners, for their part, complain that newcomers are spoiled by socialism and shirk work. One major Hong Kong contractor told me, "The people from China still have that attitude from socialism that whether or not you do your work you get paid. They're not aggressive. A few years ago, they like to have a nap in the afternoon." She shook her head in strong disapproval. "In America, you have to work very hard. Malaysia, Thailand, it's hot in the afternoon, so they shut off everything. I can't have that here. Influence others. Malaysians, Thais, mainland Chinese don't like to work long hours. I tell them no nap or I lay them off." Police report that when called to some garment factories after robberies, they can't get through the door because eight or nine workers, all illegal immigrants, are sleeping on the factory floor, locked in by the factory owners.

At all the factories I saw—the four in Chinatown, and ten others around the city—children were either working or waiting for their mothers after school. The union is loath to enforce prohibitions against children in factories because the workers fear that if their children go home to empty apartments with no adult supervision after school, they'll fall in with the gangs. At a factory on Broadway, four or five children were playing among the fifty-five workers on the day I visited. They ran in the aisles or sat on piles of finished clothing and did their homework. In one corner, a baby slept in a carriage. Bi Lui Chen, playing by her mother at the end of a row, told me she was eleven years old and in the fifth grade. She jigged around in a pink cotton outfit. Every day, she waits four hours in the factory after school for her mother to finish work, she said, and sometimes she sews. "I can do it, I can do it!" she exclaimed proudly, pointing to the high-speed machines. "The factory is afraid the inspectors come. So sometimes, when I have work to do, I do it here, a little sewing. Sometimes not. Just for fun," she reassured me. Bi Lui evidently knew that she shouldn't say she sewed for money.

Both of Bi Lui's parents are garment workers. Her father, a steam presser, works in midtown and earns more than most steam pressers in Chinatown: 40 cents a shirt, 60 cents a cheongsam—the traditional Chinese silk dress, slit at the sides—and a dollar, the top rate, for complicated clothes. Chen declined to tell me his earnings. I met him for dinner in a restaurant, and in Cantonese he said he "was fiddling with the taxation problem"; in other words, he was underreporting his income—a ubiquitous practice in Chinatown. Many immigrants from the People's Republic, where most people pay no income tax, or Hong Kong, where the maximum rate is seventeen percent, cannot bear paying the IRS. Mrs. Chen works sixty hours a week, Monday through Saturday, for between $200 and $300. Together, the Chens probably earn about $24,000 a year, to support a family of four.

"Life here is simple and boring," Chen told me. In the six years he has been here, he has left the city only twice, to see entertainers at Atlantic City. He enjoys getting together with other garment workers at an association on Canal Street for an hour or two after work, and playing a friendly game of mah-jongg before dinner. Membership is $3. "They have no political talk at all," he said. At home, he watches TV, usually English-language programs, because he can guess the words. Bi Lui likes Hong Kong soap operas.

"I am poor, but I save money," Chen said. "This is one of the virtues of Chinese culture. The Chinese care about the bankbook, the blacks care about the four wheels, and the whites care about the apartments." He grinned, pleased with his joke. Chen judges himself poor because he doesn't own a home or a business. "Of course no one is satisfied with being poor," he chided me.

At first, Chen told me he had emigrated from Canton to make money, but as he relaxed he said that the real reason was that his father had been declared a non-person in China, and he was afraid his children would suffer as he had. Chen's father's sister had married a military officer and defected to Taiwan. Consequently, his father was jailed, and Chen was not allowed to continue his schooling to upper secondary school, the equivalent of high school. He began farming rice and wheat, living, as his family had for generations, on remittances from relatives in Chinatown. "It broke my heart," he said quietly. "I was the brightest in my family." Chen's family circle here comprises about fifty people, among them his father, one grandmother, all his brothers and sisters, and their families. Only five speak English, and none of them leave Chinatown. His grandmother supported Chen for several years so he could adjust to America and learn English, but he has given up. He complained about having to work longer hours than he did on his farm in China, and said he was too tired in the evening to go to English classes. He said he did not expect he would ever become a citizen, because he wouldn't learn English. Bi Lui translated for the family. The bright, funny, buffeted little girl told me she remembered that her first-grade teacher, angry at her slow progress in English, pinched her cheeks till they bled. Her parents approved: the teacher is the most respected figure in China. "Harsh is the tradition in China, harsh can make more obedient and capable children," her father said. Some days when I saw Bi Lui, she was in a rage and wouldn't talk to me in English. Those were the days when her teachers had criticized her as too slow.

"Many adults are illiterate in Chinatown," I was told by David Chen (he is not related to Bi Lui's family), the executive director of the Chinese-American Planning Council, the neighborhood's largest social service agency. "So the kids run the households. It contradicts the Chinese way of life, which is to respect the elders. It leads to a lot of problems: the kids hang out; there's not enough bilingual instruction; there's not enough housing; there's not enough parental guidance; and at the same time, there's too much pressure for performance in school. They're all supposed to be stereotypical whiz kids.

And those who aren't end up in gangs. Face comes into it: 'Mr. Lee's kids did well, why didn't you?'"

I met many prisoners of Chinatown like Bi Lui's father—isolated, upset about the community, but resigned to making a buck and to always being strangers in America. Over and over, I heard how frightening Chinatown was, how bad crime was. But residents feel trapped. They don't know enough English to deal with the police, they are too frightened to try to fight crime alone, and they are too suspicious of American authorities to help them improve Chinatown.

3
GAMBLING

One of the few relaxations that Chinese enjoy is gambling. *Low faan* can't get into Chinatown's illegal gambling parlors, so at eight o'clock on a Monday night—waiters' night off—in November Connie Pang and I boarded a bus outside the Silver Palace for a trip to Bally's casino in Atlantic City. Chinese are some of the casinos' best customers. Every evening, about a hundred people leave Chinatown in buses to gamble all night, and every day four hundred or five hundred depart to gamble all afternoon. In 1988, during the Chinese New Year—the principal holiday of the year, and the one day when most Chinese don't work—eight thousand people went to Atlantic City, in a giant snake of one hundred and twenty buses. About the same number have gone every year since then. The casinos are so eager to have these Chinese players that they pay a bonus of $10 to each customer, and subsidize the running costs of the eight Chinese companies that operate the buses. Some casinos have Chinese marketing managers as well. Their job is to think up new ways to keep the buses loaded and the players betting. Like the regular market managers, they analyze secret videotapes and computerized records of the big players' games and decide who are big enough spenders for the casinos to lay out money to bring them in often. The casinos send limos to drive them or helicopters to fly them; put them up free in fancy suites; and extend them large credit lines. At the casinos with the most Chinese business—Caesars Boardwalk Regency, Trump

Castle, the Tropicana, the Sands—some players who are regulars have million-dollar credit lines.

Outside our bus windows, all of Chinatown was hurrying by; people were shoving, yanking children, bumping each other with lumpy bags of groceries in the fierce cold. A dim sum peddler stirring his sizzling bits of dough wore huge stiff mittens. Barbecued ducks hanging in the windows of the Cantonese restaurants looked tough and red. There were twenty-four people scattered around the bus, all Chinese except me and another white woman.

A scowling man opposite us turned out to have an impish sense of humor. "I'm a noodle-maker," he said. "I make rice noodles on Green Street in Brooklyn for last two years. I was born in Guangdong Province. I come to Atlantic City once every two weeks." He was dark-skinned and had thin legs like matchsticks under his jeans, and a sparse mustache. Under a blazer and a red V-neck sweater he wore a T-shirt. He told me he was twenty-eight years old. "I come for the blackjack," he said. "I can only gamble at night, because I work during the day. I can't be tired tomorrow, because I have a lot of noodles to make." He giggled. He would get back to Chinatown tomorrow morning at seven and go straight to noodle-making, he said, having had at most three hours of sleep. And he was losing one of those hours talking to us.

His eyes twinkled as he explained why Chinese love gambling. "Chinese are born different from *low faan*," he said. "Born to like gambling. Chinese do not have other forms of entertainment for their leisure time. *Low faan* like to picnic or take trips. Chinese don't picnic or travel, because they don't know English to read the signs and maps, and they don't know the way home. Plus the Chinese like to eat more. When they have a little money, they like to eat it all up. And the third reason is that going on trips is spending money, and going to gamble is getting money back." He said emphatically, "Chinese *like* money, and they *like* to gamble."

I thought a minute and ventured a question that had been bothering me. "Do Chinese like money more than Americans?"

"Yes," he said, again much amused. "Americans don't have to invest as much in their children. Once their children grow up, they go away. If Americans are broke, they can ask the government for money from Social Security and welfare. For Chinese, it is completely differ-ent. Once we have some money, we save it, invest it, and think how to put the money into our child, because we expect our children to stay in our home until after they are grown up. They live with us until they are married—and the men, after they are married, take care of their parents."

He yawned, then giggled. His wife and son didn't know he was on his way to Atlantic City, he said. He and his brothers share an apart-ment in Chinatown. His wife, his parents, and his sisters live in Jamaica, Queens, and other parts of the borough. He pays for the apartment that his wife and parents share. The Chinatown apartment is an old family asset bought by his parents long ago to save the family breadwinners a commute. Sometimes he sees his wife if he gets off work early. Otherwise, he spends Saturday night with her.

Then he told us about his betting. The most he had ever bet was $1,000 on blackjack. Usually he plays the minimum allowed by the casino, which is $5. If he feels lucky, he might hazard $200 or $300 on a bet. Occasionally, he wins the same amount. Once in a blue moon, he wins over a thousand bucks. He plays until he begins to lose. In Hong Kong, he gambled frequently and won often at the racetrack. He also gambled in China.

Out of his pay of $1,400 a month, he said, he can afford to use between $500 and $600 for gambling. Sometimes he stays away from gambling three months in a row. "Chinese have a saying: Nine out of ten gamblers are broke, and none can buy a piece of land." Gambling has a stigma in Chinese culture, he assured me, contrary to what oth-ers had said. But he didn't think that he was addicted. "The feeling is odd. Sometimes the idea comes into my head that I want to gamble, and I just go. I make no plans in advance, so I don't think I am addicted."

We wished him luck. He nodded and thanked us ceremoniously.

We asked the same questions of a jolly soul carrying two stalks of "rich bamboo," a thick-leafed green considered a good-luck charm. "Chinese people work very hard and they want some relaxation," she said. "Chinese like to gamble because they like to earn money and they like to bet a little—thirty or forty dollars—on the chance they will earn more." Sometimes she is so caught up in the game that she forgets the names of her parents, she said, rolling her eyes and laughing with shame.

Sui Moi Hor, a Malaysian, told us that her game was roulette. She said that she had visited the United States the previous year, discovered that money was plentiful here, and stayed. She rents a corner of her brother's sister-in-law's living room, partitioned by a screen, for a bedroom. She cleans restaurants and sews part-time in a garment factory. Recently, she told us, she started gambling in the evening. Now she comes to Atlantic City once a week. Her luck varies, but if she wins, she gambles several times a week.

We arrived at Bally's an hour and a half late, and all the passengers dashed off into the crowds. The huge casino resounded with the frenzied clanging of slot machines. Connie and I had to keep moving. The pit boss gave us the eye if we watched one table a long time. We were also being observed through the ceiling, which had one-way mirrors in it. Video cameras, some of them overhead, were taping the tables, so casino employees seated at computers could keep tallies of the bets of big winners and losers.

Chinese, we noticed, went for big payoffs. They clustered at the baccarat, roulette, and blackjack tables. Blackjack, for instance, paid off three to two. Table after table of blackjack were all Chinese. They didn't bother with craps or the wheel of fortune. Large parties of Caucasians at these tables whooped it up and egged each other on. The Chinese played silently. A number of Chinese women in their thirties were gambling in groups. They looked prosperous—like businesswomen, not Chinatown women. One, in a pants suit and pearls, was playing alone, and very successfully, at blackjack, with thousand-dollar chips in every rack.

Well into the morning, we spotted the noodle-maker, concentrating darkly. We watched from a few feet away, and he played steadily, cautiously, without acknowledging us. We didn't find Sui Moi Hor or the woman with the rich bamboo. Finally, Connie and I waited out the last hour at the bar, glassy-eyed.

At four-thirty A.M., we got back on the bus. Every seat was taken now, and the gamblers lighted cigarettes to shake off the anxiety of the night. We asked the noodle-maker how it had gone. He had not had luck tonight. He was considerably diminished, and curled up like a snail inside his blazer to sleep. The tour guide accompanying the bus, an ethnic Chinese with a sad story of escape from Vietnam in a boat attacked by pirates, admonished me. "It is bad manners to ask how someone has done," he said. "These are the hard core. They never show any emotion when they lose."

The bus of sleeping gamblers pulled into Chinatown at dawn. The gamblers woke with a start, stamped their feet, and filed out.

The more I talked to Chinatown residents, the more fascinated I became by their drive to gamble away money they have spent hours of toil to earn. The Off-Track Betting outlet at Chatham Square, one of two outlets in Chinatown, is the top revenue producer of ninety-six in the city. It is ten years old, and it has topped the charts every year. An average of $77,800 is wagered there every day—two and a half times the citywide average. The other OTB in Chinatown, on Lafayette Street, is consistently among the top twelve highest grossing in the system. It and the Chatham Square branch together have an average of $110,000 in bets a day. Close to a thousand customers wager at Chatham Square every day. On Sundays and holidays, the crowds of men are impenetrable, the room is gray with smoke, and the lines at the windows are ten deep. Chinese bet about double on a win as everyone else in the city—an average of $16.

In Chinatown, gamblers begin with spare change. If they lose that, they go into family money. And if they lose that, they work extra shifts. Many gamblers are waiters, and since there are three thousand Chinese restaurants in metropolitan New York, they can scrounge around for an extra five to six hours of work a day. Garment workers pool their money and bet. A Chinese man who works for the OTB told me, "The OTB always looks for Italian neighborhoods first, then Chinese. The Italians are macho—they like to throw their money around. They boom out, 'A thousand dollars on a horse!' They bet fifteen thousand dollars to make five hundred dollars. The Chinese are more reserved. They whisper, 'A hundred dollars on a horse.' They put down one hundred to make a sure five dollars. They'll go for the long shot, too, but they'll hedge with the favorite."

Over and over again, I heard Chinese say that they have no other recreation. "Look, gambling in our culture is not illegal. It may be illegal in America, but we didn't make those rules!" one Chinatown resident exclaimed. Many are wary of movies because gangs have shot innocent moviegoers. They don't much patronize the arts. The community has few libraries, only one park, and just a handful of nightclubs and bars; private nightclubs where Chinese sip Rémy and dance with bar girls are in midtown. Non-gamblers offered sociological explanations for the Chinese obsession with gambling. A Chinese nurse in a neighborhood clinic laughed when I asked her why so many Chinese gamble. "All they know is work, work, work—seven days a week. Gambling is the only means they have to relieve their stress," she said. Another Chinatown native told me, "Chinese are used to working in dirty, dingy old Chinatown. Atlantic City is like Shangri-La to them. One day away from the grind." The labor organizer Wing Lam says that Chinese gamble because they are exploited. "The Chinese see they can't get rich working long hours," he explained. "A lot give up hope. They need a painkiller. They spend $600 on baccarat the way the Irish spend money on alcohol. It's not in their blood—it's poor people escaping reality." David Chen, of the Chinese-American Planning Council, offered a similar reason: "You work so hard, no time to spend the money or invest it wisely, you gamble and see it double—so they hope."

Chinatown's illegal gaming halls are a sort of mini–Atlantic City. The difference between Atlantic City and Chinatown is that the tongs run or sanction most of the illegal parlors, the police periodically bust them, and they are not plush or safe. Sometimes the gangs who guard them, or gangs from other cities, rob them. Most of the illegal halls are permanent, but a few float: a humid basement parlor with brown-paper-covered metal tables and Formica siding on the walls can be a flower shop next week. They are expensive to run but very lucrative, because they are open sixteen, or even twenty-four, hours a day. One Chinatown resident broke down the costs for me: "They pay rent, they pay their employees—they have a pit boss, hosts who know everyone and can get them to come in. Investors and partners put up a cage, but they can't get Wells Fargo to pick up the proceeds, so you have gangs. You got to pay the tong a percentage of the gross, you maybe got to pay the local gendarmes—they know exactly where you are. Why do they not hit them all the time? Then, how do you keep the gang members guarding your place happy? Apartments, girls, lawyers, guns. You need a kitchen and a chef, so when a guy hits it big he can stop and celebrate with a meal. Every once in a while, you need a Shanghai sailor to come in and do a hit, so your guys don't get burned out. It's convenient that a sailor can get on a ship and get lost. It's been happening like this for the last forty years—every three, four, five years, there's a murder. You sit there with your brow furrowed, but a Chinese from the community will hear about the hit and say, 'Ah, the guy was probably dipping.'"

In the illegal joints, mah-jongg, thirteen-card (a variant of poker), fan-tan, *pai gow*, and *tein gow* are the most popular games. *Pai gow*, which is played with thirty-two dominoes thrown like dice, is so popular that Caesars Palace has added tables for it. Other casinos have also approved adding it to their entertainment. *Pai gow* has serious betting—a thousand-dollar minimum in some games, and sometimes $400,000 is on the table at once. Fan-tan can make a gambler a fortune in no time. Any number can play. A random number of buttons are put in a bowl and are then removed four at a time. Players bet on the number—three, two, one, or none—that will be left at the end. Depending on the type of bet, there are three rates of winning, and in less than an hour $50 can explode into thousands of dollars.

Hundreds of thousands of dollars are in play any night in Chinatown's basements. Some players gamble all day, and some dealers, after work, stay on to gamble all night. According to police, the extent of gambling in Chinatown has no comparison anywhere else in the city. Law enforcement officials have unconfirmed reports that in Fujianese gambling parlors profits run to a million dollars a week. Losses are also steep. Loan sharks prey on gamblers. Many stories circulate of Chinatown restaurants sold to pay fan-tan debts. Working-class losers pay off debts by becoming prostitutes or couriers smuggling heroin on flights from the Far East.

"No matter where they go, Chinese gamble," Justin Yu, a former head of Chinatown's journalists' union, notes. "On horses, dogs, chickens, numbers, sports, elections, bicycles, motorcycle competitions, whatever you can think of—they will bet on who will cross the street. I'm from Taiwan. There they gamble on everything—sometimes losing their wives, because they lose their houses and their wives split."

Why, though? Chinese have been gambling for centuries—Marco Polo, the first Westerner to visit China, observed the craving in the thirteenth century. I concluded that Chinese gamble for the same reason that they work to accumulate a pile of money: It brings "face." "Face" is probably the second most widely used expression in Chinatown. "We got a big face tonight"; "Don't break my face." Face is one's stature in the community, one's prestige. Success at fan-tan in the back of barbershops or in Atlantic City is a means of acquiring that prestige.

Face can be acquired in other ways, too: many children, a long life, high status through education, or prominence in one's profession, for instance. Wealth, however, is a form of face open to all who work hard or who have luck at the tables.

The real-estate broker Dean Lui is a wise observer of Chinatown life. "Chinese gamble because they think it is the fastest way to earn money," he confirmed. "Without a doubt, Chinese like money more than Americans do. Americans enjoy traveling, sports, a vacation. They don't care about money. They make it and they spend it. But not the Chinese! They really care about it. Every Chinese likes to be very proud. Chinese really want to help friends and relatives. It's for face. Big face. 'You have a great big face,' we say. Chinese like to address someone as 'Big Brother' or 'Big Sister,' or even 'Big Brother Big' or 'Big Sister Big.' We mean those people are on a higher level: I earn twenty thousand dollars; you earn two hundred thousand dollars— you big shot. Got big face.

"If you have money, you send some to mainland China to your relatives. Every year before the New Year's festival, you'll see long lines at the bank of people sending money out. Sometimes they send a hundred dollars, sometimes a thousand dollars. Banks charge from five to ten dollars per transaction. Myself, I received a letter from my aunt and uncle in the country in China. 'I want to buy a new house. Can you please send us several thousand dollars?'" Lui laughed. "I sent them five hundred dollars only. We are from Far East. If you don't send money, you will feel that your relatives think you are not successful."

David Chen of the Chinese-American Planning Council put the drive succinctly: "Chinese don't get famous, they get rich."

4

HISTORY

Old Chinatown exists only in traces. The shops are gone, the people are gone, and few records were ever kept. Chinese are ashamed of the bad old days of racism, and few wish to rake up Bachelor Society Chinatown, the culture that arose under anti-Chinese laws in effect between 1882 and 1943—a salty, raw, chauvinist society, made up almost exclusively of laundrymen and laborers. Some of the fifty old-timers who recently taped oral histories for the Chinatown History Museum, the one local institution dedicated to documenting the past, felt compelled to ask the museum not to release the tapes before their deaths.

Two forms of racism created Chinatowns: Chinese and American. The clash set the pattern for future discrimination against other Asians. In the mid-nineteenth century, when the first Cantonese came to San Francisco in the gold rush, there were no immigration quotas. By and large, the Chinese never intended to stay long—just long enough to get rich and go home big shots. Most were peasants; a few were members of secret triad societies, outlaw groups formed by warrior monks in the seventeenth century and dedicated to overthrowing China's Manchu rulers.

At first, Chinese were welcomed, but soon their willingness to work for very low wages enraged white miners. The miners killed a few, ran some off the mines, and taxed the rest. Still, more Chinese immigrated, lured by American labor brokers and stories of extravagant wealth in Gam Saan, the "Gold Mountain"—the Chinese term for California. After building the Central Pacific Railroad, they competed for jobs as canners, fishermen, and industrial and agricultural workers in California, and endured many forms of discrimination: They were even forbidden to walk on the sidewalks with the bamboo poles they used to transport goods; and in San Francisco, ordinances aimed at preventing communal living prescribed the cubic feet of air space that a Chinese must occupy while asleep.

In his book *Chinatown, N.Y.,* Peter Kwong, a Taiwanese immigrant and a political scientist at the State University of New York at Old Westbury, explains that organized labor laid the blame for the depression of the 1870s on the sixty-five thousand or so male Chinese in the West. Chinese were easy to scapegoat: they worked for any wages, at any job, subsisting on nothing, it seemed. They lived apart in Chinatowns to avoid white barbarians, and they smoked opium, wore their hair in queues, burned incense before idols, and didn't bother to learn English, because they were only here to find fortune. "They refused to be naturalized lest they lose their rights as subjects of the Manchu empire," one Chinese historian noted. "They had no desire to be called 'foreign devils' upon their return. Furthermore, they considered themselves far more civilized than the 'foreign barbarians' on the Pacific slope. Consequently they were more Chinese than the Chinese, and maintained their customs stubbornly. They gave themselves no chance to be understood; they were untouchable." The term "heathen Chinee" entered the vocabulary around 1870 with a Bret Harte poem about a dishonest Chinese worker. Riots and assaults on Chinese increased, and, in San Francisco, politicians took up the cry, "The Chinese must go!"

Across the West in the 1870s and 1880s, Chinese were murdered and their homes were burned. White mobs from the Cherry Creek Diggings, near Denver, beat Chinese and looted their stores while a lone gunman defended the immigrants, saying, "If you kill Wong, who in hell will do my laundry?" The historian Shih-shan Henry Tsai chronicles the riots that exploded in the region in *The Chinese Experience in America:* In Montana, Chinese were expelled from the mines; in Tacoma, vigilantes hauled them from their homes and ran them out of the city; in Rock Springs, Wyoming, miners, enraged that Chinese would not join a union, murdered twenty-eight of them; in Los Angeles, nineteen were lynched. In some places, Chinese were killed for sport. Cowboys bound Chinese to steers and drove them out of town. Some newspapers thought the violence hilarious, invariably caricaturing the Chinese as rats with sharp, bared teeth, slanted eyes, and long, tail-like queues. In a cartoon of the period, Uncle Sam inveighs, "I hate the nigger 'cause he's a citizen, and I hate the 'yellow dog' because he won't become one."

The Chinese Exclusion Act of 1882 barred Chinese laborers or their wives from entering the United States. It excluded Chinese from most occupations, including manufacturing and mining. It also forbade them from becoming citizens. President Grover Cleveland supported the act, declaring the Chinese "an element ignorant of our Constitution and laws, impossible of assimilation with our people, and dangerous to our peace and welfare." Some states denied Chinese the right to testify against whites in courts. Many states prohibited them from owning property or from marrying whites. Twenty-five states required that Chinese children be taught in separate schools. After 1924, an American woman who married an "alien ineligible for citizenship" lost her own citizenship, and another law that took effect the same year barred the immigration of all Chinese women.

Such laws persuaded many Chinese to go home, but some dived for safety into Chinatowns until the Second World War, when the Exclusion Act was repealed. In Chinatowns, men lived without wives or children. Most became laundrymen, though nowhere else in the world had Chinese washed clothes for a living; they did so here simply because laundries were permitted under the act and were cheap to open. The segregated ghettos of men were, inevitably, tenderloins, with gambling halls, opium dens, and prostitutes. Police stayed out of the ghettos and let Chinese settle their own affairs. In that way, too, American racism turned Chinatowns in on themselves.

Family associations, composed of people with the same surname, provided newcomers with jobs and loans. In district associations, composed of people from the same area, elders settled disputes, since Chinese did not use American courts. The Chinese Consolidated Benevolent Association governed every Chinatown. Its word was law, and it urged Chinese never to become Americanized. It didn't have to teach Chinese to distrust outsiders and authorities; they knew they risked beatings if they left Chinatowns. "Chinky, Chinky Chinamen, eats rats, Chews 'em up like ginger snaps," white children taunted, sometimes pelting Chinese with rocks.

The tongs served as police in Chinatowns, since white cops stayed out or were bought off. But tong fought tong; these protection societies for weak family associations, first formed in San Francisco about 1850, committed most of Chinatowns' crimes. Merchants began the On Leong tong; criminals and working-class Chinese formed the Hip Sing tong. These and five or six other prominent tongs carved up the streets of every Chinatown into business districts where only their members or approved non-members could open shop. A Hip Sing walking on an On Leong street could provoke war: Hired assassins, usually members of the triads, avenged the insult with murder. The arrangement was oddly delicate: the assassins, called hatchet men, after the weapons they used, fought proxy wars. These allowed enemies to greet each other on the street, knowing that they'd been avenged but had not risked their own lives. Tongs also controlled the gambling halls, opium parlors, and prostitution. Tong bosses owned slave girls, young prostitutes smuggled in from China, and lived off their earnings. In New York City, tong wars were a rite of spring from about 1910 until the early 1930s, when the United States Attorney in Manhattan clamped down. During the worst bloodshed, children had to be escorted to school by armed tong guards, and business was at a standstill.

Tourists in those days went to Chinatowns to ogle vice: guidebooks warned of the immorality and filth of the quarters. The sightseers hired guides to show them opium dens, slave girls, and sites of lurid tong murders. Bohemians visited to smoke opium and drift away on hazy dreams. Chinese encouraged the tourism; unable to leave the ghetto, why not bring outsiders to it to spend money? Restaurants changed their menus to suit American tastes, inventing chow mein, thought disgusting by Cantonese—"tea leaves and leftovers," one cackled. Entrepreneurs built phony Buddhist temples and opium dens so they could charge admission to tourists. Today, liberal Chinese, influenced by the Asian-American movement, skip over this period or ridicule it as an invention of white journalists for the titillation of their readers. Stories of Chinese slavers kidnapping white women, the subject of Frank Norris's famous tale "The Third Circle," were probably salaciously exaggerated, but there is no question that Chinatowns were tough.

And riddled with fear. Many residents were "paper sons," illegal aliens with false identification papers. Any child born to an American citizen was automatically also a citizen, even if the child was born in China. Laborers who had entered the country before the Exclusion Act and had obtained citizenship, or merchants who were exempted from the act, invariably told the United States Immigration Bureau when they returned from visits to China that they'd fathered sons there, whether they had or not. That opened up a slot for another Chinese, often a nephew or a cousin, or perhaps a stranger from another district, to pose as the son. Immigration grilled Chinese entering the United States—with so many originating near Canton, it became expert in Cantonese village life and family genealogies. "How many steps from the peach tree in back of your house to the village shrine?" inspectors asked. "How many sons did your mother's aunt have?" Paper sons studied these typical questions in their "coaching books," bought with their fake birth certificates, and had ready answers. Hundreds managed to fool Immigration and take up residence under false names this way. After the San Francisco earthquake in 1906, some Chinese succeeded in emigrating by claiming that they'd been born prior to 1906 in San Francisco. There was no way to know; the earthquake and fire destroyed all municipal documents in City Hall. Others slipped in over the Mexican or Canadian borders.

In New York in the 1890s, in the three-block colony of Mott, Pell, and Doyers streets, which was settled by Chinese fleeing anti-Chinese violence in the West, shops overflowed onto the sidewalks. Colorful paper lanterns fluttered from storefronts. Toy sellers, shoemakers, flower sellers, pipebowl menders, and fish and produce sellers suspended their wares in giant wicker baskets from bamboo poles. The ratio of men to women was twenty-seven to one. Men in dark tunics and dark leggings, with dark felt hats over their black queues, thronged the streets. The few children (born to merchants or scholars, who were exempted from the Exclusion Act and allowed to bring in Chinese wives) glowed in citron and fuchsia silks against the monochromatic men. Slender, beautiful slave girls, striding alone, eyes downcast, were the only women allowed on the streets. Christian missionaries battled to rescue them before they reached puberty and were sold as concubines or prostitutes. According to one journalist's count, Chinatown in 1898, with a population of some three thousand, had seven hundred gamblers, four hundred and fifty hatchet men, one hundred and seventy-five merchants, seventy-five cigar makers and seventy-five vegetable growers, forty-five restaurateurs, forty-five pastry chefs, at least twenty opium dens, one annual opera, and yearly poetry writing competitions. All but eighty-four of the male residents were bachelors. Thirty-six had Chinese wives; the rest were married to white prostitutes or common law wives. Hip Sing, led by the gambler Mock Duck, battled On Leong under the leadership of Tom Lee, a former president of the Chinese Consolidated Benevolent Association, for control of the lucrative gambling and opium rackets. Doyers Street, called "Bloody Angle" because of its crook that made it an ideal ambush spot, was the site of more murders than anyplace in America.

5

THE LEES

There is only one shop left from the early days of Chinatown. Paul Lee, a hip forty-two-year-old actor and an operator of gambling-bus tours, owns Quong Yuen Shing & Company at 32 Mott Street, a store that his grandfather Lok B. Lee, a pillar of Bachelor Society Chinatown, managed in the 1890s. Lee showed me around, grousing about the preservationists in Chinatown who want to mothball the place as a museum. "The store started in 1891—it was a general store and a mail drop for the old sojourners," he said. "They changed money here, sent money back to China, got their supplies here. Many people lived here. When I was a kid, in the basement we had cages of wild animals—deer, raccoons. We'd slaughter them for the antlers and the claws for the old medicines. Then the American Medical Association attacked Chinese herbalists, and we took the stock off the shelves."

Quong Yuen Shing, which has its original fixtures, is dark and dusty, as though it were already a museum. A fifteen-foot-long gilded screen of peacocks and chrysanthemums, carved in China a century ago, frames the former herb pharmacy. Behind it, a salesman uses an abacus. Bare wooden floors creak. A few paper lanterns hang from a flaking tin ceiling. Old wooden counters on one side display tea sets, and in cabinets behind them are Buddhas, mah-jongg sets, pictures of butterflies and peonies made of wheat straw, and, tucked away in drawers, silk handkerchiefs such as the laundrymen, the store's first

customers, sent their best clients at Christmas at the turn of the century.

"Let's go in the back. I'll show you that this place hasn't been
changed in a hundred years," Lee said. We squeezed down a narrow
corridor, passing small rooms stacked to the ceiling with cardboard
boxes of goods from the People's Republic. "We won't sell the store—
we'll just be driven out," he said, looking at the incredible disarray.
"I'm big in Chinese vegetable seeds." Nodding toward what looked
like piles of Monopoly money, he said, "That fake paper money is
ghost money for ancestor worship. If someone dies, you burn it. The
burning appeases the ghost."

At the far end of the corridor is a large room filled with a jumble
of boxes and crates, and to one side a bathroom is enclosed in a closet
that reaches three-quarters of the way to the ceiling. "This area was
open, if you can imagine," Lee said. "At a table, we'd have twenty
guys, coolies on staff, eating. They slept here." He pointed to a loft
bed on the roof of the bathroom. "That's a luxury spot—that guy had
the whole nine yards. We had workers downstairs, too, on racks like
bunks in a submarine."

Lee introduced me to his aunt. "She knows all the family history,"
he said.

His aunt, eighty-three years old, begs me, out of modesty, not to
identify her. "Please don't make me stand out like a sore finger," she
said. "Chinese would consider it boasting if I gave my name." She
went on to tell me, "Chinese were nobodies in the old days. You
couldn't fight for naturalization. There was a great deal of discrimination. When I made a reservation for my honeymoon at a hotel, I wrote
ahead and said that I was Chinese, so I wouldn't get up there and be
told there was no room. Otherwise, I wouldn't have been certain of a
welcome. That's why many Chinese boys and girls in the old days
never applied to a university—because the parents said, 'What's the
use? You'll end up in a restaurant or a laundry.' In the twenties, thirties, forties, there was no point in going uptown for a job. If it was an
important job, someone else got it.

"My father and mother wouldn't have let me marry a white person. All my social and professional life, I knew Chinese—the only
white people I ever met were at college. They didn't ask me out.

At the time, it was forbidden in our community to marry whites.

"My parents had never been to school. They had no idea what a library was. My mother asked me, 'What kind of place is it where they let you borrow books freely?' She sent my father out with me to see what it was. She thought I was making it up. My best friend, a Jewish girl, asked me to concerts. My father said okay, but only because her family was good. I don't think he knew what a concert was. He never went to these things. He just worked from the day he came over to the day he died, and yet, comparatively, he was Westernized." Her father, Lok B. Lee, confounded Chinatown by sending his six daughters and his son, Peter, to college. "Women in Chinese culture were rarely educated—his attitude was very advanced," his daughter said. "My father was king. I never dared express my likes or dislikes. No, I didn't long to. We never rebelled. Chinese are taught to hide their feelings, respect their elders. My parents didn't tell us their parents' names. They didn't reveal their pasts, or even their birthdays. They were superstitious. Chinese in general don't discuss birthdays. Their belief is that if you talk about something good all the time, the evil spirits, the *yein*, will overhear you and cause harm. We never knew, for example, the year my father emigrated.

"I couldn't join the Girl Scouts or any clubs. My mother didn't want me to go. See, the trouble was she didn't know anything. She had bound feet and couldn't walk. They said in China no one would marry you otherwise. The original purpose was to keep wives at home, keep them virtuous. But who would want to marry a woman with bound feet who couldn't go anywhere? I was Westernized, you see. You know, foot binding deforms you. Your bones are crushed. We had to go to Coward's to order custom-made shoes. What a cruel world it was!

"If I ever took Mother outside, she'd forget how to find the apartment, because she went out extremely rarely. She couldn't go alone—you'd have to go with her. Once, she got out," said her daughter, unconsciously using the term for an animal escaping a cage. "I took her to Roxy's and Radio City Music Hall. We were on line at Radio City with hundreds of people, and I said, 'Now what do I do?' My mother couldn't stand. I told the usher. He took us ahead of everybody and found us a seat. I was telling the truth. She couldn't stand up in that line.

Racism in the West during the 1870s and 1880s drove Chinese who came to California to pan gold across the country to New York City. Anti-Chinese riots escalated to mob lynchings and murders. Cutting off queues of Chinese men and other outrages were sport for hoodlums in 1865 in San Francisco, and at Rope Walk (*above*) several Chinese were murdered. (*Courtesy of Bancroft Library*).

A raid in New York's Chinatown—police searching the headquarters of On Leong, at 14 Mott Street, for its leader, Tom Lee, during war with Hip Sing in 1905. (*King's Booklet, 1908, courtesy of Yoshio Kishi*)

Opposite: By the 1890s the three-block area of Doyers, Pell, and Mott Streets was a thriving Chinese empire. Lok B. Lee (*behind counter, center, with mustache*) ran Quong Yuen Shing & Company—an importer-exporter of porcelains, teas, and Chinese groceries—with twenty coolies.

In Chinatown's union garment shops like Waylon Sportswear (*above*), salaries average $9,500 a year. However, new immigrants at Waylon earn $7,500 a year for fifty to sixty hours of piecework a week. (© *1991 Harvey Wang*)

Opposite: Today grandson Paul Lee and his wife Janny own Quong Yuen Shing, now Chinatown's oldest store. Even the photos over the former herb pharmacy (*rear*) remain the same as in Lok B. Lee's day. (© *1991 Harvey Wang*)

Chinese fleeing American racism and fearful of contact with white "barbarians" formed self-help groups that still dominate Chinatown. This family association, called "The Four Brothers," is for the Quan, Chao, Liu, and Chang families. Anyone whose surname is one of these four is automatically a member; the society will bury those too poor to afford funerals. *From left to right, foreground*: Kwok Wai Chiu, social club president, and Ning Fan Quan, co-president; *rear*: Wah Lick Chiu, co-president, and Chuck H. Lou, vice president, represent the four brothers today. (© *1991 Harvey Wang*)

Above: In *gong si fong*, or public rooms, bachelors like Mr. Ng (*above*), live cheaply. Ten to fifteen people live in the one-bedroom apartments, usually partitioned with plywood into small sleeping cubicles. (© *1983 Robert Glick*)
Right: After decades of separation, Sit Sau Fong Chiu was permitted to join her husband when the United States repealed anti-Chinese immigration laws barring Chinese wives in 1945. Mrs. Chiu's happiness was short-lived: her husband died soon after she arrived. (© *1981 Robert Glick*)

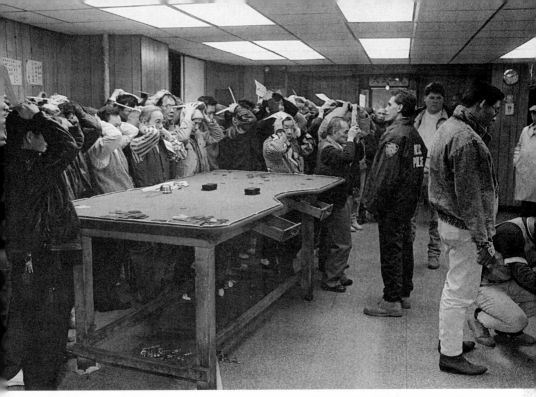

Gambling is Chinatown's main pastime: hundreds of thousands of dollars are in play each night in illegal casinos like this one, the Tsung Tsin Association, here raided by the New York Police Department's Public Morals Division. (© *1991 Harvey Wang*)

Eighty-four-year-old Benny Ong, adviser-for-life of Hip Sing, is Chinatown's "Godfather."

Chinese Connection hub Peter Woo (*lower right*) pleaded guilty in 1990 to helping broker the second largest heroin haul in U.S. history. (*FBI surveillance photo, courtesy of U.S. Attorney, Eastern District*)

Funerals in Chinatown are elaborate: banners and mourners fill the streets. (© *1983 Robert Glick*)

Chart of tong-gang affiliation (*Courtesy of Permanent Subcommittee on Investigations, U.S. Senate, Washington, D.C.*)

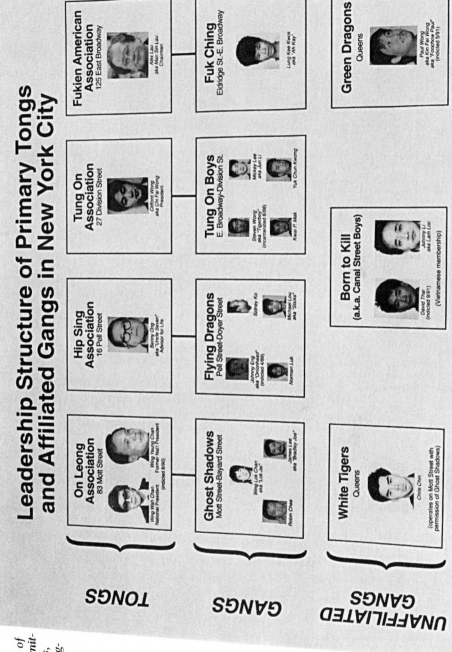

Leadership Structure of Primary Tongs and Affiliated Gangs in New York City

TONGS

On Leong Association
83 Mott Street

Wing Wah Chan
National President

Wing Yeung Chan
Former Nat'l President
(indicted 8/90)

Hip Sing Association
16 Pell Street

Benny Ong
aka "Uncle Seven"
Advisor for Life

Tung On Association
27 Division Street

Clifford Wong
aka Cha Fai Wong
President

Fukien American Association
125 East Broadway

Alex Lau
aka Man Sin Lau
Chairman

GANGS

Ghost Shadows
Mott Street-Bayard Street

Wing Lok Chan
aka "Lok Jai"

Robin Chee

James Lee
aka "Bradley Joe"

Flying Dragons
Pell Street-Doyer Street

Johnny Eng
aka "Onionhead"
(indicted 4/90)

Norman Luk

Sidney Ko

Michael Lou
aka "Sticks"

Tung On Boys
E. Broadway-Division St.

Steven Wong
aka "Tigerboy"
(incarcerated 8/88)

Kwai P. Mak

Mickey Lee
aka Jun Li

Yuk Chun Kwong

Fuk Ching
Eldridge St.-E. Broadway

Lung Kee Kwok
aka "Ah Kay"

UNAFFILIATED GANGS

White Tigers
Queens

Chris Chin

(operates on Mott Street with permission of Ghost Shadows)

Born to Kill
(a.k.a. Canal Street Boys)

David Thai
(indicted 9/91)

Johnny Li
aka Lam Loc

(Vietnamese membership)

Green Dragons
Queens

Paul Wong
aka Kin Fei Wong
aka "Foochow Paul"
(indicted 5/91)

Burmese warlord Khun Sa, seen here inspecting his troops, oversees production of approximately 50 percent of the world's heroin and is the source of the Chinese Connection. (© 198 *Bernard Genier/Sygma*

Above: Children, like these playing at the Garment Industry Day Care Center, are the grace and balm of Chinatown. (© 1992 *Harvey Wang*) *Right:* Herb doctors Mrs. Ng and Mr. Liang mix a prescription of ancient Chinese remedies. (© 1992 *Harvey Wang*)

"Father thought of buying a house in Brooklyn, so we could have a back yard. 'Go yourself,' Mother said. 'I don't speak English.' She'd have been a prisoner. At least on Mott Street she could look out the window. What she enjoyed most was all the activity of the Catholic church across the street. They had baptisms, weddings, Sunday school—always activity to watch. In a country place, she wouldn't even have been able to speak to her neighbors. My father realized she was right. She couldn't even get out of the house to shop. She telephoned the orders to Father in the store, and a boy ran and did her shopping. People don't know anything about these matters now, because after 1912, when Sun Yat-sen overthrew the Manchus and established a republic, no one in her right mind would bind her feet. All the men cut their queues, too."

Peter Lee, Paul's father, is a mild-mannered man with a small frame, younger by a decade than his sister. One morning, as he watched over the store, he told me, "Until the 1940s, we were confined here. We couldn't buy a house outside. New York had no law against it, as some states did—it was just discrimination. Our father barely beat the Exclusion Act. He was twelve years old when he came over, as a coolie. Originally, the store was a purveyor to laundrymen— half the population here in the 1890s. There were supposed to be ten thousand laundries in the area. The laundrymen came in on Sundays, their one day off, for their supplies, including dried foods, soap, and Colgate toothpaste. We also shipped supplies to Chinese laundries around the country—buttons, laundry tickets, irons."

Lok B. Lee took over in 1894; he was chosen by the store's founders because he spoke English, his son said. He paid a thousand dollars to have his identification papers upgraded from coolie to merchant, and, with his higher status, he was exempt from the Exclusion Act—allowed to have a family and to travel to and from China. "My father's favorite story was that John D. Rockefeller taught him English," Peter Lee said. "About the time they were calling Rockefeller a robber baron, he came to Chinatown and taught Sunday school to five kids. My father was one of them. He was very ingenious. He was basically illiterate in Chinese, because he came here so young. He always carried a Bible and a *New York Times*. Two of the hardest things to practice your English on!"

Quong Yuen Shing's staff were shareholders in the store—the

Chinese way of forestalling jealousy and unions. "They paid two hundred or a thousand dollars per share, and received dividends from yearly profits," Lee explained. "All the stores were owned in this way by many shareholders."

American banks refused Chinese, so stores like Lee's acted as banks. "That's how they opened all these laundries—the stores lent money," Peter Lee went on. "This store helped Lees. Other stores helped other families. To open a laundry cost two thousand dollars. My father took no collateral. You told him what district in Canton you were from, and he'd lend you five hundred dollars at six percent, exactly like the bank, and you got the rest from relatives. Laundrymen deposited with him, too, like a credit association. They only spent for their everyday needs. The rest my father would bank, and, if they wanted, send it to their wives in China. It was a very lonely life for them. When they'd piled up a thousand or two thousand dollars, become rich men, they'd retire to China, because they had no wives here. We paid out two hundred and fifty thousand dollars over that counter." Lee pointed to an old wooden counter, over which mostly tickets to Atlantic City and entertainment events pass now. "We had just fifty thousand dollars in bad debt.

"My father was head of Chinatown's independents—on the outs with all the tongs. The tongs were putting too much pressure on him one time, so the police captain here got him a gun. He went to On Leong, pulled the gun on them, and demanded peace. The cops had the place surrounded, and I saw it and asked the captain what was going on. 'Your father's inside, making peace,' he said. 'He has no bullets in his gun and we put the safety catch on it!' My father was very stern— people were afraid of him. They called him 'Jesus' because he was a Baptist and didn't gamble."

Showing me an old piece of cloth covered with metal campaign buttons and medals, Peter Lee said, "Here are my father's medals. The Chinese-American Alliance raised a million dollars for the First World War. My father headed the fund drive here. We're really talking about laundrymen donating their savings—it's amazing they could raise that much. And they weren't even citizens! This yellow-and-red button, 'Bowl of Rice Party—Call to Arms,' must be from the thirties, when Japan invaded China and the United States wasn't getting involved. Chiang Kai-shek was *the* man here. Mao was from the west of China, and the Cantonese here naturally favored the Nationalists in the south, in Nanjing. We raised several million dollars for the Guomindang—because that was the only party we knew. Sun Yat-sen started the Guomindang, you know, and he lived at 10 Mott Street when he came to New York to raise funds for the 1911 Revolution. He went to all the Chinatowns—San Francisco, Honolulu. New York was then the smallest one, but we backed him up, and later we backed up Chiang Kai-shek, his successor.

"My father had two dreams: to send all of us to college, and to become an American citizen. He died a year before Chinese were granted citizenship. We were finally accepted, because the Japanese bombed Pearl Harbor and the U.S. allied with Chiang Kai-shek. Washington let Chinese in because we were allies. One hundred and five a year! My father never gave up on America. He bought a cemetery plot here. 'Don't you send my bones back to China,' he said. 'This is my country.'"

But, Peter Lee added, his father pushed him out of Chinatown. "The only reason I'm back here is that my son and I forced our way into this store. I had my own business until we came back and bought out the shareholders. I figured we had to protect our interests. See, my father said, 'Make your living outside.' People figured that their sons could make a better living with an American company—better pay and a pension, for example. That's why this is a first-generation community, unlike San Francisco, which is into its fifth and sixth generations—the first families kept it that way. They were always getting people from the other side to run the businesses, and pushing their children out. The children wanted to go. They remembered the cold tenements, the hall toilets—all the bad things."

The Chinatown that Peter Lee returned to in the seventies had changed radically since the 1940s. The racist immigration quotas had been lifted. The United States had diplomatic relations only with Taiwan, so immigration was largely from Taiwan and Hong Kong. Students who wanted to "drink Western ink" flowed in. Some of them, together with the sons and daughters of the laundrymen of the thirties and forties, formed the Asian-American movement. A radical movement inspired by the civil rights movement, it viewed all Asians as brothers and sought to liberate them from American racism. Young militants saw the Vietnam war as racist and were shocked that GIs couldn't distinguish politically between Vietcong and Vietnamese. Asian studies courses, and writers like Maxine Hong Kingston, for the first time examined American history from the point of view of Asian-Americans. Many assimilated Chinese moved back to Chinatown and organized Third World solidarity movements, storefront social service and political education programs, and food co-ops.

In New York in 1969, some leftists took the name I Wor Kuen—after the anti-Western paramilitary group that was prominent during the Boxer Rebellion—and shook up the community. In Chinatown, the Communist flag had not been raised since the fifties, when the United States began an embargo of goods from the People's Republic. Anti-Communist leagues, backed by the Guomindang, had made taboo even profession of loyalty to the People's Republic. Some residents had been deported during the McCarthy era for sympathizing with the enemy or sending money home, and families had lost touch with relatives in the mainland. In his book *The New Chinatown*, Peter Kwong explains how I Wor Kuen was the first to import movies from the People's Republic and sell Communist party magazines in Chinatown after the embargo was lifted. The group's members agitated for the establishment of diplomatic relations with the People's Republic and the dropping of recognition of Taiwan as the sole legitimate government of China. They demonstrated against tourist buses, denouncing tourists for ogling Chinese as though they were animals in a zoo. They charged the conservative elders with exploiting Chinese, ignoring social problems, and being Uncle Toms. And they organized the first unions among restaurant and construction workers, helping immigrants to resist the power of Chinatown's right-wing Cantonese old guard.

All this rubbed off on Paul Lee. In the seventies, before he became an actor, he was a social worker who counseled gang kids and advocated establishing diplomatic relations with the People's Republic. Lee and his father have a typically Chinese, strained father-son relationship. New immigrants would consider Paul Lee a *juk sheng* ("hollow as a bamboo pole")—one who betrayed Chinese culture. He cannot read or write Chinese, and embracing individualism inevitably brought him into conflict with his father. "We have an expression in China—a mountain cannot have two tigers," he said. "That tells the whole story. In Chinese culture, the old guys are revered when they get old. The modern Chinese aren't playing that, and the women aren't, either."

Paul Lee went on to explain, "Here, it isn't asked if you've done enough for your community. I used to be on the board of a social welfare agency, and people said, 'What? You're crazy.' It's asked if you've done enough for your family. My family's about ninety people—when you have taken care of your mother, your father, your wife's mother's father, your brothers, your sisters … The list goes on and on. If they come free of debts, they want me to buy them a house. As an American-born Chinese, I'd give them a one-time cash payment. I'd talk to my wife and determine the size of the payment. In my family's terms, I'm obligated. You're supposed to give freely and be happy. If I had a cousin on the other side getting married, I'd be supposed to raise her dowry. It's never okay to marry out of the Chinese family—don't let anyone tell you different.

"We used to be a little neighborhood. Chinatown is now an integral part of an international financial center—Hong Kong, Taiwan, Toronto. We may be small next to Japan, but we have a lot of big money moving around, and legitimate money. Chinese are into every field you can think of now. When I was a kid, I used to be pissed off that we were locked into math or science. I couldn't be in history or the arts or political science. Chinese want their children to be scholars or professionals. No one wanted me to be an actor. Gerald Tsai, the CEO of Primerica—that's awesome. Our self-image today is much better. I used to be a little store on Mott Street. Now I can dream in other areas. I was a consultant on *The Year of the Dragon*, and then MGM hired me to represent it. They put me up in the Beverly Wilshire, on Rodeo Drive. My customers couldn't care less about my film career. That's something I'm so proud of." Paul laughed, greatly amused.

"Hollywood stars could come here and be completely anonymous," he went on. "A vast, vast majority of Chinatown wouldn't know them. I bring the Chinese superstars here to perform in Atlantic City. For instance, Danny Chan, the singer. Roman Tam, the top performer in Hong Kong. Fifty dollars a head." Paul clapped his hands. "Our showtime is one A.M." He laughed again. "I get more for my tickets to these shows than Frank Sinatra gets. I'll tell you what this place is like. How many people do you know who would not want to work in a

Woody Allen movie? Nobody in Chinatown has ever heard of Woody Allen. I had to get some extras for his film *Alice* and I asked a room full of a hundred people. 'Please do me a favor.' Zero. The film people were, like, 'Don't they know this is a Woody Allen film? They should be happy to be in it!' I said, 'If you want them to be happy, don't tell them it's a Woody Allen film, tell them it's a film for that nice little man over there with glasses.'"

From Lee's store, I went to the Chinatown History Museum to see Charlie Chin, who, until recently, was its community education director. I asked Chin why second- and third-generation Chinese like Paul Lee call themselves Asians and wince at the term "Orientals." "'Oriental' is now considered to be almost a slur," Chin told me. "After the Asian-American movement, there was a wholesale clearing of racist terms. 'Oriental' is a Western point of reference: it means anything east of Jerusalem. But 'Asian' is the term people in Asia use to refer to themselves relative to each other. There have never been so many Asians in the United States as there are now. Although we're only three percent of the population nationwide, non-Asians feel quite threatened."

6

MYRIAD ASSOCIATIONS

The institutions that sprang up in the nineteenth century to protect Chinatown against American racism still dominate it and still isolate it. The family associations, more than forty strong, are the social fiber of the community. The Chinese-American Planning Council and other social service groups that came out of the Asian-American pride movement of the late sixties and seventies offer more sophisticated services—job training, legal advice, health care, day care, translation services—but the family associations remain influential because they provide the Chinese equivalent of Social Security, a system to care for members in distress and in old age.

The two largest family associations are those of the Chens and the Lees, and they are boisterous rivals. About twenty-five thousand Lees live in metropolitan New York, making their association, which is housed in a modern six-story white marble building on Mott Street, a power in Chinatown. The past president of Singapore and the current premier of the People's Republic are both Lees, and when government officials visit Chinatown, they all go to the association. M. B. Lee, its elder and a former president of the Chinese Consolidated Benevolent Association—the informal government of Chinatown—is a kingmaker who bridges old and new Chinatown.

The fifth floor of the Lee association's building is a modest place. There are tables with a few dilapidated chairs, which, on the afternoon I visited, were occupied by sleepy old men. One pretended to read a Chinese newspaper; one was motionless, ash accumulating on the end of his cigarette. Near a window flanked by some desiccated palm plants, a man blew dust off his desk before sitting down at it. The wall above him was papered with fluttering orange slips representing donations received from members at New Year's. Lee, a courtly sixty-six-year-old, came out of his office and invited me to sit down at one of the tables. He nodded toward the slips and said, "We get about sixteen thousand dollars each year, almost enough for general expenses. This is a clearing house. We can tell you where your cousins are. You new, you don't know, you come here. We locate them. We still occasionally settle disputes in the community. Also we chip in money to bury elders." Lee explained that since the founding of the People's Republic, the association no longer disinters the bones of members, in a ceremony called *jup gum*—"the picking of the gold"—and sends the remains, polished by professional bone polishers, to China for burial. That custom, which kept a dead person's ghost from sorrowing in an alien land, has faded because immigrants refuse to be buried in Communist soil. "If there is money left over from the collection, we send it to that person's relatives in China," Lee said. Unlike the Chens, the Lees do not have their own cemeteries, so every April, in observance of Qing Ming, the ancestor worship ceremony, Lees drive to municipal cemeteries to tend the graves of their relatives and pay their respects with offerings of food and ghost money. "If you don't do this before Easter, they may come out and give you trouble," Lee said. "You don't take care of them, of course they get upset." He smiled.

Lee is also the treasurer of the association's credit union. He explained that because many Chinese don't use banks and frequently underreport their income, they lack credit ratings and therefore often turn to their family association. Over the years, such funds have enabled many Chinese workers to become entrepreneurs without the aid of "outside" banks. "You look at these people's financial statement, you wouldn't give them a loan," Lee said. "Law is law—these guys don't look able to pay off the loan. We have this problem every year to explain to the examiners. They look at the books, and they say, 'Income so low, how come you make them the loan?' So I tell them, 'He makes more than the books.' Now, they accept that, because for last fourteen years, you look at our write-off of bad loans, and it is very low. You go to the bank and try to borrow, you have all that red tape. Here, I know the borrower and the guarantor."

A stylish young man in a leather jacket entered the room, followed by a young woman with teased hair and high heels. Lee explained, "This fellow is paying an installment on a twenty-thousand-dollar loan to start a car-courier service in Brooklyn. Car services are popular new business among Chinese. They serve the corporations and law offices, go Atlantic City. Most people borrow to open restaurant, garment factory, or for bridge loan. To open factory, cost you over one hundred thousand dollars. You buy the floor, renovate, put in heavy machinery. Initial investment is forty thousand to sixty thousand dollars. Rest is installment. And, of course, people need small amount of money, ten thousand to fifteen thousand dollars, to go back to China, Taiwan, or Hong Kong to get married. New immigrants go back for their sweethearts."

As of March 1991, the credit union had $5.78 million in assets. Last year, the fund made three hundred and twenty loans, totaling nearly $2 million. Since the fund began in 1965, it has made some twenty-three hundred loans, totaling $32 million and has charged off just over one percent of them as bad debts. This is a better record than other credit unions attached to district and family associations. In the 1970s the funds of three Chinatown associations were embezzled. The associations are tempting targets—many are very rich from rents received on buildings they own, and some allow gambling on their premises.

Accompanied by a Chinese friend, I visited Lung Kong Tin Yee, on Division Street. The name means the Four Brothers Association, but it is actually a multifamily organization, representing the Liu, Quan, Chang, and Chao families, whose ancestors, according to legend, made a famous pact in a peach garden about A.D. 200 in a vain attempt to save the Han dynasty from collapse. Ning Fun Quan, a formal, correct man in glasses, wearing a dark suit, who is one of four co-presidents of the association, led us up past the second floor, where there was a mah-jongg parlor, to the third floor. There, he unlocked a door and took us through an antechamber into an imposing room. A long, central table, like a banquet table, capable of seating fifty, dominated the room. Around the walls, thirty teak chairs with mother-of-pearl inlay on the arms were ranged side by side. Several men were seated at the enormous table, talking in Cantonese and flicking cigarette ashes into a large stone ashtray. Behind them bulked an elaborate, flag-decked golden shrine. On one wall, an oil painting showed the four ancestors who had made the long-ago pact; they were surrounding the Han emperor, clad in imperial yellow. On another wall, a giant black and white scroll proclaimed the four classic Chinese virtues: honesty, loyalty, kindness, bravery.

"I have never been up here. See, you are very special!" my friend exclaimed. "This is number one Chinese association, this is tops! You see this! I never knew they had such a beautiful room."

He deciphered the shrine for me. "This is patriarch shrine with titles of the ancestors and their emperor. This smaller altar in the middle on top is dedicated to their prime minister. Six hundred years ago, the Lung family allied with these families in Lung Kong, a place considered to have good *feng shui*." *Feng shui*, he explained, is a system of geomancy which takes into account the alignment of natural things in guiding life. "For instance, a particular arrangement of mountains, or rivers, creates good *feng shui*. But living across from a sharp angle on a roof in a city—that angle could be an arrow, and hurt you—bad *feng shui*. So, these families allied in a place with good *feng shui*. These candlesticks are Ming dynasty, made six hundred years ago. The carving in this shrine is very elaborate, well done. You see the lions, all the birds, the little gods. This carving is Qing dynasty, about ninety years old. Here, the paper scroll says, 'God and Men Are Happy and in Harmony.' The two scrolls on the left and right of the shrine say, 'The Emperor Is Respectful and the Statesmen Are Loyal, and Their Story Lasts Forever,' and 'The Elder Brothers Are Kind and the Youngest Brothers Are Righteous and Their Story Lasts Forever.' The Taiwan flag indicates support of this family association for the island."

"You notice," my friend whispered, "no women here, except in the mah-jongg club. This is a chauvinist society. It meets to greet every visitor from China and to support the Chinese Consolidated Benevolent Association."

"Our association more than one hundred years old," Quan told me proudly, in clipped English. "We are worldwide organization—

Singapore, Hong Kong, mainland China, Taiwan. Costs thirty dollars to join. Annual dues are optional—could give ten dollars. It's up to you. We have three thousand members in New York, and it's growing. Every night, we have free dinner. Old people, young people, come here and eat. Our members only. Every night, at least thirty people. Only pay a little bit for dishwashers. We got two cemeteries. Everybody donate money, and we fix them up nice. Any member without a family, we have to bury them. This is our brother. So we all put up money, one dollar okay, thousand dollars okay. Nobody ask you— whatever you can give. If not enough, the association gives the rest. We help each other—do whatever we can. Sometimes help find jobs. No longer lend members money. We still settle disputes. We decide what's right and wrong. Our word is law. But sometimes it can't be settled, sometimes members have to go to court. Not always easy." Depending on the crime, Quan added, the association might raise bail for a member in jail. He went on to say that, like all the associations in Chinatown, Lung Kong Tin Yee celebrates Chinese holidays—New Year's, the arrival of spring—with a traditional banquet in a restaurant. And it buses its members to the cemeteries for Qing Ming.

The Chinese Consolidated Benevolent Association, to which the majority of Chinatown's family associations, more than ten of its district associations, and three of its six tongs belong, is constantly fighting for leadership with the new guard—members of the younger generation who run the Chinese-American Planning Council and other social welfare agencies. The CCBA styles itself the supreme voice of Chinatown, though its word is no longer the absolute law it was a hundred years ago. It has not acted as a criminal court in many years, and its president, the unofficial mayor of Chinatown, is elected from one of two Cantonese associations that no longer represent most of the community. Nevertheless, the CCBA, which is housed in a building on Mott Street, in the heart of old Chinatown, still operates as a city hall. Politicians and journalists turn there whenever they need to know what Chinatown is thinking, and new immigrants who get lost are taken there. Many Chinese consider it retrograde because its leaders advise Chinese to preserve their culture and not assimilate.

The CCBA conducts all its proceedings in Chinese. It will not discuss its inner workings with outsiders or reveal how its members are chosen. Those are private matters; it is not a public organization, I was told repeatedly by its president, Paul Yee. Nor will it accept funding from outside sources, although it has made one exception—a grant from the city for a summer youth program. And it will not let in city-funded Asian-American associations, which criticize its conservatism, or such organizations central to the community as the International Ladies' Garment Workers' Union. The CCBA owns several buildings on Mott Street, and rent from five stores in these buildings provides an income of about $300,000 a year. It has only four full-time, paid staff members: the president, two secretaries—one bilingual in Chinese and English, and one Chinese-speaking—and a janitor. The CCBA runs the largest Chinese school in Chinatown, offering instruction in Chinese culture and language on afternoons and weekends, and an English school.

The CCBA's main purpose, however, is to promote Taiwan. It has been pro-Taiwan ever since 1949, when Chiang Kai-shek fled to the island after the Communist Revolution. Most of its members ally themselves politically with Taiwan. And Taiwan has a representative on the CCBA's executive council, whose seven permanent policymaking members also include delegates from three tongs (Hip Sing, On Leong, and Chih Kung); the Chinese Chamber of Commerce; and two district associations dominated by Taiwan's ruling party, the Guomindang. The president of the CCBA frequently doubles as a representative in Taiwan's legislative Yuan, or governing assembly, and other CCBA leaders, who are presidents of member associations, are also overseas members of the assembly. For voting in the legislative Yuan and promoting Taiwanese interests in Chinatown, they receive many benefits, including, it has been reported, salaries, free transportation to and from the island, apartments in Taipei, and monopolies on foodstuffs imported from Taiwan, such as mushrooms. The anomaly of American citizens voting in another country's assembly came about because Chiang Kai-shek held to the traditional notion that Chinese are Chinese first, no matter how many generations they have been citizens of another country. And Taiwan, unlike the People's Republic, allows dual citizenship.

To promote Taiwan, the CCBA throws an annual party for Chiang Kai-shek's birthday, and on October 10th, the day Sun Yat-sen declared the establishment of the Republic of China. "The Chinese

Community of New York celebrates the Double Ten Anniversary of the Founding of the Republic of China," the banner stretched over Bayard Street proclaimed several years ago. In the basement of the CCBA, about three hundred people, many of them senior citizens, waited patiently. The CCBA president led the *kiu lings,* or "big shots"—the heads of its major family associations—to reserved seats near the stage.

The stage was decorated with bunting, flowers, the American Stars and Stripes, and the white sun of Taiwan. Camera crews from Taiwanese television stations stood by, filming the proceedings for broadcast in Taiwan. They trained their cameras on several beauty queens in the audience wearing tiaras and capes.

A woman in a white rhinestone dress appeared onstage and belted out "The Star Spangled Banner" and the national anthem of Taiwan. The president of CCBA gave a brief welcoming address, followed by four or five city and state politicians who congratulated the community on seventy-eight years of Double Ten Days. A visiting state senator noted, "Chinese have the oldest civilization in the world and have nothing to prove to anybody because they've shown it in their illustrious history. If the world doesn't know, it's the world's fault, not the Chinese peoples' fault."

Then, a small, stooped, gray-haired man crept to the stage. George Young, one of the finest calligraphers in the country, read a long formal poem from Teng-hui Lee, the president of Taiwan. Some of the audience listened, but many people dozed. The back of the room was a ghetto of sleeping gray heads, nodding over miniature Taiwan flags tucked into shirt pockets.

Miss Republic of China was presented. She wore a collar of purple silk roses draped over a short black cocktail dress, and her hair was in a pageboy. Behind her, a chorus of two boys and ten girls in pretty cheongsam sang a popular song called "May Flower." A Chinatown newspaperman whispered to me, "This troupe—the Hawa-ha Goodwill Tour—is sent by Taiwan on a propaganda tour around the country. Many of these performers are pretty good—they have albums in Taiwan or are television entertainers. They go or else. They have no choice."

At the finale, the reigning Miss Republic of China crowned her successor to polite applause. The English-speaking secretary of the

CCBA, nodding approvingly, advised me, "People are here to show support for the Nationalist government because they're angry about the Beijing massacre." The newspaperman, his eyebrows ironically raised, shook his head. "They're here because they get free food," he whispered. "Secondly, because they're upset by Tiananmen Square."

The crowd waited as the *kiu lings* in the first two rows ate their lunch of pork rice, spare ribs, noodles, and bean cake desserts from Styrofoam bins. Then the senior citizens got their free lunch, and some said later there was a melee for the food.

The parade assembled on Mott Street, which was closed to traffic. The captain of the local precinct stood at the parade's head, along with the president of the CCBA. Behind them, a representative from Taiwan's informal embassy, the Coordination Council for North American Affairs in Washington, led the presidents of the pro-Taiwanese family and district associations, and tongs, including Ning Fun Quan from Lung Kong Tin Yee.

The rest of the parade consisted of small cohorts: one banner in red Chinese characters said, "The Freedom-Loving People of Hong Kong and Macao." It was held up by about ten men in jackets and red ties. A few waved small Taiwan flags. The delegation from the "Chinese Memorial Post No. 1291—Department of NY—American Legion" was dressed alike in caps, sport coats, blue pants, black raincoats. Behind, Chinese students wore masks of imprisoned Tiananmen Square student leaders. A female troupe waved banners identifying them as "The Republic of China Association of Amer. East." The "City Hall Senior Citizens Center—Chinese Golden Age Club, City of New York" were a motley bunch without banners or buttons, carrying plastic flags. A troupe of artists, costumed as elephants, tigers, acrobats, and Chinese maidens, brought up the rear, whirling and cavorting to the accompaniment of cymbals and drums.

Three stretch limos, driven by Italians, inched down Mott Street, and the parade began. A Chinese marching band played "Yankee Doodle Dandy" and "The Battle Hymn of the Republic." The Taiwanese beauty queens in fur-collared coats waved to the few waiters watching outside restaurants. A giant Statue of Liberty on stilts, carrying a lighted torch, lumbered ahead.

"Down with the Communist party of China," the paraders shouted as the drum corps passed the central bank of the People's

Republic of China on East Broadway. Employees on the sidewalk in front of the bank laughed at the jeering and the parade flowed past. "We have two Chinas," a shopkeeper told me. "The mainland and the island." A Buddhist monk in orange robes strolled by, unfazed.

"Get rid of the Communists!" paraders shouted in Cantonese along Pell Street. Merchants and shoppers leaned out of stores, applauding, and shouted back, "Get rid of the Communists!"

The parade wound down Canal Street and back into Mott Street. On the balcony of On Leong, several men in dark suits and dark glasses slowly waved Taiwanese flags. A white limo passed, and from its sun roof, the beauty queens blew kisses. "Celebrate the national day and down with Communism!" a speaker truck rolling behind them squawked. Later, in the evening, the Taiwan council, which acts as an unofficial embassy for the Republic of China, hosted a reception for a thousand people at the Vista Hotel.

Chinatown's leftists had celebrated a week earlier, on October 1st, the day when Mao Zedong declared the founding of the People's Republic. At its mission, the People's Republic had hosted a reception and, later, a banquet for eight hundred well-wishers in Chinatown. Both were attended by many members of Chinatown's new guard, second-generation liberals and leftists, most of them veterans of the Asian-American movement.

In the 1970s, when the United States moved toward establishing diplomatic relations with the People's Republic and dropping recognition of Taiwan, the two camps in Chinatown, pro-Taiwan and pro–People's Republic, battled in the streets. Some family and district associations broke ranks with the CCBA and flew the colors of the People's Republic. Conservative, pro-Taiwanese merchants became pragmatic and signed contracts with the People's Republic for merchandise. Those without good contracts in mainland China suffered. Now, so many members of the community depend on the People's Republic for their livelihood that the two camps are holding their fire, and most merchants cultivate both Taiwan and the mainland.

The Chinese-American Planning Council, with offices on the fringes of Chinatown, are derisively called the new guard Chuppies—Chinese yuppies—by some residents. Virginia Kee, one of the council's founders, outraged Chinatown when, in the 1960s, she broke the code of silence and argued that the community was a poverty zone, like Appalachia or Harlem, and needed assistance. Kee now sits with her back to the wall in public places so she can watch who comes in; like most reformers, she is fearful of gangs allied with the tongs that are members of the CCBA. "This was a community of old men," she says. "My mother couldn't stand near the window in the forties, because she'd have been thought a loose woman. The Second World War changed that—after it, we were allowed to be citizens. I do many things that challenge the establishment here. I realized in building the Chinese-American Planning Council, knocking on doors, that until we got political power no one would listen to us. We still have to educate each wave of immigrants. Where overseas did they ever get into the polls? They didn't vote in China or in Taiwan, and certainly not in Hong Kong."

Charles Wang, who is the president of the China Institute, an uptown center for Chinese culture and study, and was the executive director of the Chinese-American Planning Council, also blames the CCBA's leadership for isolating Chinatown. "This community, because of its early history—the fear and the racism—was reluctant to have anything to do with the outside," he said when I spoke with him at his office. "It was designed so that those in power at the CCBA were the go-betweens, and the rest of the people would have to rely on them. Outsiders didn't take much interest in us unless there was a gang war, and our leaders didn't want outsiders to know what was going on. Therefore, few articles were written about us, and no one knew about our problems. Partly, we are at fault. We are so quiet, we don't complain, and so we tend to get shortchanged. As more Chinese register to vote, and return census forms, more of us will be counted."

Most people in Chinatown aren't interested in American politics, and the neighborhood has only eight thousand registered voters. Only a quarter of them voted in the last mayoral election. But among the twelve thousand who in June 1989 marched in the rain to the United Nations to protest the crackdown in Tiananmen Square were many people who live in Chinatown; at that time, too, thousands boycotted a pro-Beijing Chinese-language newspaper in Chinatown that was funded by the People's Republic, forcing it to fold.

Among Chinatown's new guard, the feeling is growing that Chinatown must give up fighting Chinese politics and instead speak out, demand its fair share of federal funding, vote, join America. "Pro-

China or pro-Taiwan really split the people," says Lee association leader M. B. Lee. "We don't have to do this every day. First we need to get the rights." Businessman Sherman Lee agrees. "We should learn from the Jews," he urges. "Get the money first, get the political positions, and fight among ourselves later." Harold Ha, a jeweler and one of Chinatown's behind-the-scenes younger leaders, also expressed similar views. "The new generation is getting much more mixed with the U.S. culture," he told me. "Chinatown will be part of the city—not so isolated as before. Before, it was really, really isolated. Now it is more and more open. I hope it will become like San Francisco—more open, cleaner, prosperous." Miriam Friedlander, who represented Chinatown in the City Council from 1975 to 1991, also notices a difference. "The stereotype that Chinese are quiet and submissive has been broken by their own leadership," she said to me not long ago. "We're going to hear their demands for housing, for city services, for help against crime and gangs. The Hispanic community, as a contrast, is basically set. It is more advanced politically, and more a part of the American system. It has more people interrelated with speakers of English. But the Chinese are developing this now. Yes, the language barrier is more difficult. And inexperience is a factor. There is not one elected Chinese legislator in the entire state, for instance."

7

TONGS

The tongs are even stronger now than they were fifty years ago, and are doing their best to keep Chinatown isolated. They overwhelm the community, influencing every aspect of its life—business, politics, journalism, tourism. The reason is simple: some of their members sponsor crimes that terrorize and cow the community. Some crimes are the traditional ones—smuggling of aliens, prostitution, extortion, loan-sharking—but now, instead of smuggling opium, which faded around the Second World War, members of tongs import gargantuan quantities of heroin, generally through Bangkok or Hong Kong. Along with independent traffickers, they have in the last six years taken over from the Cosa Nostra the business of smuggling the drug.

The tongs' influence is pervasive partly because of their open structure: anyone who pays $30 can join a tong and will be inducted in an elaborate ritual that includes the burning of paper vows; chanting oaths before Gung Gong, the god of war; offering incense to the gods of hell; and swearing blood brotherhood to avenge all wrongs done to other members and to die before cooperating with police. Not all tong members are criminals, of course. Thousands of waiters, merchants, laundrymen, businessmen, seamen, garment factory workers, even journalists belong to tongs for the muscle to enforce their business deals, for protection, and for revenge: any member of a tong can call on a gang's services in a dispute. A tong member in trouble doesn't have to ask. He receives a telephone call. The message is simple. "Do you need help?" the voice says. A Chinatown elder explained why people join tongs: "You have so-called peace of mind. You think the tong is behind you. That's the psychological reason. You think also maybe it will help your business: You know more people, you will meet all the other members. As a member paying thirty-dollar dues a year, it's okay. But if the tongs tap you to become part of their hierarchy, then you have to deliver." One tong member told me, "When people look at me, they have more respect. The respect is fear." While it is true that tongs also do some good—for instance, they translate for new immigrants, sponsor the dragon dancers at New Year's, and sports leagues, and housing for some elderly—their crimes far exceed their beneficence. Their power is such that no one in Chinatown wants to discuss tongs—especially with outsiders.

Nearly all of the Chinatown tongs are national groups with chapters in cities throughout the United States, and each has tens of thousands of members. Their New York chapters are often the largest because New York has the largest Chinese community in the country. For the same reason, several tongs have their national headquarters in Chinatown. The top men in a tong (women are not permitted to join) are its board members and its elders—the wealthy and influential in a community. Board members are elected because they are prominent: they may own a large business, or give to charity, or simply have charisma. But power resides in a tong's elders and its presidents, whether or not they are important outside the tong.

The so-called godfather of Chinatown is Benny Ong. (His real name is Kai Sui Ong, which means Good Prophecy Ong.) He is the adviser-for-life of Hip Sing, Chinatown's most powerful tong. Ong is eighty-four years old, a thickset man with a sagging moonface and hands like square blocks. He is often called Uncle Seven, because he was his parents' seventh child. Born into a poor family in Harbin, he emigrated at age twelve, worked in a Chinatown laundry, and became a Hip Sing in the 1920s. He spent the years from 1935 to 1952 in jail for second-degree murder, and thereafter resumed active membership in Hip Sing, which was then under the presidency of his brother Sam. After Sam's death in 1974, Benny took over. He was jailed again briefly in 1977 and 1978, for bribing police and government officials;

in conversations recorded by investigators, he boasted that he was *the* payoff man in Chinatown and had numerous friends among district attorneys, police inspectors, and chiefs of detectives.

Hip Sing's big rival is On Leong, which has its headquarters in New York and is run by the national president, Wing Wah Chan, and the local president, Albert Moy. Tung On, headed by Clifford Wong, is a new group, with headquarters in Chinatown. In addition, there are the Chinese Freemasons, Chih Kung, and the Fukien American Association, run by Alex Lau; the last was formed in the early eighties by people from the Chinese province of Fujian, and is said by law enforcement officials to be heavily involved in heroin trafficking and the smuggling of aliens. It is pro–People's Republic, unlike the other tongs, which support Taiwan. Except for Chih Kung, each tong is affiliated with a gang, and it is the gangs—the equivalent of standing armies—that carry on the tongs' power struggles.

The tongs' turf is rigidly divided. Law enforcement officers assigned to cover Chinatown and others working on Asian crime have maps of Chinatown with streets colored to indicate tong control. Hip Sing controls Pell Street; On Leong controls Mott. A tong member on the wrong street is a provocation, just as it was in the 1890s, and a gang member ripping off another tong's gambling parlor still starts a war.

"Chinese invented the Mafia, and then Marco Polo took it to Italy and the Italians reinvented it," a Chinatown insider explained to me. "The tongs are the families—everyone knows who's a member. You don't want to cross them. Each has about fifty prominent members. Real bosses, about ten each. They post elected officers. If you're a Chan or an Eng, it's quite possible you belong to one of them. Chans or Chens are On Leong; Engs or Ongs are Hip Sing. The tongs run the gangs and the gambling houses, and they settle disputes in the old-fashioned way: you give me face, I'll give you face; if you don't listen to me, I'll break your face. Uncle Seven is the elder statesman of the underworld, but his power has been eroding for some time. He's from the previous generation, and many mavericks have been challenging the structure. Also, there are the Vietnamese gangs—the tongs have no control over them."

The Vietnamese gangs, new to Chinatown crime in the last few years, are greatly feared in the area; they are considered more violent and vicious than Chinese gangs, who hire them as muscle. They are mostly young refugees who have dropped out in frustration at being unable to learn English or have run away from foster homes. As refugees, they can't be deported. Members of the most notorious gang, Born to Kill, are often tattooed with the initials BTK above a coiled snake. Born to Kill has upset the longtime order of Chinatown organized crime because it is not backed by any tong and because its members speak dialects none of their victims understand, and prey on merchants who have already paid tongs anything from $50 to $1,000 a month in "lucky money," or protection money.

"It's chaotic now," Mrs. Kong, who owns a large family-run retail soybean business in the center of Chinatown, told me. "Different gangs come to store and ask for protection money. Usually, a store has to pay the tong, and then its gang doesn't bother them. But now the Vietnamese gang shakes the store down, and other gangs do, too."

Mrs. Kong's daughter Tina added, "We know a policeman who is more powerful than the gangs, so we don't pay. It depends on your business and who your friends are. We pay lucky money at New Year's, but it's nothing—fifty or a hundred dollars. Of course it's a bad problem. People is very afraid about it. To set up some business if they know no friends! I just try to protect our interest—not stop it. A lot of people complain, but they never do anything to stop it."

Another merchant told me, "It's cost of doing business here. Maybe one percent of places getting extorted are unhappy. It's status quo. I'm upset now because we're in first phase of disorganized crime. It's so serious it's terrifying. Those kids come in. We have no one to negotiate with. You can't b.s. your way out, or make a deal. This is new. In eighty years, this is new. We don't know who they are—it's not the same guys each time. We think it's free-lance kids. Vietnamese don't respect anybody. Things are changing."

This same merchant explained why he preferred the organized crime of the past, when gangs extorted weekly or monthly payments for themselves and the tongs with clockwork regularity: "If it's organized crime, and one wild kid says, 'I want to sell you an orange tree'—you know, extorting me, demanding a lot of money for the lucky New Year's plant—I say, 'Don't break my face, are you kidding?' I know the management of the tong that controls my street, its general, and its lieutenants. To save face, I'll complain to its second rung, not the top. The kid gets taken care of. If I have a really big problem, I go to see the top people: on Division Street, I go to see Clifford Wong. On Pell Street, I go to see Benny Ong. On Mott, I see Wing Wah Chan. I'm for tranquillity. I'm not looking for reform. I'm typical, I think. Chinese are the richest people on earth, you know. All these guys out there are getting rich. They don't view themselves as enslaved by gangs and associations. The IRS enslaves me, not the gangs."

Further complicating turf in Chinatown are several gangs from Queens—the Green Dragons and the White Tigers—which are allowed by Chinese gangs to operate on some streets and run some gambling parlors. Neither Queens gang is affiliated with a tong. But probably most feared in Chinatown are members of the Hong Kong triads, here in advance of China's takeover of the colony.

Crime is worsening in Chinatown. According to a study published in 1991 by Ko-lin Chin, a sociologist at Rutgers University, and two colleagues, eighty-one percent of the restaurants and two-thirds of all the businesses in Chinatown are victimized by gangs.

Everyone knows who the gang kids and the tong bosses are, but no one revolts and turns them in. Those who do make complaints won't testify in court. Few crimes are reported; fewer still go to trial. Police make cases only with great difficulty. A sergeant in the Fifth Precinct, which includes Chinatown, said, "Chinese don't cooperate—although the little they're doing now is better than the nothing they did before.

"Let me give you some examples," the sergeant, who spoke to me on the condition that he remain anonymous, went on. "Here's a double homicide that went down at four fifty-five P.M. on a warm afternoon at 277 Canal. All our witnesses are American. Canal Street is wall-to-wall people at five P.M.! And there were no Oriental witnesses? It took us a year and a half to find the guy—Lam Trang, a Vietnamese, Born to Kill. He shot two Chinese-Americans, sixteen-year-olds, Flying Dragons. It was a turf war. Trang jumped across the country. The Vietnamese have no roots—they jump from community to community.

"The situation with the Chinese is unique. I've had them come into the precinct house to do lineups, and look at the floor. They never cooperate in identifications when we go out canvassing. Off the top of my head, I can think of only one complainant who has gone to court for us. She's the only one.

"Here's another example. We had a witness in a homicide four years ago but she was so fearful of reprisals that it took us three weeks to get from her an identification of the suspect and then she moved away." The witness was a poor Burmese-Chinese woman, a cook in a restaurant, the sergeant said. "A Burmese guy strangles a twelve-year-old Chinese girl from down the hall in her building and stuffs the body in a sleeping bag in this woman's closet. She sees the body. The killer calls and says, 'I have something of mine in your closet, don't open it.' The woman is here illegally. He threatens to report her to Immigration. She's terrified and leaves the apartment to stay with a friend. Her building on Eldridge has no heat, so no one found the body for a while, and the Burmese guy eventually threw it out the window. The witness is an acquiescent type. She's used to being browbeaten. There is no women's lib in Burma, you know. She didn't report the crime.

"How many Americans do you feel if they found a body in their closet would not call the police?" the sergeant asked.

"They're funny people to deal with—they're used to having the government shoot criminals. That's how the Communists deal with them in China. The perpetrator isn't going to come back and haunt anyone. All the time, they ask when I say so-and-so is in jail for a few years, 'In jail for only two years?'

"Finally, we got an ID by appealing to this woman's religion. We got a former police commissioner from Burma to sit with her, we put Burmese music on, and he sat patting her hand. He told her, 'You're a Buddhist, you have to assist the police if you know something.' She actually jumped up and fell at our feet and started kissing our feet, saying, 'I understand.' The burden was off her—it was like repentance."

Nancy Ryan, the chief of the Trial Division in the Manhattan District Attorney's office—she is known in Chinatown as the Dragon Lady—adds, "In fifteen years, I have had less than two dozen merchants testify in open court. Not until 1983 did we have any civilian testify in a murder case. We had to arrest him to get him to court. And I've had just one civilian identify the murderer in a homicide. It's a very complicated problem—the Chinese are deeply frightened. They know there are armed thugs on the street and they can't have twenty-four-hour police protection. They don't understand our system, and they can't conceive of a system where cops know who the gang members are and let them roam the street, or a system where if someone is charged with a crime he's out on bail in a week. They don't trust public officials. Chinese have many proverbs that exhort people not to trust public officials. They come here with their shirts on their backs and their dreams, and they struggle in a way we can't conceive of, because we are too spoiled by affluence. I find it hard to imagine that anyone else in these very adverse circumstances would be more noble about testifying."

William Calhoun, who until the beginning of 1991 was the captain of the Fifth Precinct, added, "It's not 'Will there be retribution?' but 'When?' Ten years is not too long for Chinese to wait, I'm told. This community is faced with people bent on havoc. It's organized retribution."

In one of the latest instances, in the spring of 1990, a beauty shop worker and her boyfriend were murdered and their bodies dumped on an estate on Long Island. The woman, a former girlfriend of a gang leader, had testified five years earlier in a gang-related trial in Brooklyn.

"We go crazy with this stuff. We make the Sicilian vendetta look like nothing. We'll wait twenty years to get you back," says a young Chinese.

Chinatown has four Chinese-language daily newspapers, but most of them don't report such crimes. Journalism in Chinatown is a warped, submissive creature, as emasculated as it is in China. Journalists risk firings and death threats for reporting the news. Ying Chan, who has been one of Chinatown's most respected reporters and is now on the staff of the *Daily News*, told me, "There's no tradition of independent journalism in Chinatown—everyone is so scared. The papers represent political interests, which are tied to economic interests. You can't cover the tongs—we did the best we could. Every time we tested the limits, people got beat up. The gangs called me in the early 1980s and told me they were waiting for me on the street. In 1988, my publisher told me that Benny Ong had asked him to fire me and said he would give him thirty thousand dollars' worth of advertising." This sort of intimidation, Chan added, was standard practice in Chinatown. "The publisher didn't fire me—he asked me not to cover Chinatown. The unwritten rule is: No names of tong members or gang members. We print their English names, or use phonetic Chinese to confuse everyone, or give just their Chinese surnames. Or we blank the name out—it's standard to put 'XXX' for a witness's name."

In 1978, Hsin Yuan Cheng, then a Chinatown columnist, was badly beaten on the street one night by five young men. He is sure he was attacked because he wrote so many stories about the community. "At that time, I am young, and I try to correct everything," Cheng told me. In 1984, a member of Hip Sing's gang, the Flying Dragons, walked into the Chinatown office of the editor of *Sing Tao Jih Pao*, a large Hong Kong–funded daily, and demanded at gunpoint that a reporter who had written about a dispute over an extortion be taken off the story. She was. In 1987, the now-defunct *Center Daily News* dropped its coverage of a landlord-tenant dispute involving the gangs when its reporter was harassed. In 1989, a reporter from *Sing Tao* did not observe the unwritten rule and wrote up the testimony of an On Leong boss in a murder trial. The reporter was fired but was rehired after he apologized personally to the On Leong boss and the paper, in abject apology, sent the tong a roast pig, a traditional offering of respect. A Chinese TV reporter who shot footage of an On Leong gambling joint in the late eighties was told he would be killed if the story was shown.

Another incident that occurred outside Chinatown still has a chilling effect on news gathering in Chinatown. In 1984, San Francisco journalist Henry Liu was murdered after finishing a critical biography of Chiang Ching-kuo, the son of Chiang Kai-shek, who was then Taiwan's president. A United States federal appeals court, upholding the sentences of ten members of United Bamboo, a Chinese gang from Taiwan, called the murder a political assassination. The court ruled that the international boss of United Bamboo had flown to San Francisco "so as to be able to provide Taiwanese government officials with support here in the event that those officials needed to flee their country and be safeguarded in the United States ... Additionally, at the suggestion of Taiwanese officials," the boss "planned to murder Henry Liu, a Chinese journalist who had become an American citizen, because he was considered to be a traitor to Taiwan. In addition to eliminating Henry Liu and silencing his critical writing, the murder was designed to serve as a warning to others in the United States whose acts were considered subversive to the interests of officials in Taiwan. . . . In return for his efforts to develop the United Bamboo gang as a base for putative fleeing Taiwanese officials, and for the murder of Henry Liu, [the boss] and the United Bamboo gang were to receive 4 billion Taiwanese dollars as well as political patronage, protection and prestige in Taiwan."

A reporter for the *Center Daily News* in San Francisco, who wrote an accurate story suggesting that the murder was ordered by Taiwan intelligence agents tied to the president of Taiwan, was transferred. So was her editor. Other reporters who might have investigated the connection between certain tongs, gangs, and Taiwan did not take up the gauntlet.

Peter Lee, a Chinatown journalist, pointed out, "If an American journalist was censored, there'd be outrage. Here, the community says we shouldn't have written that story. It's in Chinese culture to be careful of what you say, not to humiliate someone in public, to avoid confrontation. This is why tongs threaten us so freely. As the tongs see it, they have a legitimate beef when we cover them or print their names. It's a vicious cycle. The longer people tolerate this, the less freedom they have." Perhaps having second thoughts himself about talking to an outsider, Lee added, "If one day you read that Peter Lee is found dead somewhere, you can pretty much draw the conclusion that I have a big mouth. I'm only half joking. I know there is that possibility. I hope the Justice Department and the FBI will open an investigation into censorship and infringement of the First Amendment in Chinatown."

Quo Chen, a Taiwanese reporter who has worked in Chinatown, doubts whether anyone will ever do "the inner story" of the tongs and the gangs. "The damage would be too great—the dirt would be spread on everyone's head," he told me. "I mean community leaders. It's a nasty statement, but it's true. This is such a small community. We meet each other every day. No way to escape, no way. Suppose you are a publisher, you know someone who is a good friend of a tong member who's doing drug trafficking, prostitution. Because you write about it, take sides, you may lose money. Take my former paper, which comes out as a weekly in New York and as a daily in Taipei. It has enough money and manpower to investigate the tongs and the gangs—why doesn't it? Let me put it this way: these things are not a significant disease. Some of the tong members traffic in drugs, some launder money, but what is their relation to one another? We don't know. And we are not that interested in finding out. 'You have your way to survive, I have my way'—that's the dialogue among Chinese. You may belong to a tong, but I do not. I understand you, and you understand why I don't see you as a criminal—your acts don't hurt my interests."

Additionally, some Chinese see tongs as legitimate, even admirable, because they provided financial backing for Sun Yat-sen's 1911 Revolution and then for the Guomindang. Chiang Kai-shek used triads, secret criminal societies on which the tongs were modeled, to assist the Nationalists in the civil war against the Communists. After 1949, many triad members fled with him to Taiwan. Others formed the underworld in Hong Kong, maintaining ties to their American cousins, the tongs. "It would take a dissertation to explain the admiration for these people," Quo Chen says. "They're not looked down on: they're always against the government, which in Chinese history is always corrupt. The connection between the Guomindang and the gangs has its source in Sun Yat-sen. In a feudal society, to make a revolution you have to have organizational power and the triads—also called the Green Gangs—were it. So you see it in the government. In China and Taiwan, they say, 'You are in the black way, the dark root.' That means gangs. Now, Uncle Seven, tongs, overseas Chinese—all are attached to the Guomindang. It's nasty but it's understandable if you know our history."

"Tongs have shut down journalism in Chinatown," another journalist told me. "You can say that. I can't, it's too dangerous."

One story the Chinatown press stayed away from was a bitter dispute several years ago between City Hall and the CCBA. In the early eighties, Mayor Edward Koch had proposed an addition to the Manhattan Detention Complex, known as the Tombs, a prison on the western edge of Chinatown. The community rose against it. As a compromise, housing for the elderly and several shops were added to the proposed addition. Representatives from the community, including the CCBA and the Chinese-American Planning Council, were elected to the board of a corporation overseeing the construction and management of the addition. When the CCBA arranged the election of several tong members to the board, howls of protest from the Chinese-American Planning Council and other board members reached Richard Mei, Jr., an adviser on Asian affairs to Mayor Koch. Mei led a fight to remove the tong members.

Mei told the Koch administration in a memo that the city could no longer support the project if the tongs remained members. Mei recalls, "We were afraid that they'd control the community space in the project or charge rent or protection money. Also, we had some fear that they'd monopolize the selection of tenants. One of the problems is that it has always been very difficult to gather evidence against the tongs." The city tried to shame the tongs off the board, saying that the CCBA had elected "unacceptable" members, including some associated with organized crime. Manhattan District Attorney Robert Morgenthau read the riot act, charging that the police believed that the tongs were connected to youth gangs that served as enforcers for criminals controlling gambling, drug dealing, and extortion in Chinatown. "Ridiculous," the CCBA responded, in the *New York Times*. There had been fighting among the tongs' youth "groups," it admitted, but "now all that has changed." Benny Ong shot back, also in the *Times*, that the CCBA "will not lower its head to this evil" or "tolerate this type of defamation."

The city won on a technicality—it took the CCBA to court for stacking the board. Richard Mei, who is now with the State Department, said, "I was vilified in the Chinese press. They said I was a yellow dog and a traitor to the community. The CCBA put a notice on its door banning me from its premises." The project is finally going forward after years of delay.

Another subject that Chinatown journalists have avoided is the tightening of the tongs' control over the CCBA itself. The tongs have long been able to dominate the CCBA through its executive council, but until recently a gentlemen's agreement barred them from electing one of their members president. In February 1990, however, Benny Ong, the Hip Sing elder, and Wing Yeung Chan, the former national president of the rival On Leong, shocked Chinatown by voting as a bloc at the CCBA's annual election. "It's time for a change," Uncle Seven said. "All the past presidents have been corrupt. None of them have spoken English." He proposed raising the president's salary and extending his term from a year to two years. A former president of the

New York City chapter of On Leong nominated a former president of the New York City chapter of Hip Sing. This nomination was seconded by the national president of another tong, the Chinese Freemasons. Wing Yeung Chan nominated Paul Yee, a businessman close to On Leong, and Yee's nomination was seconded by the national president of Hip Sing. Several hours later, the other candidate withdrew, citing "health reasons," and the CCBA, over the objections of its outgoing president, who reminded members that they weren't permitted to vote on only one candidate, elected Yee.

A Chinatown reporter observed, "It was the first time these rival tongs cooperated and endorsed the same candidate and forced him down our throats. Usually, they don't cooperate and no one votes for their candidates. The *World Journal*"—one of Chinatown's newspapers—"and *Sing Tao* sanitized and glamorized the election and said it was great for Chinatown. That is ridiculous. You have a puppet handpicked by the Chinese Mafia running the CCBA, Chinatown's governing body. Imagine if the mayor of New York was handpicked by John Gotti!"

After the election, journalist Ying Chan noted, "Everyone knows there is a story here—but it's hands off. People don't want to get into trouble."

Within a few months of the election, Benny Ong flexed his muscle over CCBA. He proposed expelling twenty-four members of the organization, thereby eliminating many of the staunchest supporters of Taiwan. Paul Yee called a general meeting without the twenty-four members that Ong wanted expelled, and the motion passed. Once again, breaking precedent, On Leong and Hip Sing voted for the explosive change. Much later, after threats of litigation by the ousted members, Uncle Seven withdrew his proposal. "In the CCBA, who has the right to expel any members?" one representative fumed. "It is almost the twenty-first century in the United States and we have this dictator! You look at the Mafia in the 1890s, and they ran over their own people. It's the same here. But what can you do?"

8
—
POLICE TOUR

Chinatown's police, most of whom are white, have their own view of the area and its crime. To get a sense of how the tongs divide up their turf, I accompanied police officer Mike Wagner on his rounds. Wagner, a bachelor in his late thirties with a ruddy face, strawberry-blond hair, and a mustache, worked in gang intelligence in the Fifth Precinct for five and a half years, and is now a sergeant in another precinct. We were starting a week later than we had planned, because the previous week a businessman had been kidnapped by one of the gangs, and Wagner's unit had had to go out searching for him. Wagner's sergeant, Michael Collins, told me, "It happens down here. It was a business deal gone sour. His partners called the tongs and arranged for the gangs to get him."

From the front seat of an unmarked Chevrolet, the community, with its jagged neon signs, looked seedy and dangerous. We passed the headquarters of On Leong ("Peaceful and Virtuous Association"), and drove slowly down Mott Street. "There's Number 66," Wagner said. "Down there, in the basement, that's On Leong's gambling place. It's thirteen-card and *pai gow*. See that white piece of paper on the door? It says *hoi p'ei*, or 'open skin'—it means open for business. The skin is the surface of the tables. Number 63, another On Leong joint, was padlocked by the Police Department's public morals squad, and it never opened up again.

"It's crazy here," Wagner went on. "These people strangle each other. Factories pay lucky money. Even the ones on the third floor pay. But to arrest for extortion we need a threat of violence. The gangs know that. So they say, 'My brother needs fifty dollars,' with no direct threats."

We turned up Bayard Street toward the Bowery. "This all belongs to the Ghost Shadows gang," Wagner said. "Mott is controlled by one of its factions, Bayard by another. They do extortions, robberies, and some kidnappings and homicides."

A 1988 Justice Department report on Asian organized crime says: "The Ghost Shadows gang is attached to the On Leong Tong ... Money from gang extortions, a traditional source of revenue, still flows up to the Tong leadership and is subsequently redistributed according to existing agreements. In many respects, however, the Shadows is an independent organization that works with, rather than for, the On Leong Tong ... Members of the Shadows are known to work as mid-level heroin couriers, travelling frequently to Toronto, Boston, Chicago, New Orleans and Miami. At least some heroin distribution occurs in collaboration with New York and Chicago LCN [La Cosa Nostra] families."

As we drove down Pell Street, a narrow passage through overhanging tenements, our car practically brushed the restaurants lining the sidewalk. "That's Number 9—a Hip Sing gambling parlor," Wagner said, pointing to a nondescript entrance. "It's open two eight-hour shifts a day. Uncle Seven's cut from that is a hundred and thirty thousand dollars per month, an informant told us. Might not be gospel." Wagner slowed the car in front of the Chung Shing Tea Parlor, a Flying Dragons hangout. A gang member in jeans and a parka, a street boss, came outside and greeted him. Inside, about fifteen *sai low*—"little brothers," as gang members are called in street slang—played video games.

The Justice Department report: "There are three powerful Tongs in New York: Hip Sing, On Leong, and Tung On. The leadership of each is believed to be controlled by [Chinese organized-crime] figures ... Formal leadership of the Hip Sing is a complex arrangement of co-presidents, chief officers, executive staff, coordinators, external relations and assorted administrators. Informally, the power resides in Hip Sing's 'Advisor-in-Chief for Life' ... Benny Ong ... The Flying Dragon Gang ... is attached to the Hip Sing Tong. During the last three years, the Dragons have recruited heavily among Vietnamese youths who now comprise about one-quarter of the … gang members. The Dragons operate from Pell and Doyers Streets in Chinatown and are reported to have branches in other major cities, including Dallas, Houston, Atlanta and Washington, D.C."

On Division Street, opposite the statue of Confucius put up by Chinatown's right wing, Wagner showed me the Tung On headquarters, a three-story brick building. "This association has ties to the Sun Yee On triad, over in Hong Kong," he said. "That's the biggest triad in Hong Kong. The triads are banned in Hong Kong, you know. Tung On brought back some twenty-five-year-olds from Sun Yee On to guard its gambling houses. The street gang, the younger kids, do the robberies and shootings." Clifford Wong, the handsome, dynamic thirty-nine-year-old leader of Tung On, Chinatown's third most powerful tong, is known as a "legitimate" businessman. In 1989, the New Jersey Division of Casino Gaming Enforcement revoked Wong's "junket license" to bus gamblers to Atlantic City, charging that Wong was an organized crime leader. A year later, it banned him from the tables. Wong's brother Steven, who is known as Tiger Boy and is the leader of Tung On's gang, was convicted on federal narcotics charges three years ago.

"On this corner here, at the head of Catherine Street, is the Tsung Tsin Association, one of Chinatown's wealthiest businessmen's groups," Wagner told me. "The winner of its election is easily moved, shall we say, by Clifford Wong. Number 1 Catherine and Number 1 Division are the same building, and in the basement is the Tsung Tsin gambling house—two shifts, noon to eight P.M., and eight P.M. to four A.M., a multimillion-dollar business any given time. All the houses are."

Going down East Broadway, Wagner said, "This is Tung On turf— used to be a Jewish neighborhood. Number 7, here, is a Fujianese gambling house occasionally." Farther on, he pointed out an unlit, five-foot-long neon sign running down the side of a building: THE GOLDEN STAR BAR, it said. "They used to call it Grandpa's—that was the owner's nickname. There was a shoot-out there in 1982. The restaurant never reopened." I knew the story, which is famous in Chinatown. Herbert Liu, an immigrant from Hong Kong, defected from Hip Sing and, with backing from the Chinese Freemasons, challenged Benny Ong's power. The challenge ended when four masked men carrying automatic weapons walked into the Golden Star Bar, a Freemasons hangout, and opened fire, killing three diners and wounding eight. Liu accused Benny Ong of ordering the shootings. Freemasons surrounded Hip Sing and briefly took over Pell Street. Liu held a press conference. Benny Ong said nothing. Several weeks later, he told a reporter from *New York* magazine: "Sixty year I build up respect and he think he knock me down in one day?" Liu apologized to Benny Ong, and Hip Sing then took control of the Freemasons.

Wagner pulled up in front of Number 65 East Broadway, one of Chinatown's many merchants' associations. We watched a woman hurry to the door, glance around furtively, be buzzed in, look up at a mirror in the hallway ceiling, and be buzzed through a second door into the gambling parlor. A second later, a man entered the same way.

As we drove under the Manhattan Bridge into the Wild West of Chinatown, where few people were about, Wagner said, "Down here, when a gang comes in, it tries to show its power and do a lot of extortions and robberies. When you see a GRAND OPENING sign, it's only a matter of time before the store gets an extortion. The going rate here for a grand-opening extortion is three hundred and sixty dollars. Protection money is divisible by threes and sixes. And eight is lucky. It could be a thousand and eighty dollars—three times three hundred and sixty. Anything divisible by three, they like. But never four itself— the number four means death in triad numerology."

The Fukien American Association, Wagner told me, has its headquarters at 125 East Broadway. Two stone lions out front scare away demons. "Their territory is Forsyth, Eldridge, and Grand streets," Wagner explained. "The top guys in their gang, the Fuk Ching, are heavy into importing heroin. In the last five years seems like almost all heroin in the country goes through New York City." We headed up Eldridge Street, which looked especially shabby. "Three Mountain Association is another Fujian tong. Here's their gambling spot, Number 7. During the summer, they were so blatant. They'd open the door for air and there'd be a whole shitload of them in there. I guess there are about half a dozen permanent gambling spots in Chinatown—a lot less than there used to be.

"A lot of parents save their children from the gangs by sending them back to Hong Kong or the mainland to live with their grandparents. We know of three in the last month. We tell parents we can't babysit their kids—eventually, they're going to get locked up or dead.

Immigrants are the ones with the runaways. The American-born Chinese, the wife stays home with the kids. You can't blame the new immigrants—they work so hard. The mother works eight to eight in a garment factory, the father works twelve to twelve in a restaurant, and who's home when the kids are? We had one runaway whose mother and father live in Brooklyn. They told me they put him in Chinatown in his grandmother's apartment. Come on! Everyone puts it over on Grandma!"

Wagner pointed out the window as we swung down Mott again. "See that?" he said. "Those two bullet holes in the back of the pay phone? That was an ambush of Ghost Shadows by some Flying Dragons, but Born to Kill is our worst problem. The Vietnamese came here five, six years ago and opened up the malls on Canal Street. That was the only place they could go; old Chinatown is full up. Vietnamese are a problem in every major city—Houston, Washington, Philadelphia. Everywhere, there's a problem with them hitting Oriental jewelry stores. They also rip off the Chinese elders because they know the elders won't report the crimes. Our robberies were going sky-high. Now it seems like the shootings between BTK and the Dragons for being on each other's turf are slowing, and the shootings are for other reasons—drugs, mostly.

"We're seeing a lot of old gang members coming back, hanging out on the street, vying for the leadership of the Dragons. They don't fight—they have their followings on show and let Sidney Ko look them over. He's the *dai low*—the intermediary between the gangs and Uncle Seven. Eventually, Benny Ong decides who's the boss."

Cruising down Baxter Street past the Tombs, Wagner yelled, "Hey, wait a minute!" and braked before two men in their twenties wearing black jackets and punk haircuts. "What's up?" he said, rolling down the window. "How's everything? What are you doing here?"

"Visiting my father," one said. Wagner waited till they walked away and then grabbed my notebook, noted the license plate number on a car disappearing up the street, and jumped out of the car to find a pay phone to call the precinct.

"They're old gang members come back," he said when he returned.

On our way up Bayard Street, we passed a number of stores shuttered with heavy metal screens. "See those big expensive locks on the gates?" Wagner said. "The gangs Krazy Glue 'em if the stores don't pay."

We cruised by the Pell Street tea parlor again. "Look at 'em all in there, they're all Dragons," he said in amazement. "Twenty, twenty-five Dragons. The Chinese gangs have taken in a lot of Vietnamese for muscle. Vietnamese are crazies. They shoot anyone the gangs want."

The next time I saw Mike Wagner was amid bedlam at Chinese New Year—the Year of the Horse. Plumes of smoke rose from Mott Street, visible for blocks. Even underground in the moving subway, one could hear the firecrackers and smell the brimstone.

All of Chinatown had spent the night up, banqueting on choicest delicacies—shark fin, pressed duck, dried oysters—and exchanging visits and gifts. Today the dragons were out, five tackling different sections of town so all the new Chinese could be included.

The dragons worked hard. In Chinese cosmology, the dragons are the symbol of beneficence: they guard the gods' treasures, do their bidding, and drive away the evil spirits for the New Year. On Mulberry Street, two dragons gyrated back and forth before the Sun Chung Lee supermarket. The owner and his staff watched them kneel before an overturned plastic milk carton and take off a red envelope—a gift of money—and an orange, the good-luck fruit of the New Year. Then there was terrible, terrible gut-shaking thunder as a seven-foot-long string of firecrackers hanging before the store detonated. All the spectators put their fingers in their ears. A group of Chinese Freemasons kept the crowds away from a black cart, in which several young men beat drums. The cart, pushed by several Freemasons, followed behind the dragons, making a din. Inside the dragons, teenagers, also Freemasons schooled by kung fu masters to imitate the soul of the dragon, worked themselves into a frenzy.

Mott Street was insanity. People stood on fire escapes, firecrackers exploded, and smoke billowed. The end of the block was obscured by the thick smoke. Boys with punk haircuts clanged cymbals; from store to store the dragon hopped; the firecrackers went off; children on balconies cringed. The drumbeat became more wild. People on sidewalks and stoops laughed and snapped pictures.

Firecrackers ahead and firecrackers behind. Big bombs. Chinese with shreds of red paper in their black hair. "It's like a war!" a tourist exclaimed. The dragon danced among the firecrackers going off around his feet, enveloping him in smoke. He blessed each store and brought luck. All over Chinatown blue and green and black dragons danced.

Pell Street was forbidding—an alley without sunlight of neon signs advertising restaurants. Cold dark street of empty restaurants.

The dragon made its way up the street. People carrying oranges shuffled behind the dragon in the red curled firecracker shreds blanketing the street. No one noticed a man in a doorway. The hood of his sweatshirt was pulled down on his forehead, hiding his face, and he focused a telephoto lens on the Chung Shing Tea Parlor at a bevy of *sai lows*.

Children danced in and out of popping firecrackers, cowering, giggling, with fingers in their ears. "Wee-hee-hee," said a Chinese man in delight. I ducked into a door for refuge and watched the firecrackers that rose in the air and dropped to the street and hopped, like frogs, turning red, pink, and yellow.

The dragon whirled by. Stepping back into its wake, I passed the photographer and nodded. "Those kids are so young," I whispered to Wagner.

"Yeah, but for face, they'll shoot you," he said, and snapped another surveillance shot.

In the crowd, hidden in the smoke, Wagner's partner memorized faces.

THE CHINESE CONNECTION

PART TWO

9

ONTO CHINA WHITE

People who know Chinatown have different ways of explaining why the tongs, which were relatively quiet after the 1930s, when a series of tong wars ended, have had a resurgence since 1965. The most common explanation is that the new immigrants flooding Chinatown since the change in immigration laws gave the tongs new life: more people meant more gamblers, and the tongs needed muscle to watch the pots. "We don't have Wells Fargo to watch the money, so tongs hired kids," one resident said. "The kids rapidly outgrew the tongs. Now the tail wags the dog."

Nancy Ryan, who began working in Chinatown in 1976, after graduating from Yale Law School, is, as much as anyone, a historian of the gangs. She has prosecuted more of their members than anyone in the city, and her version of gang history confirms the conventional wisdom. "People who were made gang members in the seventies tell me very similar stories," she said. "They were twelve-, thirteen-, fourteen-year-olds, new immigrants from Hong Kong. They didn't know English, their parents were off working, they could look forward to rising to the level of waiter, maybe, or being a garment worker forever, and they were being picked on by other ethnic groups. At first, they banded together for self-protection, no heavy artillery. Then they began associating with an older group—men doing a lot of robberies. They got bolder and acquired guns from elders in the tongs, and claimed territories. In the early seventies, we had a lot of gang warfare—kids facing off across city thoroughfares and just shooting madly. Somehow, around that time, in a way that's not clear to me, they took up with the tongs. The relationship is symbiotic. The gangs use the tongs to enhance their own prestige. They also make money collecting payoffs from the tongs' gambling houses and acting as lookouts for the police. The tongs protect the gangs and use them to enhance their prestige, because the gangs inspire terror.

"There were a lot of drugs in the early seventies in Chinatown, and the story I got was that On Leong was not happy with the drug trafficking of the gang that controlled Mott Street then—the White Eagles—so in 1974, it replaced them with the Ghost Shadows. A lot of the Ghost Shadows and the Flying Dragons are members of the tongs. Hip Sing denies it, but that's a lot of nonsense—the gang's activities can be traced to the tong."

In the mid-seventies, Ryan went on, the gangs grew more independent, graduating to organized crime, and extortions and robberies, on their own. "The stores paid without hesitation," she said. Then she broke off to tell me about Eddie Chan, who ran On Leong in the late seventies and early eighties. A former staff sergeant in the Hong Kong police department, he had left Hong Kong, along with some forty other policemen, in the early seventies, during an investigation of corruption in the department. Chan was said to have made millions from illegal activities by then. He arrived in New York in 1975, opened a jade and antique store, and rapidly acquired a funeral parlor and interests in a chain of movie theaters, several restaurants, a gold exchange, and a Hong Kong commodities company. He engaged the services of Michael Nussbaum, a New York political consultant, who introduced him to senators and congressmen. Chan was called Fast Eddie by the police, for his swift ascent to the national presidency of On Leong.

By the late seventies, crime and gang warfare had become rampant in Chinatown. Alarmed by the situation, the New York Police Department authorized a group of detectives to investigate Asian crime. The group, which became known as the Jade Squad, was led by Sergeant James A. McVeety, who retired in 1990 after thirty-three years of police work. The squad was given jurisdiction to work anywhere in the city, and began making inroads into Chinatown. Those inroads led to the first federal prosecution of a Chinatown gang.

"In 1984, we indicted twenty-five Ghost Shadows for racketeering," Ryan told me. The case had its beginnings with an anonymous tip indicating that a white woman whose body was dumped in the precinct in 1982 had been killed by the gang.

"The detectives went out with photos of the victim and asked a group of kids on Mott Street if they'd seen her," McVeety said. "Our informant was with them. He noticed one kid shy away, and later he asked him why. He said, 'Because we killed her.'"

Ryan, who prosecuted the case, recalled, "They picked the victim up in a bar, and she went to one of their apartments, not knowing they were Ghost Shadows. She had sex with one of them. Gang apartments, by the way, are little pigpens. They are filled with hundreds of take-out Chinese food cartons, cigarettes, trash. The rest of the gang came up to the apartment, and she refused to have sex with the others. One of them rushed at her with a cleaver. Eventually, seven raped her, then they sat around playing a kid's game—rock, paper, scissors—to decide who was going to kill her. They left their lighters around the body, providing a flickering light. It turned out that gang rape was not uncommon."

The same informant helped the Jade Squad and Ryan develop the 1984 case. The Ghost Shadows were charged with eighty-five crimes, spanning more than a decade—among them thirteen murders, forty-three acts involving murders, nine acts involving extortion, and two acts involving briberies. The investigators tape-recorded two extortions; negotiations between a gang leader and a gambling house about money; and a gang-initiation ceremony. A government summary of the charges alleged that proceeds from crime were used for "lawyers' fees, bail money, and other legal expenses; entertainment, meals, and spending money for the 'kids' ... and—of critical importance—gang apartments and guns." It also described recruitment tactics: in schoolyards, for example, teenagers were beaten by gang members while others recited the advantages of membership—girls, money, cars.

Among the eighty-five alleged crimes were the abduction and murder of a rival gang member; the extortion of $2,000 from Eddie Chan when he was new to Chinatown, even though Chan signaled through placement of chopsticks, salt, sugar, and other table implements that he was a triad member; the robbery of $30,000 and an equivalent amount of shark fin from a store with the cooperation of its owner; and the gangland abduction and murder of two students who happened to be strolling down Mott Street.

Somehow, Eddie Chan got away; he left the country secretly about a month after the indictment of On Leong's gang was made public in 1985. "We were trying to develop a case against him," Manhattan District Attorney Robert Morgenthau told me. Three months before Chan fled, the President's Commission on Organized Crime had identified him as the leader of organized crime in Chinatown. A rumor spread that he was going to be arrested, and in the space of a few days Chinatown depositors withdrew $6 million from the United Oriental Bank, in which Chan was a major shareholder. By the time Chan disappeared, he had become a prominent Asian-American spokesman, feting politicians at banquets, testifying before Congress, lobbying for larger immigration quotas, contributing to Ronald Reagan's 1984 reelection campaign and to the campaigns of local Democrats, among them Donald Manes, Geraldine Ferraro, and Mario Biaggi.

With Chan's rout, and with half the Ghost Shadows in prison—all twenty-one who were caught pleaded guilty—Hip Sing was riding high in the mid-eighties. Around that time Robert Stutman, then the head of the Drug Enforcement Administration in New York, grew concerned about the rise in purity of heroin on the Lower East Side, in Harlem, and in the Bronx. China White, a variety of heroin whose street purity is as high as 100 percent, was inundating the streets. The drug comes from the Golden Triangle, the area where Laos, Burma, and Thailand meet, and makes its way to Chinatown through Hong Kong—the Chinese Connection. "We were missing the boat—we knew nothing about Chinese traffickers and their organizations," Stutman told me. "I requested an agent. We were very lucky. Richard LaMagna, our agent, happened to be fluent in Chinese—one of the real experts in the country on China. I asked him to form a group and find out what was going on."

Police around the country were coping with an increase in Chinese crime and had begun to wonder about the involvement of the gangs, which exist in every city with a Chinatown and in some other cities as well; the tongs, which have chapters in many cities; and certain other international criminal groups—Big Circle, for instance, a

Chinese gang in Hong Kong with a branch in New York City, and the Wah Ching, one of the most powerful Asian organized crime groups on the West Coast, headquartered in San Francisco, with ties to several triads in Hong Kong. The feeling grew that these organizations were in some way interrelated and that the new wave of crime was the doing of groups as methodical and dangerous as the Mafia.

The realization was a decade late, federal authorities now acknowledge. In the 1970s, New York, like most other cities, had only token Chinese in its police department: in 1978, out of twenty-four thousand six hundred officers, fewer than twenty were not white, black, or Hispanic. Chinese didn't sign up—"No good Chinese join the army or the police," an old Chinese adage has it—and police departments made no effort to recruit them. (Even now, uniformed officers who are not white, black, or Hispanic make up less than one percent of New York's police force.) Without Chinese-speaking police, authorities couldn't possibly understand Chinese criminals. China has nearly two thousand dialects—three hundred in Guangdong Province alone—and Chinese names are confusing. Chinese have a family name and two given names, and all three are necessary to identify someone. But, since classic Chinese has only a hundred surnames, the same names recur in millions of combinations. And they are pronounced differently in Chinese and written differently in English depending on the dialect: Ng (or Ong or Eng), a Cantonese name, is Wu (or Woo) in Mandarin, and Ngoo in Fujianese, for example. Police departments were mystified by all this, especially since they couldn't find translators. "If the suspects switched to Fujianese on you—forget it," one New York policeman said. But the overriding reason that the feds were lost was that understanding and controlling Chinese crime had never been a priority. In the seventies, the FBI and the DEA were busy learning Sicilian and investigating the Cosa Nostra, and in the eighties they were fighting the crack epidemic. And non-Chinese police obviously couldn't go undercover in Chinatown.

Not until the mid-eighties, when Chinese began selling heroin outside Chinatown to other ethnic groups, could a few cases be made—mostly by Italian and other white cops, aided by the smattering of Chinese detectives who had been added by then to the force. But in the last five years, thanks to the task force that Richard La-Magna supervised at the DEA, the number of cases has soared. Connections between Chinatown gangs and Asian crime networks and Hong Kong triads have been exposed by LaMagna's pioneering group, called Group 41, and by prosecutors in the New York Eastern District, who have made national reputations as the first to prosecute a "new" crime.

The connections began to surface when a Chinese woman tried to haul picture frames stuffed with heroin through customs at Kennedy Airport in 1986. One hundred and sixty-five pounds of heroin and a million dollars in cash were discovered at the airport in December 1987. A few months later, an equally large bust took place. Then, in March 1988, Group 41 nabbed its number one drug fugitive, Johnny Kon, in a New York City hotel. Kon, one of the largest heroin traffickers in the world, lived in Hong Kong and owned $20 million of real estate in the United States, a watch company in Paraguay, and a fur company and many trading companies in Hong Kong. He was charged with smuggling eight hundred pounds of heroin into the country concealed in ice buckets, T-shirts, and vases. "I've never seen LaMagna's eyes light up as much as when Johnny Kon came through this office," recalled Charles Rose, the former head of the Eastern District's organized crime and drug enforcement task force, who is now the district's executive assistant United States Attorney. "He knew Kon and had worked on him a long time." Then King Man Lai, another major Hong Kong smuggler, drove too fast on an upstate New York thruway and was stopped by a twenty-two-year-old state trooper who'd never seen a Chinese before. But he'd seen cash, and there was too much of it, he thought, in boxes in the car's back seat—about half a million dollars. The trooper remembered having heard a talk by LaMagna about Chinese organized crime and called Group 41 in New York. "We gutzed our way through that one," said Rose. "We had nothing on Lai. We called Hong Kong over the weekend and built a case against him." In another case, a Thai police general, the former head of Thailand's SWAT team, was convicted of drug trafficking.

Group 41's cases have involved a staggering sixty-five hundred pounds of China White shipped through New York City since 1987— enough to last America's estimated five hundred thousand heroin addicts a year and a half. "We believe the impetus is 1997, Hong Kong reverting to China," says Rose. "We see many people trying to get their goods and money out of Hong Kong before the Chinese take over."

❈   ❈   ❈

Not long ago, I went to the DEA's offices on West Fifty-seventh Street to find out what Group 41 thought about the extent to which Chinese organized crime now controlled the heroin trade. Several agents there and LaMagna's successor, Al Gourley, filled me in.

The veteran of the group, a man in his fifties with a diffident manner, said, "In the early eighties, the Sicilians brokered heroin. No longer. Opium production in the Golden Triangle has doubled, and the Chinese have jumped in with both feet.

"Here it is in a nutshell," he continued. "The opium is grown in the Golden Triangle, mostly in Burma, and production is booming. Chinese there sell it to Chinese brokers in Bangkok or Hong Kong, and they deal with Chinese in Chinatown. That's the Chinese Connection. The usual route is from Bangkok trawler to Hong Kong trawler to Hong Kong speedboat to the harbor."

Al Gourley interrupted to say, "But it also can be transited through Vietnam, Malaysia, Singapore, the Philippines, and—this is new—the People's Republic. It's from ninety to a hundred percent pure. Street heroin used to be five or ten percent pure. You had to mainline it to get a high. This stuff is generally cut to thirty or fifty percent pure on the street. It's lethal. We're very worried because it's so pure you can smoke it. That's going to addict a lot more people because they don't have to worry about getting AIDS from injecting it. Smokable heroin is widely used in Asia."

The veteran said, "We're getting killed on mail parcels."

"The gang kids wait in an empty apartment, sign for the package, and leave," Gourley explained.

"The new guys in this are Fujianese," the veteran noted. "And Big Circle people. Boy, they're wackos. They're carry-overs from the Cultural Revolution—former student or cadre leaders. They got out of China and in Hong Kong went from robberies to drugs. They're worldwide now, and their members belong to triads."

"Tell her about the ethnic discount," Gourley directed.

The one Chinese agent present said, "From Chinese to Chinese, heroin is one price—between sixty and eighty-five thousand dollars a unit. That's one and a half pounds. If Chinese sell to Dominican or Puerto Rican distributors, it's between eighty-five thousand and a hundred and forty thousand dollars. Dominicans are the major buyers in this city."

"We've had the rubber case," said Gourley, "the umbrella case, the bean-sprout case—the stuff in that one was hidden inside the cylinders of machines that wash bean sprouts. Most of these cases involved large quantities—a few of them eight hundred pounds and up. Years ago, you were King Shit if you imported two hundred pounds of heroin. The largest seizure in the French Connection"—the heroin-smuggling route from Turkey to New York via Marseilles—"was only two hundred and twenty pounds."

The veteran: "We've found people working in kitchens in Chinatown, where you don't ordinarily make much money, who have little ruby-and-diamond Christmas presents and three or four thousand dollars in their pockets. They invest in the jewelry stores. The stores launder the money back to Hong Kong."

Gourley: "The most common means of money laundering is to have couriers carry the cash on planes. A person can carry as much as a million dollars. One suitcase holds half a million. Money is heavy—they use hundred-dollar bills if they can. Or they 'Smurf' it back—send it in money orders under ten thousand dollars, the limit for reporting to the government. Smurfs are ... what the hell are Smurfs?"

No one in the group knew exactly. Little gnomes, someone said. The chief nodded. "Yeah, gnomes who go to the bank to deposit the cash."

The veteran: "Normally, gamblers with debts become the couriers."

Gourley: "The approach of 1997 is flushing out the animals. A lot of the traffickers are triad members, but the public has got it wrong—triads don't run this business. It's not like the Mafia. Some of their members traffic, but when they do it's their own show. They have no obligation to kick their profits up to a godfather." He looked glum. "The traffickers run to Taiwan. We have no extradition treaty with Taiwan."

The veteran: "Taiwan has fugitives from all over Southeast Asia. As a matter of course, it doesn't turn anybody over."

10

ONIONHEAD OF THE FLYING DRAGONS

When Group 41 started, it picked as targets eight or nine top heroin dealers in Chinatown, among them Johnny Eng. Also known as Onionhead and Machine Gun Johnny, Eng had taken over Hip Sing's Flying Dragons in 1983, after its leader was murdered. He traveled often to Hong Kong, and authorities suspected he was smuggling heroin. Eng, who was chunky for a Chinese, wore aviator glasses and a mustache. A self-possessed man in his mid-thirties, he greeted cops by name on the street and held to the code of silence. Shot in a robbery attempt while carrying a bag of cash to buy a restaurant once, he refused to cooperate with police.

In the winter of 1986, Robert Lee, who runs the Asian American Arts Centre, an art gallery and dance studio occupying a loft on the third floor of 26 Bowery, knew nothing of Group 41's objectives, and in some ways that was fortunate, considering the nightmare events that followed the day when his landlord, one of the last Jewish landlords in Chinatown, introduced Lee to representatives of his new landlord—three casually dressed Chinese men in their twenties and thirties. They invited Lee to a restaurant, where two other men and a young woman joined them. "This is Johnny," one said. The man named Johnny sized Lee up without saying anything while the others made their pitch: They asked him to move his arts center—which was also his home—from 26 Bowery to a building they owned on Mott Street, where the rent would be the same. They explained that they planned to open a fancy Hong Kong–style restaurant on the two floors below the loft that Lee and his wife, a choreographer named Eleanor Yung, occupied, and that they needed the loft for the restaurant's banquet room. Lee said that he couldn't decide.

Later, a stranger called, and said that his name was Ngarn and that he represented the new landlord. Lee asked for proof that this new landlord owned 26 Bowery and the property on Mott Street. Ngarn came to a meeting at the loft. Lee and his wife demanded to know the name of their new landlord, but all Ngarn said was that unless they vacated their loft they might run into trouble on the streets. "I'm a good guy," Ngarn said, "but the landlord is bad-tempered and is associated with the Pell Street Boys"—another name for the Flying Dragons. He told Lee, "You sat next to their leader— Onionhead, Johnny Eng, the biggest gang leader in Chinatown—at the restaurant several weeks ago."

"We were then very frightened," Lee told me.

Nonetheless, Lee refused to move. Ngarn offered him $250,000 if he would vacate and persuade the other tenants to do so, or $80,000 if he would get rid of the fourth-floor tenants and move upstairs. Ngarn would not talk to the tenants himself, Lee noted, because they were *low faan,* and he dealt only with Chinese.

Eleanor Yung told the New York City Loft Board later, when she and her husband filed a complaint against their landlord for harassment, that they were in a difficult position. "To have accepted the offer would mean that we would have to begin associating with Hip Sing, and we would have to bring gifts to Uncle Benny," she testified. "And then we would be in their hierarchy of operation, we would have to listen to them." But, she said, she and her husband were trapped. "I couldn't turn it down immediately, because we were afraid it would backfire and they would set the gangs on us."

Friends urged them to resist. Their lawyer told them to forget it— they were up against Chinatown's biggest gang leader. Lee thought of people who had resisted: the lady who tips the ducks in a Catherine Street restaurant had picked up her cleaver and chased a gang when it tried to extort lucky money from her; the owner of another restaurant had held a press conference rather than give in to extortion. Those were the only two resisters Lee could think of who were still alive. He and his wife nevertheless decided to resist. Ngarn informed them that their landlord, still unnamed, would do things his way.

Soon after Lee and his wife announced their decision, construction began on the restaurant and odd things happened: the hall lights went off; the hot water functioned only sporadically; and one day the façade of the building was gone, the arts center exposed. The lights were still not working when the restaurant opened the following winter, and Lee and Yung had no intercom and no mailbox. By that time, they had lost two-thirds of their students, and Yung had done no choreographing for the season.

In the pictures of the restaurant's New Year's opening party that were published in Chinatown papers, Lee recognized one of the men he'd met a year earlier. He was a thin, goggle-eyed man, identified as Shu Yan Eng, the owner of 26 Bowery. Lee remembered that Shu Yan Eng had sat next to Johnny Eng and had said very little.

A couple of weeks later, a man from Hip Sing paid a visit to Lee's father, a retired laundryman who lives in Chinatown. Telling me this part of the story, Lee lost his composure and covered his eyes to wipe away tears. He explained that, though his surname was Lee, his father was one of Chinatown's many "paper sons" who had entered the country with false papers, and that his actual surname was Eng. "My father has lived in the United States since he was thirteen," Lee said. "He was part of the all-male Bachelor Society. The men went back to China once in twenty years to see their wives and make them pregnant. My father still has his old friends, though there are fewer of them each year. They hang out in the back of barbershops, continuing their calm existence. This man visited him and said, 'Tell your son that everything is okay—okay to take his time, look for another place to move to, and we'll help him move.' My father is an Eng. Hip Sing is an Eng society, you see—this man came on behalf of the tong. They said, 'Oh, he's an Eng, let's be nice.' I had no way to protect him. My father didn't feel threatened—he was trying to help me, passing on the message. This man was his old chummy. They had now made it clear to me that they knew my father and where he hangs out. By this I knew they were threatening the life of my father."

Shortly after the visit to his father, Lee broke Chinatown's code of silence and reached out to the white world for help. He held a press conference and accused his landlord, Shu Yan Eng, of using the gangs to intimidate him into vacating his loft. The *Daily News* covered the conference, but the one Chinatown paper that sent a reporter stopped investigating the story when the reporter was threatened. Rumors spread that Lee and his wife were obstructing business, and merchants' contributions to their arts organization dropped.

In the spring of 1988, Lee and Yung began testifying before the Loft Board in their case against Shu Yan Eng. The case pivoted on Johnny Eng—who he was, and whether he was threatening the couple. Shu Yan Eng's lawyer bore down: Had his client ever threatened Lee? Had Johnny Eng? Had Hip Sing? No, not directly, Lee had to admit. The lawyer suggested that Onionhead was a term of ridicule for Lee, not the name of any person present at the restaurant meeting in the winter of 1986. And he forced Lee to concede that 26 Bowery wasn't his sole residence—the Lees occasionally shared a nearby apartment with a relative. "You've lost the case," Lee's lawyer told him. "You can bring a suit only if 26 Bowery is your home."

As Lee struggled to make the hearing officer understand how dangerous a threat involving Onionhead was, Johnny Eng, unbeknownst to Lee, had fled Chinatown, leaving the Flying Dragons in disarray. His sub-boss, Michael Yu, had been arrested on narcotics charges and Eng feared he'd be next. According to affidavits filed later by the government for Eng's extradition, Yu's downfall was a result of gambling.

Yu's girlfriend, Wah Tom Lee, loved to gamble. She was often found at the parlors on Pell Street that Yu ran for Johnny Eng and Hip Sing. Her debts rose into the thousands of dollars. At Eng's suggestion, she earned $50,000 by arranging for two friends to pick up heroin brought by Eng's couriers from Hong Kong to a washroom at Kennedy Airport. Several months later, Eng asked her to find people in Chinatown willing to receive packages mailed from Hong Kong. Inside each package, among tea and toys, spices and peppers, was at least fifteen pounds of heroin. For the first delivery, Wah Tom Lee earned $30,000 and the receiver earned $20,000. More packages arrived and more profits were collected. Yu and Wah Tom Lee sold some of the heroin themselves and made even greater profits. In September 1987, together with some friends, they flew to Hong Kong with about $600,000 of profits in their suitcases for Johnny Eng. In appreciation, Eng treated the couple and one of their friends to five days at Club Med in Indonesia.

Customs and DEA agents intercepted the eighth package and

arrested Yu and Wah Tom Lee on March 1, 1988. The heroin that they and their friends had received was valued at some $48 million to $64 million.

That fall, Robert Lee pressed his complaint again, this time with a new lawyer and an expert witness to identify Johnny Eng. Peter Kwong, a Taiwanese immigrant who is a professor at the State University of New York at Old Westbury and the author of several highly regarded books on Chinatown, explained to the Loft Board that the Hip Sing tong was "an organization in some ways similar to the Mafia," which intimidates Chinatown with violence. "Either you move out of Chinatown, don't do business in Chinatown, or you basically shut up," he testified. "The code of silence is that it's understood we resolve things within Chinatown."

A year later, with the complaint still not settled, Lee one day looked up and saw five United States marshals in bulletproof vests running through his loft with guns drawn. They had arrested the landlord Shu Yan Eng for heroin trafficking, they announced, and were confiscating the building. One of them told Lee to send his rent checks to George Bush. "Bush has his problems, but at least he's fair," he said.

"It was like the cavalry coming to rescue us from our tormentors—absolutely surreal," Lee told me two months after the government took over his building. Lee is aware that revenge for resisting the gangs could come at any time, but he is not leaving Chinatown. "We love this community," he says.

Shu Yan Eng was recently acquitted of the narcotics charges, but he was sentenced to three years for tax evasion and is appealing. The Loft Board found him guilty of four counts of intimidation, performing renovation without notice, interference with tenant's business, and failure to provide adequate safety at 26 Bowery, and fined him $4,000. Johnny Eng, who is charged with buying heroin from Shu Yan Eng and also with smuggling several hundred pounds of heroin himself, has been extradited from Hong Kong and will be tried in 1992. In a related case in Boston, four people, some of them members of the Chinese Freemasons, the tong controlled by Hip Sing, pled guilty to laundering more than a million dollars of drug and gambling profits from New York and Chicago for Johnny Eng after he fled Chinatown. Eng is expected to stand trial in that case, as well as a third, a narcotics charge in New York. Prosecutors are hoping that Eng, in the face of these multiple charges, will cooperate and provide the break they need to assemble a racketeering case against Hip Sing on a gamut of charges, including heroin smuggling. "It comes down to whether we can ever show that Johnny Eng had to pay grace money to Uncle Seven," one United States Attorney told me, referring to profits from crimes.

A Chinatown elder confides, "The next two or three years will be the worst, until a successor to Uncle Seven is chosen."

11

PETER WOO AND THE RICO INDICTMENT OF THE ON LEONG TONG

As prosecutors go after Johnny Eng, one link in the Chinese Connection has been broken: Tai Pei Liquors, at 53 Mott Street in the heart of Chinatown, is gone. The sign has been removed, the stock sold, and drygoods have replaced the overpriced liquor. Peter Woo, who was its owner, is gone, too, awaiting sentencing for his part in what at the time was the largest heroin haul in United States history—eight hundred and twenty pounds, worth a billion dollars on the street. It was this case, more than any other, that alerted authorities to the rise of a new Chinese Mafia.

Woo was also part of Bachelor Society Chinatown, the community of men who grew up together in the thirties and early forties without Chinese women, knew one another's business, feuded and traded with one another, and slowly took over the positions of power in Chinatown's family associations and tongs. Woo, a man of medium height, with a round stomach, had an aura of self-satisfied bonhomie. After he began to grow bald, he wore a cap with a little brim, like a Greek fisherman's cap. He looked as though the world were his oyster, and for many years it was.

Woo came to this country from Guangdong Province in the 1930s. During the Second World War, he fought in the Asian Theater. When he returned to New York, he became conspicuous in Chinatown: he was a leading shrimp and lobster wholesaler, a landlord, and a restaurateur, and he had contacts with City Hall. Because he spoke English, he was one of the few who could operate outside Chinatown. "Woo was the first Chinatown person to become involved in politics," a resident who had known him for many years told me. "He was very important from 1950 to 1965. He knew everyone in city politics. He got a lot of things for the Chinese community—jobs, and help from City Hall—without receiving any pay. He just built up his reputation."

Woo cultivated several New York mayors, starting with Robert Wagner in the fifties, and in 1960 turned out the Chinese vote for John F. Kennedy. Woo reportedly ran a gambling parlor in the American Legion hall in Chinatown. The Chinatown Democratic Club, which Woo started in the basement of his liquor store, doubled as a gambling hall and made him a millionaire in the sixties. Some said he paid off City Hall to make sure his gambling joint was the only one in Chinatown at the time. But he was so tightfisted that the lion dancers, who bless each store at New Year's, could get little money from his store. Estranged from his wife, he lived for a time with an actress from Hong Kong. He traveled often to the racetrack, to Las Vegas, and to the Far East. At nightclubs in Hong Kong, he was introduced as a big shot—the worldwide head of the Eng Association (Eng is his surname in Cantonese), and an overseas political leader who had been recognized by President Jimmy Carter for his contribution to the American Legion.

In the late seventies and early eighties, however, Woo seemed to be semiretired. He became strangely inconspicuous, though he still spent hours at the liquor store, most of them on the phone. Then, toward the end of 1987, a Chinese immigrant from Hong Kong, a thirty-seven-year-old importer-exporter, gambler, and kung fu expert named Simon Au Yeung, walked into the FBI office in Chicago with a tale that was of great interest to the agents there. Au Yeung said he had spent a small fortune to infiltrate the operations of top Southeast Asian traffickers. The names he dropped were all Group 41 targets— among them Eddie Chan, the former On Leong boss, who had been a fugitive in Asia since 1985, and King Man Lai, the major Hong Kong heroin trafficker.

The FBI knew far less than Group 41 about Chinese traffickers. It had started later, and found Chinatowns nearly impenetrable. Only once had an Asian citizen volunteered to go undercover in an FBI investigation. "The Asian community is so tight-lipped," I was told by Jules Bonavolonta, a former assistant special agent in charge of the organized crime and drugs divisions of the FBI in New York. "There's an ethnic code of silence, the way there was with the Italians for years. Au Yeung's offer to go undercover was virtually unprecedented."

Robert Shaw, the head of the Asian crime squad in the FBI's Chicago office, said, "Usually, working a case, you're at the lower or middle levels, reaching for the top. Au Yeung's information put us at the top immediately." To the FBI, Simon Au Yeung was a godsend—a Chinese Rambo.

Au Yeung told the FBI that the drug dealers had asked him to join their operations and use the Taiwanese import-export company he headed to smuggle heroin into the United States. He said he had met Eddie Chan at an international meeting of On Leong in Taipei in 1986, and Chan had liked him enough to have him introduced to King Man Lai. Au Yeung and Lai had gambled together, and one night in Manila, Au Yeung recalled, Lai had lost $750,000 in a single hand. Au Yeung also said he'd gone on shopping expeditions with Eddie Chan for presents to give Taipei bar girls. To cultivate Chan further, Au Yeung said, he'd given him twelve bottles of rare Louis XIII cognac, which cost $600 a bottle, and a Xerox machine. The FBI, which had been investigating links between the Cosa Nostra and the tongs, was also interested to hear about a "juice" loan—a street term for money lent by a loan shark—that Au Yeung had received from a Chicago member of On Leong who was known to collect "street taxes" (protection money) in Chinatown for the Chicago mob. In September 1987, Au Yeung got a second juice loan, of $50,000. Au Yeung told the FBI he had planned to use this money to buy drugs and further ingratiate himself with the drug dealers, but had then lost it gambling in Hong Kong with them.

By the time Au Yeung turned up with his improbable tale, he had spent seventeen increasingly disillusioned years in Chicago. The son of a Hong Kong merchant, he had come to the United States on a student visa, hoping for a college education and a better life. Instead, when his student visa lapsed he became an illegal alien, surviving by working as a bartender, busboy, and waiter while studying off and on at the University of Illinois. Somewhat later, he had founded a kung fu association and had managed several well-known Chicago restaurants. Au Yeung was apparently not new to the FBI: for four years, he had reportedly been a free-lance informer for its foreign counter-intelligence unit, which monitors espionage in the United States, and had provided information about Taiwan's political activities in Chicago. (The FBI will not comment on this.) Although the FBI's Asian crime unit did not entirely know what to make of Au Yeung (for one thing, he had a minor criminal record), the bureau decided that his information checked out, so it gave him a contract, for $2,500 a month, to gather evidence against Chinese traffickers. As part of the investigation, the FBI made payments on Au Yeung's juice loan.

The first person Au Yeung got in touch with was Peter Woo, to whom he had been referred by an old army buddy and Eng cousin of Woo's—the Chicago loan shark. When Woo sold Au Yeung a pound of ninety-two-percent-pure China White for the bargain price of $35,000, the FBI took notice. "The amount and the purity were a clue that Woo had connections to a source in the Golden Triangle," Shaw explained, and Bonavolonta added, "We knew we had something big."

"At this time, I don't think Woo is a biggie," Au Yeung told me in January 1990. "He's an old-timer. He likes to brag a lot. He's kind of broke. He doesn't have the potential to buy cheap and sell dear. His aim is to get a commission from each sale, maybe three thousand dollars a transaction."

Au Yeung was right and wrong about Woo. Woo was often broke, but he was a hub in the Chinese Connection—a broker who brought Asian sellers and American buyers together. Occasionally, he bought a small amount of a shipment himself, and to sell it he turned to his partner, a meat market owner two doors from Tai Pei Liquors. "Don't distribute through Chinese or the tongs, especially not Hip Sing and Johnny Eng," Woo warned his new customer, Au Yeung. "Uncle Seven may be a stoolie. Sell only to blacks and Italians."

For months, the FBI tailed Woo, to and from the OTB in Chatham Square, where he bet daily, and Atlantic City, and the racetrack, and it listened in on a wiretap of the liquor store phone as he made deals in code with Chinese suppliers in Singapore, Hong Kong, and many cities in the United States and Canada. Charles Butera, a New York police detective who, with FBI supervisory special agent Geoffrey Doyle, was in charge of the case, told me, "Woo was a wheeler-dealer, always looking for a way to make a buck. He did legitimate deals, too, bringing people together for his wholesale seafood business. He'd mix the truth with lies to better his position, or to make a buck. He played both ends against the middle, constantly. As he got the money, he'd gamble it away. Sometimes he spent it before it came in. He was always meeting with people. People in Chinatown respected him and went to him for help. Every afternoon, when he walked back from the OTB after checking on his bets, people would stop him in the street to ask for his advice. He always had a smile." The FBI also tailed Woo to Little Italy and Staten Island for meetings with Mafia associates.

After months of waiting for more heroin, the FBI began to wonder if Woo was a dead end. Gradually, agents listening in on the wiretap realized Woo never had more because he owed $70,000 to a Hong Kong supplier who refused to deal with him until he repaid his debt. To gain time, Woo for months mixed truth with lies, telling Au Yeung that the next shipment was his, telling the supplier that he would repay him shortly. In an opera buffo played out on international phone lines, agents heard Woo explode in fury when he learned that his meat market partner had double-crossed him and had pocketed the $70,000 that Woo owed the supplier in Hong Kong. Woo, partner, and supplier quickly fell out: Woo threatened to hunt down his partner; the supplier threatened to kill Woo. "You were being followed," he accused Woo angrily after an aborted deal. "You are crazy," Woo countered. "I am just an ordinary person. Nothing on me."

After Woo partly repaid his debt, he flew to Hong Kong, where he again promised Au Yeung more heroin. But instead, Woo's partner offered Au Yeung "domestic ginseng," explaining that he was out of "imported stuff." The ginseng turned out to be cocaine, and the FBI rounded up several buyers and twenty-two kilos.

Then, in late August 1988, the investigation took a decisive turn. Woo suddenly suggested that Au Yeung meet his new supplier in Hong Kong. Once again, the FBI flew Au Yeung to Hong Kong. The small, skinny young man with the mark of the unicorn—a large mole between his eyebrows, considered good luck by some Buddhists—who knocked on Au Yeung's door in the Excelsior Hotel introduced himself as Hok Pang Chan. Over dinner and later at a massage parlor, Au Yeung and he compared vouchers in Hong Kong's underworld. Au

Yeung's was impeccable: He was vetted by the formidable King Man Lai and another major heroin trafficker, an old friend from high school. "Chan doesn't say very much," Au Yeung recalled. "He thinks slow. You can see him use his brain. He's very watchful, very cautious."

After verifying Au Yeung's credentials, Chan offered to do business. He said that he was planning to hide a small amount of heroin on a United Airlines flight from Bangkok to San Francisco and asked Au Yeung to remove the cache when the plane left San Francisco. If the plan succeeded, Chan said he would use it a second time, adding that he and his boss had smuggled over four hundred and fifty pounds of heroin into the United States in 1987—about half the amount the Drug Enforcement Administration had seized that entire year.

The FBI scrambled to learn about this new face. Hong Kong police began a check of Chan's phone records, and, secretly, Au Yeung checked with acquaintances in Hong Kong's triads. At the same time, Au Yeung bought heroin from another man, Chuk Ling Leung, who was a regular supplier of Woo's partner.

When Au Yeung contacted his new business partner again, Hok Pang Chan said that the airplane smuggling scheme was off, but he would still sell heroin to Au Yeung. The following day, Au Yeung tried to settle the deal, but Chan denied knowing anything about it and, enraged, retorted that he did not deal in drugs.

Before the FBI could sort out what had gone wrong, Canadian police arrested six associates of Chuk Ling Leung. Two were stopped at the Niagara Falls border with heroin hidden in their car, and four others were picked up in Toronto. Peter Woo and his partner, in Toronto also to buy from Leung, were allowed by Canadian police to escape so the investigation could continue.

But with Hok Pang Chan, it could go nowhere. Dan Bellich, the agent in Chicago who was closest to Au Yeung, recalled, "Chan had been very willing to deal, and then, suddenly, he hung up. We knew of nothing that should have caused him to drop out. Simon didn't seem himself. He just said, 'Chan won't deal with me.' We went back to the Chinese agents in New York who were translating the wiretap, and looked again at the translations of all the conversations between Chan and Au Yeung. There was nothing to explain it. Robert Shaw and I met numerous times with Simon. 'There's got to be something wrong,' we kept saying. 'Chan doesn't just hang up on you for no reason at all.'"

Weeks later, Au Yeung admitted that he had dropped a code word in his conversation with Chan. "Chan did what I expected—he took that as a warning, and refused to talk," Au Yeung said. He explained that through his acquaintances in Hong Kong's triads, he had learned that Chan belonged to Sun Yee On, the largest triad, and was linked to Khun Sa, the warlord leader of the Shan tribe, in Burma. Khun Sa oversees the production of fifty to sixty percent of the world's heroin and is the source of the Chinese Connection. Au Yeung claims to have seen Khun Sa's headquarters—a mountaintop stronghold, defended by a private army of several thousand men and by surface-to-air missiles. "When I learn Chan is working for Khun Sa, I am reluctant to go after him," Au Yeung said. "That's just a little bit too big. He's offended, he'll kill you in seconds. We all have our limits. That was mine."

Au Yeung's withdrawal threatened an international investigation that had already absorbed several millions of dollars of taxpayers' money, involved hundreds of investigators, identified five different smuggling organizations in four countries, and yielded a lode of intelligence for future cases. It was already more successful than the FBI had imagined possible, and it appeared to be leading the bureau to the most wanted man in heroin—Khun Sa.

The FBI persuaded Au Yeung to go on. "Getting to Khun Sa was a dream," I was told by Dan Bellich, who convinced Au Yeung that he should press ahead. "We did not force him since his life was at stake," Bellich added. "His main objective was to get Khun Sa."

But, in the months following, Hok Pang Chan refused to trust Au Yeung, or to do more business with him. Chan particularly got the wind up when Au Yeung would not pay "flash money," or up-front money. (Requiring flash money before delivering drugs is one way dealers smoke out agents.) Finally, after many twists and turns in the case, Chan agreed to meet Au Yeung in Hong Kong in the New Year.

That Christmas, in Singapore, Chan shook hands with his boss, a Thai-Chinese from Bangkok called Anan Detchinambanchachai. Detchinambanchachai, Hok Pang Chan, and a crew of ethnic Chinese had gathered in Singapore to discuss a shipment of golf cart tires. The tires, in transit from Bangkok to Singapore, were on their way to New

York. Inside many of them was a bonanza of China White—more than any law-enforcement agent in the United States had ever seen.

Before the tires left Asia, Detchinambanchachai, Chan, and his crew met again in Korea. Detchinambanchachai's instructions were explicit: Sell the drugs in Chinatown to Chinese brokers like Peter Woo; hide the proceeds in the tires, and ship them back to Singapore if the normal money-laundering channels were not open; rent several houses and pay a few people $50,000 apiece to move the heroin into them for safekeeping. Detchinambanchachai also reminded Peter Poh, the boss of the crew, to dress nicely when he collected the tires' bill of lading from their destination, an import-export company in midtown Manhattan.

In the New Year, as the shipment approached New York, Hok Pang Chan met with Au Yeung in Hong Kong and offered him some heroin from an otherwise unnamed shipment that he said he was going to the United States to supervise. In return, he asked Au Yeung to provide him with a visa. The State Department shipped the visa in a diplomatic pouch overnight to Hong Kong, and a DEA agent, masquerading as one of Au Yeung's workers, copied down Chan's biographical particulars. The FBI at last learned his correct Chinese name.

In February 1989, Hok Pang Chan flew to New York, where he conferred frequently with Peter Woo and "some twenty Asian males unknown to us," FBI agent Geoffrey Doyle told me. "We began to call them by the color of their jackets—Black Coat, Blue Jacket, White Jacket, Red Jacket. Over the next three weeks, we had round-the-clock surveillance on Chan." From a remark of Peter Woo's overheard on the wiretap at Tai Pei Liquors, the FBI learned that the heroin had arrived, but was inside round metal containers difficult to cut. Twenty-four agents from the FBI and the New York Police Department working three shifts out of a Queens hotel figured that the containers must be oil drums. "Then, on February eighteenth, we came to the stark realization that Chan wasn't going to take us to the heroin," Doyle said. "We realized that the right person could be any one of the twenty-odd individuals he'd been meeting with. We identified Blue Jacket as the most likely, and focused on him exclusively."

On the damp night of February 19th, Blue Jacket, who turned out to be Peter Poh, the boss of Detchinambanchachai's crew, led agents to a Queens restaurant and picked up White Jacket, Brown Jacket, and Gray Jacket. The group drove to a two-story home in Corona, Queens, where they met with Red Jacket. Poh then drove to a brick house on Booth Memorial Avenue in Flushing. All evening, people came and went from the house.

"At midnight," Doyle said, "we followed White, Blue, and Brown Jackets back to the house in Corona again. We observed a car pull up out of nowhere. Its trunk was opened and boxes were unloaded into the house. Then a second car pulled up and ten or so bags were taken from it into the house."

The following day, when it looked like preparations were under way to sell the heroin, the FBI descended. Inside the Corona house, there was no furniture and no oil drums—only hundreds of golf cart tires. Upstairs, in a bedroom, dozens of nine-inch-wide tires lay on a plastic sheet on the floor below an oil painting of Pope Paul. A number of the tires had been split open, their cache of heroin untouched. Fifty-eight suspects in Hong Kong, Singapore, New York, Chicago, Detroit, Buffalo, San Francisco, Los Angeles, Toronto, Calgary, and Vancouver were eventually arrested. The probable source of the heroin, Khun Sa, the Burmese warlord, was not among them, much to the FBI's chagrin. Many of the suspects pleaded guilty, including Peter Woo.

"It was an incredibly sophisticated and exquisitely planned shipment," I was told by Jacques Semmelman, a former Assistant United States Attorney, who successfully prosecuted several of the defendants. "The tires were opened in Thailand, the heroin was fitted in, and they were revulcanized. The shipment went from one country to another, making its way across the world, and not one thing went wrong. They made it look very easy, very easy to import eight hundred pounds of heroin into the United States. The breakdown occurred on the receiving end, with Peter Woo. Woo was the key to all this, directly or indirectly."

During the trial of one of his suppliers in 1990, Woo gave his account of why he had changed from brokering politics to brokering heroin. The self-described "shrimp king of the world" admitted having smuggled illegal aliens and heroin into this country and having run gambling clubs in Chinatown. Woo's double life of respected businessman and political fixer on the one hand, and smuggler and gambler on the other, is typical of Chinatown: its tong bosses and drug dealers and bookies are often also legitimate businessmen.

Woo told the court that he began dealing in drugs in the mid-eighties, after losing a lot of money trying to corner the shrimp export market in China. The defense argued that he began far earlier, after incurring losses at a casino in Hong Kong. They portrayed him as a ladies' man, with three girlfriends around the world; as a frequenter of massage parlors in Asia; and as a heavy gambler who ran up large debts in Hong Kong. Woo said that he was "pretty well known among the Chinese community as well as the American community." He also said that he knew almost every government leader in the Far East. On the stand, Woo exhibited no remorse and bridled when his prestige was impugned. When he was asked where he obtained money to start buying drugs, he snapped, "Sir, twenty or thirty thousand dollars, and I have been doing business since 1946—you don't think I have that much amount of money?"

Chinatown residents have their own ideas about how Woo became *bot fun guey,* a "white powder ghost," or heroin dealer. "Before he retires, he spend so much, and he couldn't make up," one said. "If you live that kind of life, like a rich man, you become poor, you won't be able to survive. He thought he was smart—he just do like a matchmaker. When the deal went down, he maybe was in Toronto. He didn't understand narcotics conspiracy law."

Just days before his arrest, Woo was promoting the idea of a political action committee for Chinatown. "We have to get our fair share," he was telling friends.

After Woo's arrest, Simon Au Yeung, a man who is like Woo in many ways—a gambler rumored to have large debts, an international trader, a boastful and charming con man—disappeared briefly into the witness protection program. His lawyer, a former Chicago cop named Daniel Soso, told me that there was a million-dollar contract out on him, and that Au Yeung would meet me only if I traveled to a "safe" location and paid for both his and Soso's travel and hotel accommodations there as well.

We met at a resort in the winter of 1990. Soso wore jeans; Au Yeung was in a suit, with a tie whose price tag ($37.50) he'd forgotten to remove. He had a round, smooth face and curly hair—unusual for a

Chinese. He proudly showed me an Uzi machine gun in his briefcase and two 9-mm automatics under his jacket. There was tension in the air throughout our meeting.

The Chinese Connection, Au Yeung said, takes advantage of "the government's overlooking Chinatowns and their isolation. Heroin is viewed simply as a commodity; you buy cheap and sell dear. To Chinese, they are not harming their own people. The biggest customers aren't Chinese: they're blacks, Dominicans, Mexicans, whites. And heroin trafficking is an easy way to accumulate wealth, to get a good face. So long as Chinatowns are kept isolated, the criminals can do anything they want, because the Chinese community isn't offended by drug trafficking. They will stick up for their own, they will not accept the role of the U.S. government to prosecute Chinese."

He had volunteered to go undercover for the FBI, he said, because the drug dealing and corruption in Chinatowns appalled him. "I was in Hong Kong in the mid-1960s when the Hong Kong police were corrupt and mixed up with the triads, but here in the U.S. it turns out to be some of the tongs which are criminal. First time I met with the FBI, in the seventies, no one could care less. I felt it was a common concept of law enforcement at the time that this is Chinatown business, let them handle it."

Au Yeung went on, "Taiwan has the upper hand in Chinatowns now. The immediate reason is the murder of Taiwan's foremost critic in 1984 by the United Bamboo gang in the United States. I hate it so much. No one should do that in the U.S. Plus, no Chinese should be afraid walking around or have to pay extortion money to do business. In the early years, they came here as coolies, without much education, and they had to stay together to fight the 'white devil,' their name for Americans. But time flies, and we got so many different people immigrating now, we should live by the U.S.'s rules.

"The men who make the unwritten rules in Chinatown that protect the On Leong and Hip Sing say the rules protect welfare of all Chinese. But look at New York, San Francisco, Boston. In New York, for instance, the tongs are in massage parlors, drugs, gambling associations. The streets are under control of the gangs. The victims are afraid—the ones who badly need help are those who have to rely on Chinatown and couldn't survive outside. They are afraid of reprisals, they take corruption for granted, so they just keep suffering."

In our discussion, Au Yeung unveiled another motive for his undercover work: "It was my ego trip. Put it this way—I'd like to join the bureau for a long time. I came to the U.S. with high expectations of myself. Later, because of so many personal and financial things, I couldn't achieve what I expect."

Here Soso put in, "I'll be blunt. He found himself in a situation where he was involved with a lot of bad guys overseas and he wanted to do good. He also wanted to see political change in Taiwan. And it fed his ego that he was being a star undercover agent for the government." He added that it was against his advice that Au Yeung had left the witness protection program. "He's crazy," Soso said. "He is irrationally convinced of his invulnerability."

Au Yeung declared that he'd had to leave the program because the Chinese press attacked him as a stoolie and a drug dealer who had cooperated with the FBI only to avoid arrest. He angrily insisted that he was no stoolie or criminal, and had never sold drugs. But his account of what led him to infiltrate the Chinese international drug rings before becoming a contract employee of the FBI struck me as unconvincing. For instance, when I asked him how he had first met the most wanted Chinese criminals, he replied merely, "On business overseas."

He had left the witness protection program, he said, to be able to talk to the press and clear his name, and to convince other Chinese that helping the federal government fight drug dealers and crime would not harm them. "The Chinese press say I'm going to hide for the rest of my life. I'm *not* going to hide! The bad guys have to hide. I didn't do anything wrong. Why should I hide? The way I see it, the drug dealers can get killed like me. Put it this way—if they come after me, I hope I can take out two on the way down."

As we made our way out of the resort, a tall man in a raincoat passed us. The man whipped his head around to stare at Au Yeung, who tensed and stared back at him. Soso cocked his eyebrows questioningly, and his hand went to his side, to his gun. Au Yeung shrugged. He said that he didn't recognize the man. "He's a small-time mobster." The man, still looking at Au Yeung, disappeared around the corner. "All these guys have a sixth sense about each other," Soso explained. "It's instant recognition." As Au Yeung left, smiling, and brushing aside concern for his safety, he said, "I'm a tiger."

Au Yeung and I talked several times by phone in the months after our meeting, and the more we talked, the more bizarre he seemed. His motives multiplied, becoming more complicated with each interview. He seemed to be always holding back information, to have one more veil to drop. His story was full of holes, and he often retracted things he had told me earlier. Even Daniel Soso agreed that his client was a con man. "I can't figure him out yet," he said. "I don't know why, when he's holding back. It's difficult to figure out his reactions." This elusiveness, of course, kept him alive during eighteen months of undercover work, sometimes without any FBI backup. Most of Au Yeung's stories are impossible to verify; he alone knows whether they are true.

On one occasion, Au Yeung said that he had initially called the FBI in 1983 not out of idealism but to save his skin—something that he and the bureau have repeatedly denied. He said that gambling had been his chief entertainment in Chicago. Once or twice, he gambled at On Leong's building, the gateway to Chicago's Chinatown. The brick and terra cotta building, with its red pagoda tops and painted balconies, was called the Chinatown City Hall. On its third floor, disputes were arbitrated. On the second floor were gambling tables for *pai gow* and fan-tan. In 1982, he said, he let a relative use his account with a suburban bookie. The relative lost his entire credit line—$10,000. The bookie demanded payment. Au Yeung worked out a deal with the bookie in which the relative would pay off the debt in weekly installments. The relative's wife, however, threatened to go to the police. At that point, Au Yeung said, he went to Hong Kong with his family for two months to see his father, who was ill. When he returned, the bookie again threatened him about the unpaid debt, and he alerted the FBI, thus beginning his four years of free-lance informing.

As Au Yeung told it, he decided to risk investigating the On Leong on his own, without FBI approval, and to pay for the investigation with his winnings at its gambling tables in Chicago. One night, he won $25,000; the next night, $40,000; and, eventually, a total of $225,000. "I found a trick in fan-tan," he explained. "It takes time and patience."

To further his investigation, he continued, he joined On Leong and went to Taiwan to meet Eddie Chan. Two years later, when Au Yeung was a contract FBI employee, Eddie Chan became suspicious after an FBI raid on the On Leong building in Chicago. He invited Au Yeung to Manila and warned him about betraying the tong. Au Yeung kept his composure, and Chan, mollified, introduced him to some Dragon Heads, as chiefs of organized crime and drug trafficking groups in the Far East are known. "It was like a dinner party, with fifteen or twenty people," Au Yeung said. "Eddie vouched for me. It was the biggest mistake Eddie Chan made." He laughed. "Now a lot of people think Eddie's working for the authorities."

Au Yeung's evidence against Eddie Chan and On Leong became the starting point of a second federal case, a mammoth racketeering indictment handed down in the summer of 1990 against On Leong. The Justice Department charged that the tong ran a multimillion-dollar illegal gambling operation in several of its chapters in the United States; protected that lucrative operation by means of the Ghost Shadows; and paid off, assaulted, threatened, or murdered anyone who got in its way. Twenty-nine people, including four past On Leong national presidents—Eddie Chan among them—and the organization's current national president, were indicted, and On Leong buildings worth millions of dollars in Minneapolis, Chicago, Houston, and Miami were seized. Seventeen of those indicted pleaded guilty. The case, which was tried in 1991, sought $11.5 million in illegal gambling proceeds from the tong and aimed to shut down the tong's illegal activities. The first case against a Chinese tong by the United States government, it was also the very case that the Manhattan district attorney's office did not make in the mid-eighties when it prosecuted the Ghost Shadows, and Eddie Chan disappeared in the wind. But, as it turned out, many of the questions I had about Au Yeung, particularly regarding his background and his integrity, surfaced again during the trial, and his involvement in the case and his testimony proved a liability for the government. Indeed, as became clear, Au Yeung helped the government lose its historic prosecution.

Simon Au Yeung's principal target in the case (besides Eddie Chan) was a man, who, like Peter Woo, rose to wealth from gambling parlors in New York's Chinatown. Wing Yeung Chan, Eddie Chan's handpicked successor, was charged with racketeering and running an illegal gambling operation. Wing Yeung Chan, who is in his mid-forties, was a waiter until 1977, when Uncle Seven went to jail along with a man who ran a gambling parlor on Mott Street. While those two were in jail, I was told, Chan got financial backing to open a gambling house of his own. He quickly became a millionaire. With some of the profits, he bought a restaurant on the ground floor of On Leong, and in 1987 was elected the tong's national president. His younger brother Wing Wah Chan is now the national president. Another brother heads a faction of the Ghost Shadows. Yet another brother is a Catholic priest.

The trial was held in one of the largest courtrooms in the Everett M. Dirksen Federal Building in Chicago, to accommodate the huge crowd of defendants, their lawyers, and their translators. As weeks, and then months, went by, and the trial became maddeningly protracted, the courtroom was rarely full.

Assistant United States Attorney John Scully, leading the prosecution, got off to a surprisingly shaky start, apparently unaware that in such a mammoth case, alleging numerous crimes over a large span of years by a cast of thousands, the government could lose on the confusion caused by the Chinese names alone. On the trial's fourth day, Judge John A. Nordberg several times admonished the prosecution to lay more of a foundation for its questioning and to better identify the players. "There has been a welter of names this morning," Nordberg complained after sending the jury out of the room. "There has been great difficulty in spelling them ... There are apparently an inexhaustible number of Chinese names. Some of them have two or three different names ... It is apparent to me that there are a number of Chinese that have the same name. I take it that, unless there is a reference to the fact that an individual is on trial here, you are talking about somebody else. If that's not the case, how do you expect either the Court or the jury to have the slightest idea who a particular individual is that he [the first witness] is referring to?"

The government's explanation, that the witness did identify the individuals as among those indicted, only further irritated the judge. "I note that we were having trouble with somebody called Kong Hing Fong, and is that Henry Fong [a defendant]? We also have had reference to a David Fong. Is that Moy Chang Woo [another defendant]? ... If I can't figure out who they are and what relationship they would have to this case, I know the jury is not going to have the slightest idea of what any of these names have to do with the case."

Several days later, Judge Nordberg gave the jury a list of names of people involved in the case that he had prepared for his own use, so the jury wouldn't go bonkers trying to sort out which of the people mentioned by witnesses were involved in the case and which were not. It was the first sign of the government's sloppy preparation and failure to anticipate the pitfalls in its case.

Confusion, however, persisted. The jury had to sort out which criminal acts each of the fifteen defendants was charged with, as well as which witnesses corroborated which charge—an exceedingly difficult task, as two-thirds of the government's witnesses required translators, and each witness could be cross-examined by fifteen defense attorneys.

Throughout the trial, the defense did not dispute that heavy gambling occurred at many of the On Leong's twenty chapters nationwide. Chief in the brilliant and costly defense bar engaged by On Leong was Daniel Webb, the former United States Attorney in Chicago, who represented Wing Yeung Chan. Webb admitted that his client bet at On Leong games but scoffed at the idea that he directed a racketeering enterprise. On Leong is the same sort of organization as the Lions' Club, Webb argued, and gambling is an ancient, respectable part of Chinese culture. Like all the defense attorneys, Webb maintained that the tong's chapters run their operations locally, thereby denying the charge of racketeering, which required proof that the tong's national operations were directed by New York.

Star witnesses for the government played into the defense's hands. The first, a former national president of On Leong who had been granted immunity, laid out a pattern of racketeering by the tong: gambling at nearly all of the chapters he had visited as president from 1983 to 1985; payoffs to the Chicago mob to protect the On Leong casino; payoffs to the Chicago police, also, to protect the casino and to alert the tong of raids; payments to him as national president that ranged from $200 to $5,000 a month from the gambling proceeds of many chapters; and interstate traffic in firearms at the request of Eddie Chan, who, he stated, also dispatched Ghost Shadows to resolve problems at numerous casinos. However, the witness also admitted that he had cheated often on his taxes and had pocketed most of the Chicago chapter's payoffs to the mob.

Simon Au Yeung was also destroyed on the stand. After describing taped conversations he had had with Wing Yeung Chan about the casinos—conversations that appeared to show that Chan supervised operations in the various chapters—Au Yeung hanged himself with a series of admissions, each more extraordinary than the last. He admitted to declaring personal bankruptcy before beginning free-lance informing for the Federal Bureau of Investigation; to still being desperate for money because he'd agreed to pay $600,000 to settle a fraud suit by a former partner (which was $100,000 more than the claim); to lying to several grand juries; to deceiving the Federal Bureau of Investigation by peddling a book about his undercover work without its permission, against a prohibition in his contract, and by not declaring his FBI salary on his income taxes; and to conning whenever it suited his self-interest. The declarations, elicited in a devastating cross-examination by Daniel Webb, caught Au Yeung in lie after lie. Again and again, Au Yeung denied Webb's charges, then collapsed when presented with written evidence exposing his lie. Webb bitterly mocked Au Yeung's integrity by reading from Au Yeung's grand jury testimony, in which he had stated that he was "just there to fight crimes and work for justice. That's my goal." By the end of the cross-examination, Au Yeung agreed that he often could not keep his lies straight. He also acknowledged that he had not told the FBI that he'd lied to the grand juries when it hired him to gather evidence against On Leong. In a final flourish, Webb forced Au Yeung to concede that he had fabricated some of his testimony against Wing Yeung Chan. When Webb finished, Au Yeung had so perjured himself that the government's case was considerably weakened.

With the government's first two star witnesses destroyed, its case rested almost entirely on Chicago lawyer Robert Cooley. Cooley testified that in 1980 an officer of the Chicago On Leong asked him to fix a murder case against some Ghost Shadows charged with killing another gang member in front of On Leong's building. According to Cooley, the officer agreed to pay him $100,000 to guarantee a bench trial instead of a jury trial, and an acquittal. Cooley further testified that the tong official told him not to worry about the witnesses—

they'd been paid off to recant their previous testimony. Cooley did as asked, he said, and the Ghost Shadows later went free.

He then described subsequent meetings with Eddie Chan in New York, at which Chan asked him to do all he could to defend one of the acquitted Ghost Shadows. The man was in trouble in another city because he had done "other things for the On Leong ... and ... he could cause us a lot of problems if he talked, if he got in trouble," Cooley recalled Eddie Chan saying. Other tong officials in Chicago and New York, Cooley said, told him substantially the same thing.

Cooley further said that he had been asked to represent the Ghost Shadows because for fifteen years as a lawyer in Cook County, he had subverted the legal system—bribing judges, prosecutors, clerks, and witnesses. For a number of years before that, he had done the same as a crooked cop. Then, pursued by bookies for gambling debts, threatened by the mob, and behind in his taxes, he had turned himself in. Equipped with a body mike from the U.S. Attorney's office, he had begun gathering evidence of corruption in the First Ward Regular Democratic Organization in Chicago.

The defense leapt on Cooley as an object beneath contempt. Cooley, however, could not be shaken from his main allegations. And to counter the defense's suggestions that Cooley was lying again, and had himself fixed the murder case without any involvement of the tong, the prosecution called the Ghost Shadows who'd done the killing to the stand. They testified that they'd acted on Eddie Chan's orders and had understood that the tong had fixed the case.

In the closing arguments, the defense turned the trial on its head and tried the witnesses. Attorney after attorney claimed that the key witnesses could not be believed, and implied that they, rather than the On Leong officials, should be on trial for crimes for which they had been granted immunity. All also argued that On Leong's gambling operations were harmless local affairs. To buttress their arguments, they pointed to the large number of prosecution witnesses, including a number of On Leong officers pleading guilty, who had said that the gambling was controlled locally. The exasperated jury, four months into a trial expected to last two months, sent a note to Judge Nordberg urging him to hurry up the proceedings so they could begin to lead a semblance of their normal lives.

The government's charge of an illegal national gambling operation was a shoo-in, since its existence was undisputed. But had the jury been able to keep track of the evidence presented by the many witnesses to return a guilty verdict for racketeering? The judge advised them that they could not find the defendants guilty of running an illegal gambling operation without also finding them guilty of racketeering. After ten days of deliberations, the jury was hung on every count except some minor tax evasion charges for several defendants. The defense was jubilant. The government moved for a retrial.

To date, the FBI has not hired Au Yeung. It considered giving him the Good Samaritan Award for citizens who aid its investigations but then decided not to. Instead, the Justice Department awarded Au Yeung $250,000 for invaluable help in the Peter Woo heroin case and the On Leong gambling case—before he took the stand in Chicago and admitted to defrauding Uncle Sam and lying to grand juries. Au Yeung, who is always heavily armed, now sends out Christmas cards in envelopes bearing his return address and still hopes to sell the movie and book rights to his story as the first Chinese to bust Chinese organized crime and the Chinese Connection.

12

THE WARLORD AND MISS PALMER

The Chinese Connection ends on top of a mountain in northeast Burma, several miles from the border of Thailand. All around is thick, humid jungle with plunging gorges and mountains rising 3,500 meters. There are no roads for several miles, no telephones, no airport, no government.

Here, Chang Chi-Fu, known as Khun Sa, holds the world's police at bay, protected by the neutrality of Burma, one of the poorest and most isolated countries in Southeast Asia; by the corruption in Burma's military junta; and by the roadless, mountainous terrain itself, so secluded that for years the exact location of his fortified camp was not on any map. In this part of the Golden Triangle, warlords rule eight or ten tribes fighting for independence from the Burmese government. Khun Sa, leader of the eight million Shan people (six percent of Burma's population), has been fighting Rangoon since 1958, when the Burmese government broke a promise to give autonomy to the Shan States. Western analysts are skeptical that Khun Sa heads a genuine independence movement. They believe that his private army, the Shan United Army, mostly protects his people's opium crop.

Khun Sa oversees the production of fifty to sixty percent of the world's heroin. In the Shan States, an area the size of Greece, he controls the cultivation of the poppies, the jungle labs that refine the opium paste from the poppies into China White, and its distribution through Bangkok and Hong Kong to Chinatown via the Chinese Connection. The story of his rise is a sordid one, a game of geopolitics in which first the British, then the United States, protected opium cultivation in the Golden Triangle.

The British forced opium on China in the nineteenth century in order to obtain another market for the main export crop of their Indian empire. After establishing an opium monopoly in China, they established another in Burma, which was colonized between the 1820s and 1880s. But they were powerless to stop opium growing in Burma's northern states, the only area in Southeast Asia where large-scale heroin cultivation threatened their monopoly. A dozen or so hill tribes there had grown opium as part of their way of life for years. Rather than colonize the remote, lawless northern territory, the British let local warlords rule the no man's land until 1948, when Burma gained its independence.

A year later, two thousand soldiers from General Chiang Kai-shek's Nationalist armies, fleeing defeat in China's civil war, invaded northern Burma. The incursion created a diplomatic crisis. Burma demanded that they surrender or leave. The United States refused to pressure the Guomindang, its ally. Newly independent Burma cut off United States aid and severed diplomatic relations, fearing that it might become a second Korea.

The People's Republic, however, did not invade, and the United States Central Intelligence Agency, happy for a buffer in northern Burma against the spread of Communism, rescued the Nationalist Chinese troops, shipping them supplies and arms. As more National-ist soldiers crossed into Burma, the "lost armies" grew to over ten thousand. In short order, they took over and streamlined the Shan opium crop. They set prices, increased production, created trails to transport the opium into northern Thailand, and imported Hong Kong chemists to purify the opium first to morphine, then to China White. With the profits, they mounted several failed invasions of China in the 1950s.

Khun Sa was the first Shan tribesman to challenge the Chinese Nationalists' control of the opium trade. Son of a Guomindang general and a Shan wife, he had been an minor mercenary until a misguided Burmese policy to train warlords to fight the Chinese equipped him with several hundred troops in the sixties. Khun Sa fought many battles with the Guomindang armies to assert his power, leaving hundreds dead. In the late 1960s, GIs in Vietnam were becoming addicted by the tens of thousands to such brands of heroin as Double UO Globe, and others produced by Chinese Nationalist troops in the Golden Triangle. The United States then began looking on its allies as criminals, and regretted aiding and abetting their survival in the fifties.

Khun Sa was captured in 1969 and sentenced to life imprisonment in Burma, but was later released in a weird swap for two abducted Russian doctors, engineered by one of his lieutenants. He left jail as Lo-Hsing Tan, a powerful rival heroin trafficker, went to prison. Lo-Hsing's imprisonment opened the way for Khun Sa's return to power in the seventies. He taxed the Shans and their opium caravans passing through his territory, and refined the paste in his own labs. To ensure that he could sell through Bangkok, the nearest port, he paid off a number of Thai generals, and, it was rumored, Thai royalty.

"Khun Sa became prominent in the mid- to late 1970s, after Lo-Hsing Tan was arrested by the Thais and extradicted to Burma," Richard LaMagna told me in Washington at the Drug Enforcement Administration headquarters. "Lo-Hsing's arrest left two major rival opium producers, General Lee Wan Huan, head of the Third Chinese Irregular Force, and General Tuan of the Fifth Chinese Irregular Force—both old Guomindang soldiers. They and Khun Sa were constantly at odds with one another, their shifting alliances always extremely complicated."

In 1980, the United States put a bounty on Khun Sa's head after the abduction and murder of the wife of a Drug Enforcement Administration agent in the city of Chiang Mai, in northern Thailand. Khun Sa responded with bounties of his own on Drug Enforcement Administration agents in northern Thailand. Several years later, after intense United States pressure, Thai police assaulted Khun Sa's headquarters in northern Thailand, seizing ten tons of weapons. Khun Sa escaped into the Burmese mountains. There, he survived many assassination attempts and continued to fight fierce battles with his old Guomindang rivals, including Lo-Hsing Tan, whose life sentence was commuted. In 1987, Khun Sa held a "press conference" at one of his camps to tell the world that opium production in the Golden Triangle would double to one thousand tons.

At that time, it hardly seemed possible that a bright, eager, extremely decent, thirty-one-year-old Catholic woman who looked as if she'd bailed out of the road show of *Oklahoma,* could assail Khun Sa. By a strange twist of fate, Catherine Palmer, an Assistant United States Attorney in New York's Eastern District who had become infatuated with Asian narcotics cases, saw that possibly, just possibly, she might be able to indict the source of the Chinese Connection.

The twist of fate that gave her the opening was rain in Bangkok. Torrential monsoons lashed the city for over a week in early 1988. The unusually heavy rains snarled traffic, interrupted the outdoor markets, and delayed loading at the Klong Toey port, the third busiest in Southeast Asia. There, they soaked through two hundred heavy bales of rubber strips waiting to be loaded onto a cargo container ship. Dock workers who saw a white liquid seeping from the bales called the Royal Thai police. Cutting through the bales with chain saws, they found over a ton of heroin, bound for New York City.

Within hours, Richard LaMagna, then the head of Group 41 in New York, was on the phone to Palmer's boss, Charles Rose, the chief of organized crime and drug enforcement in the Eastern District at the time. LaMagna requested a search warrant for a warehouse in Queens—the destination of the rubber bales. The ton of heroin, three or four days from the Golden Triangle, signified to Richard LaMagna, Charles Rose, and Cathy Palmer the same source—Khun Sa. "No amount of heroin in that quantity comes out of the Golden Triangle without his involvement. Khun Sa was going to be our major target," Charles Rose told me when I talked with him in his office. "This was a very, very good investigation," Palmer added, looking very pleased, enthusiastic, and charming. "We started with nothing but a whole lot of heroin. It was like fitting together a jigsaw. It was great!"

Inside the Queens warehouse, Group 41 agents found rubber bales identical to those on the Bangkok pier, strewn helter-skelter, but no heroin. They ran the bales through an X-ray machine and found nothing. They cut them open and found nothing. The warehouse, a one-story cinder block building down the street from a Burger King, did not look occupied. The heat was off, and mail was piling up at the door. The office had no signs of use—no records, no files. The agents vacuumed the warehouse and sent the sweepings and a few bales of rubber to DEA's lab for analysis.

Two sisters from Thailand, who had been in the United States for several years, paid the bills at the warehouse. "A little, fat Thai-Chinese woman came into our office with her lawyer and was quite arrogant," LaMagna recalled. "She took the attitude, buzz off—you have nothing on me. We said that we thought she was involved and she ought to take it seriously." The sisters were let go after they denied any knowledge of the heroin.

A month later, the lab confirmed that the sweepings from the warehouse contained traces of China White. "It confirmed our suspicions, because no one would run the risk of shipping over a ton of heroin without a trial run," Cathy Palmer told me. "Custom records showed that the Bangkok manufacturer of the rubber had made two prior shipments to that same warehouse. DEA was investigating in Bangkok with the Thai police where the rubber originated, where in the Golden Triangle the heroin came from, and talking to shipping brokers."

The case stalled there for the rest of 1988, the leads cooled. Palmer went back to working her networks of informants in jails and slums strung across Southeast Asia, and to her many contacts in the police departments in Hong Kong, Thailand, Australia, and Tokyo, gleaning information. She had built the contacts in the course of compiling a formidable record: since joining the Eastern District office in 1986, she had tried thirty Asian heroin cases and won them all. She worked seven days a week—sixteen, eighteen hours a day. Even Group 41 agents grew concerned. Palmer didn't know how to take a holiday. At Thanksgiving and Christmas, she was on the phone lines to Asia.

"We spend a large part of our time talking to defendants and informants," Palmer told me. "Early the following year, we started talking to three co-defendants in another case in New York. They'd been arrested in 1987 and it had taken them a year and a half to cooperate.

"Our shipping documents showed that the two previous shipments to the Queens warehouse from Bangkok occurred in March and June of 1987. There were a significant number of bales missing in the earliest shipment. We didn't know what that meant. When we were talking to these three co-defendants about distributing heroin here since 1986, they mentioned having fifty kilos to distribute in

March of 1987. It took a while for it to sink in that these were the bales missing in the earliest shipment. These defendants had come over to the States specifically to meet the earlier shipments, and were waiting for the ton-plus from Bangkok hidden in the rubber, and of course, it was seized. They identified the Hong Kong brokers who came here to distribute the stuff, and the Chinatown brokers."

Palmer also got help from King Man Lai, the prominent Hong Kong trafficker, whom she had convicted the year before and who was in a New York jail, doing time. Lai knew associates of Khun Sa's. He was a regular customer of one of Khun Sa's Bangkok distributors, and with Lai's help, Palmer traced the heroin back to several Thai-Chinese distributors.

By the summer of 1989, Palmer was sure that she could indict Khun Sa. A grand jury in Brooklyn began hearing the evidence in September. That fall, Palmer and Group 41 agents solidified the case in Bangkok. Witnesses and other intelligence linked the sodden bales of rubber on the Klong Toey port and the two previous shipments to the Queens warehouse to Khun Sa. The last piece in Palmer's jigsaw was a cooperating witness who provided a crucial link. After Attorney General Richard Thornburgh and the Justice Department and the State Department signed off on the case, the grand jury handed up the indictment around Christmas.

Working long nights for weeks had delayed Palmer's Christmas, and she was not surprised when a present arrived in February 1990 at her Brooklyn office. Two weeks earlier, letter bombs had killed a Southern judge and a civil rights lawyer. The DEA agent and the New York City policeman in Palmer's office to discuss a case jokingly offered to defuse the "bomb." Opening the package carefully, they saw the briefcase that Palmer had been expecting from her parents. A string hung from it, attached to a sawed-off .22-caliber pistol, rigged to fire on opening. United States marshals began a round-the-clock guard on Palmer.

That night on the evening news, a shaken Andrew Maloney, United States Attorney for the Eastern District, refused to bring Palmer forward for comment. The networks instead ran a clip of one of Palmer's old press conferences. It showed a tomboy-looking, petite woman with a mane of hair and oversized glasses beaming over a podium.

That month, I stopped by Palmer's office. I didn't notice the people sitting outside. They were young—students, I figured. Palmer was tired and pale. And angry. "Nobody intimidates me," she fumed. "The thing I dislike most about all this besides upsetting my parents is changing my life-style," she said, pointing to the two young marshals outside her office. "I can't even go down the hall without them." "Nothing's been found yet. There are a lot of angles to look at."

A month later, Palmer stood by Attorney General Richard Thornburgh and outgoing DEA administrator Jack Lawn for the announcement of Khun Sa's indictment at the Justice Department in Washington. Andrew Maloney laid accolades at her feet. "I have never seen a case put together like this in my twenty-five years of law enforcement," he said. "And it's thanks largely to the effect of offices of DEA, the cooperation of the Royal Hong Kong police, the Thai police, but most especially, this little lady over here."

The press was puzzled. "What are our chances of apprehending Khun Sa and could he share a cell with General Noriega?" a reporter asked. Attorney General Thornburgh replied that he "was not one to make rash predictions," but hinted that extraditing Khun Sa from a country with which the United States had no diplomatic relations could prove complicated. "We will exert ourselves to the maximum to obtain personal jurisdiction over this individual," Thornburgh said. "We begin with the process of criminal indictment. We hope to end with the process of conviction and substantial incarceration."

"This indictment is going to have tremendous impact overseas," Palmer told me excitedly when we talked in her office. "Somebody had to do something—Khun Sa had been sitting up there in the mountains for twenty-five years, thumbing his nose," she said. "The public isn't sensitized yet to Khun Sa and the problems of Southeast Asian heroin. Five years ago, they weren't sensitized to Pablo Escobar and Jose Gonzalo Rodriguez Gacha and those cocaine guys in Colombia they now know a lot about. We'll get him. I believe one day we'll get him and one day, Khun Sa will be brought to trial on those charges." Palmer just laughed about the possibility of prosecuting the man whom Thornburgh called "the Prince of Death." "People in the Shan States say he's a Robin Hood, benefiting the poor. It's clear," said Palmer, looking amused, "that he's something very, very different."

Khun Sa's indictment was, in many ways, the culmination of

Group 41's and Palmer's extraordinary winning streak, one of the most successful, sustained prosecution efforts in the war on drugs in the United States. "Group 41 was a team effort," Richard LaMagna told me. "It was one of those times in your life when everything comes together. I don't want to claim credit for having taught Cathy. She's not at all taken with herself. She has almost no ego that gets in the way; she just wants to get the job done. She's totally dedicated, probably too much so, because she has almost no personal life of her own. Charles Rose provided a lot of support and let Cathy run with it. She took it on herself to do innovative things, especially with Hong Kong, Singapore, Australia, and Thailand—extraditions, for instance, that had never been done before, and flying witnesses over here for trials. She inspired so much confidence and trust and respect overseas that they let her stretch the limits. Also, a lot of prosecutors have difficulty relating to agents and policemen, because they are on a different wavelength. Cathy's idea of a good time is to go out for beers with them."

"When Cathy Palmer began working here, I don't know if she could have picked out the parts in the world where heroin was coming from," Charles Rose said. "Within six months of her starting in this office, I recruited her for this section even though technically she was not ready. She's the most dedicated professional I've ever worked with in twelve years. Her relation with the agents is without comparison."

"Cathy *is* too good to be true," Group 41 supervisor Al Gourley added. "She uses eighty-five to ninety percent of her time in her work. She's always available. The agents know she won't tell them, 'Forget it, you haven't got a case.' She'll tell them what they need to secure it."

"This will sound really weird," Palmer told me. "I'd worked on Wall Street for four and a half years. I liked it very much, but I felt a need to contribute more. I was interested because Asia was an area of the world I knew nothing about." Plus, she added, the area gave her a chance to make her mark. "Asian drug trafficking is new. No one else was doing anything, and there are major violators out there. How often in your life do you get to work on stuff you think is great and that's making an impact?"

Since being indicted, Khun Sa has reportedly lain low. Rangoon would like to get rid of its old enemy and hand him over to the United

States, but corruption in Burma's military makes it unlikely the government will ever capture him. "I deal with Khun Sa's indictment every day," Felix Jimenez, the head of the heroin desk at DEA, told me shortly after the indictment. "The Burmese are denying that Khun Sa's in Burma and the Thais are saying he's not in Thailand. Right now, there is a lot of political pressure from us on Burma. I believe if the government is serious it will do something. The government wants to do the right thing, but corruption is out of control there." To capture Khun Sa, LaMagna estimates that Rangoon would have to send twenty thousand troops to "march several days through Khun Sa's villages, without roads, or supply planes, which can't land in that area. I doubt the junta will bother." Felix Jimenez is not skeptical. "We got Noriega, we can get Khun Sa," he asserts.

Right now, Khun Sa is under considerable pressure from his old rivals. General Wa, head of another insurgent group, which also produces heroin, has made peace with Rangoon and agreed to a gradual reduction in opium production in exchange for monies for development in his region. Wa, with Rangoon's backing, is trying to push Khun Sa off his mountain and farther south. Last year, Wa's army killed twenty-nine members of Khun Sa's bodyguard. In the battle, Thai planes for the first time strafed Khun Sa's mountaintop camp. Nonetheless, the United States estimates the 1989–90 crop of opium in Burma at 2,200 metric tons, down slightly from the previous year because of bad weather, but still double the 1987 crop.

Khun Sa's indictment pressures Thailand and Laos to extradite him if he crosses their borders. Khun Sa has half his laboratories in Laos and frequently travels across the border, but Laos seems little motivated to eradicate its opium crop, or to stop Khun Sa. Thailand long ago indicted Khun Sa on drug charges. But corruption in the army helps him evade capture. "We believe certain elements in the Thai military are corrupt—either turning a blind eye to border activities or actually facilitating his heroin distribution," LaMagna told me.

The flood of China White from Khun Sa, which continues to inundate the United States, worries Washington. With cocaine use in the United States falling, some officials fear that a heroin epidemic is quietly building, fed by the potent China White of the Chinese Connection. Distributors have given inner-city crack addicts a taste for heroin by sprinkling China White in vials of coke. The heroin eases the crash after the euphoria of crack. "I believe that drug addicts will switch to heroin and heroin will be the drug of the 1990s," DEA heroin chief Jimenez argues. Robert Bryden, special agent in charge of the DEA in New York, fears that the middle class will become addicted because China White eliminates the fear of contracting AIDS from dirty needles. "Frankly, I think its appearance in the mid-eighties was a marketing decision by the Chinese. They know that the chances of increasing the number of addicts injecting heroin is very, very small because of AIDS and HIV. So, they made the purest heroin available so that it can be smoked, and users don't have to worry about AIDS, to gain a much larger market."

Other federal officials believe this is hyperbole. The evidence that would persuade them—a jump in the number of overdoses reported at hospitals in major cities, an increase in heroin addicts enrolling in detox programs—hasn't materialized. Robert Bryden points out that because China White is smokable, it causes far fewer overdoses than less pure heroin, which must be injected. China White is so popular that now Colombian traffickers are growing poppies in the mountains of Peru and Colombia and exporting China White to the United States to cash in on the Chinese Connection multi-million-dollar profits. Another heroin epidemic, supplied in great measure by Khun Sa, would be eerily reminiscent of the 1960s, when heroin was the drug of choice, DEA administrator Jack Lawn noted in 1990 before he left office. "We believe that Khun Sa was predominantly responsible for the flow of heroin to our military forces in Vietnam and in Thailand during R&R as a means of retaliating against U.S. forces for the damages that they brought during the war in Southeast Asia."

Khun Sa is fifty-eight years old, dark-skinned, with high cheekbones, small green eyes, blackened teeth, and remarkable cupid-bow lips. In documentaries made of him by Western journalists, he wears jungle fatigues, a .45 on his hip. His camp, scraped off the top of a mountain, is a dirt enclosure ringed by jungle. Except for the Shan United Army troops, it looks like summer camp in the tropics: no electricity or running water, open-sided barracks with tin or bamboo roofs, benches laid out along flattened dirt paths, and bamboo stockades encircling compounds here and there. Most recently, Khun Sa in 1989 told correspondent Tom Gerald of ABC's "20/20" news magazine, "President Bush may have the button for nuclear bombs, but I have the button for opium. My opium is stronger and more potent than your nuclear bomb. It's enough that I just feed you this poison.

Why should I do anything else?" Then, Khun Sa laughed and laughed. It was like laughter in a fun house, full of crazy echoes. Each time in the interview that Khun Sa mentioned death or defying the United States, he laughed in the same crazy fashion. He seemed to enjoy himself. "They [the United States] have weapons to attack me. I have weapons to attack them. And I am not afraid of them," he declared. "Do you think we are your slaves? If we don't grow opium, we don't eat. They [the Shan tribesmen] don't know it goes to the United States—all they know is that after they sell it, they can buy grain." As he had previously, Khun Sa offered to dig up the Shan State opium crop if the United States would pay him $48 million over six years, and help his people learn to grow other cash crops—an offer the United States has always disdained.

In the two years since indicting Khun Sa, Cathy Palmer has been showered with honors. She was offered a high-level job in the Justice Department in Washington. She was the keynote speaker in 1991 at the annual conference of international law enforcement officials on Asian organized crime. In 1987, she received the Attorney General's Distinguished Service Award for outstanding prosecution against Asian organized crime, and in 1991, the Administrator's Award from the Drug Enforcement Administration and the Attorney General's Superior Performance Award for her unbroken prosecution record. She has been profiled in *U.S. News & World Report* and other publications, and interviewed on national television.

Palmer no longer grants interviews and has told friends that the celebrity is unwelcome. She turned down the promotion to the Justice Department, unwilling to quit the Eastern District before current cases can be wrapped up. This summer, she will testify in her own case. A Queens man named David Kwong has been charged with sending Palmer the shotgun boobytrap. The Hong Kong immigrant, convicted several times before on firearms and drug charges, reportedly wanted to kill Palmer because she was too successful.

The idea that Chinese organized crime is a loosely organized international network is now considered fact by the Justice Department, the Federal Bureau of Investigation, and the Drug Enforcement Administration. A 1991 national strategy report by the U.S. Attorney General, called "Attacking Organized Crime," states: "Chinese Organized Crime groups, not at all new to the United States, are increasingly active in many major population centers. These groups—Triads, certain criminal factions of some Tongs, and certain subordinate street gangs—include not only the principal importers of southeast Asian heroin into the United States, but also the operators of modern racketeering enterprises who utilize LCN [La Cosa Nostra] connections to penetrate the law enforcement and judicial communities through long-established LCN contacts in order to achieve their criminal objectives." The study concludes that Chinese organized crime groups, in addition to La Cosa Nostra and other Italian and Japanese organized crime groups, "pose a substantial threat to society as hierarchical, criminally diverse, organizationally mature, multijurisdictional criminal organizations ..."

The Federal Bureau of Investigation lists Asian organized crime as its number two priority after La Cosa Nostra. The bureau in Manhattan has two squads looking at the problem: one aimed at drugs, and one aimed at eliminating the hierarchy of Chinatown's street gangs. As a result, the pace of federal prosecutions has picked up: Two gangs, Born to Kill and the Queens-based Green Dragons, were indicted for racketeering in 1991. The Green Dragons gang was allegedly run by its leader from the Fujian province of China. The Born to Kill case, broken by a member of the gang who secretly tape-recorded conversations, is said to have eliminated the entire membership of Chinatown's most feared gang. The informant revealed astonishment that so many law enforcement agencies knew about his group. He'd never heard of most of them. Other cities with Chinese organized crime include Boston, Houston, Los Angeles, Seattle, Portland (Maine), Chicago, Denver, Washington, D.C., and Detroit. FBI director William Sessions soberly told the Senate Permanent Subcommittee on Investigations in the fall of 1991 that Chinese criminal groups, the most developed of Asian organized crime groups, "are rapidly expanding their operations outside the Asian community."

Congress has also sounded the alarm. In hearings before the Senate Judiciary Committee in August 1990, chairman Joseph Biden predicted that Asian organized crime groups, which he termed a potential "supermafia" and a "vast and frightening threat to our cities and our communities ... will be the dominant organized crime force in this country by the middle of the next decade."

GROUP PORTRAIT

PART THREE

13

CHILDREN

Children are the grace and balm of Chinatown. They are its remedy and consolation. Tumbling about the streets, balls of color in the slum, they bring face, a future, and sense to their parents' lives, especially to the prisoners of Chinatown.

Children are expected to live with their parents until they marry; the men, after they marry, to take care of their parents in their old age. Children are also expected to merge into the mainstream, unlike their parents, and for this reason Chinese families put great stock in education. This leads to strains and also to startling successes.

Both are visible at the Garment Industry Day Care Center, sponsored by the International Ladies' Garment Workers' Union, the Chinese-American Planning Council, and the Greater Blouse, Skirt and Undergarment Association. The center is the union's answer to the problem of children waiting after school in the factories for their parents. But the day care has room for only eighty children, and a waiting list of two hundred to three hundred. And the twenty thousand women—sixty percent of Chinatown's population—employed in the garment business have thousands of children.

The day care, located in an attractive, three-story building, serves only children of union workers. It is a fresh world for the children, compared to the tenements where their families crowd into one-bedroom apartments and they sleep in the living rooms. The center is gaily decorated with paper cutouts and echoes with childish laughter and chatter. The youngest charge is two and a half years old. Most attend for three years, until they are five and a half years old, then go to public school. Nearly half attend for free; the rest pay a nominal fee.

Karen Liu, the director of the several day care centers located in the building, explained to me that in most of the children's families, the fathers are not around. "A lot work in restaurants in upstate New York, New Jersey, and Connecticut, and live near their work on weekdays," Liu said when I stopped by one day in October. "So the children see them once a week. You see the fathers being bused home in vans around Chinatown. We don't consider these one-parent households, even though the father is absent most of the week." Liu added that precious little home life is the rule in Chinatown: mothers work until eight or nine P.M. in the garment factories; fathers work from eleven A.M. to eleven P.M. in the restaurants, so parents rarely see their children.

In the five-year-olds' class, twenty children sat at low tables making small guppy noises of eating, as they feasted on pizzas and ravioli they had cooked themselves. Many smiled at me and waved, excited to see a visitor. "They are very expressive," Renee, the teacher, said. "But when they came here two years ago, they would not even look at a visitor or talk to one. Now they are very talkative and love to play games. Last year, this class had three who went to gifted class; the year before, one.

"They have Chinese culture ingrained in them—about half go to Chinese school on weekends. They don't like it; it's too hard. We teach in English, unless it's a difficult subject, like math. Then we use Chinese. We incorporate all cultures into our classes," she said, gesturing at the paper piñatas, dragons, fall leaves, and pictures of Columbus pinned to the classroom walls.

"These children's parents push a lot more on academics than American parents," Renee continued. "Last year, one complained—why weren't the children learning multiplication tables, because she learned them in Hong Kong at their age. In the first grade in Hong Kong, they learn to add and subtract, and they learn the multiplication tables. So parents have to adjust. We give homework, but it's very simple things. The baby class at age three haven't even developed their motor skills yet.

"Parents also tend to be more disciplined with their kids," Renee added. "Some are very strict with their children when they are very young. The American way is that babies should be given freedom and allowed to explore on their own. Not in Chinese culture. And, if the child does something wrong, the parents correct them right then. In American culture, if the kid makes a mistake, you wouldn't scold them when they're very young. Chinese are *too* strict. I found that with my four-year-olds, a lot of them come from such strict families that they felt that everything they did had to be perfect. I had one little boy last year whose father placed so much academic pressure on him, forcing him to write, that when the boy couldn't get his lines straight, his father beat him. It is *not* unusual. My mom used to push a lot, also, when I was growing up in Hong Kong.

"These kids translate for their parents. They translate at the doctor's, or when Con Edison comes over. It's a lot of responsibility. I tell parents not to push their children, that they are only five years old and should be playing a lot at this age. All the teachers here have to remind the parents that this is America."

In the hall, several four-year-olds too lively to take naps—Freddy Ng, Tony Mai, Jenny, and Ugia—were pasting paper squares onto their papier-mâché pumpkins. "I'm going to put on orange!" Freddy said, very happily, menacing his pumpkin with a gluey square of orange. "Chinese New Year is very noisy and a big dragon," Ugia said. "I like Christmas," Freddy said. The others agreed. "Santa Claus brings a basket—you can put candy inside," Jenny said. "And toys," Freddy crowed.

Mary, their teacher, told me, "Parents enjoy that we have free play, that we perform *The Wizard of Oz,* but they stress that they do not understand the need for it. They would rather have their children do more reading, more math, more vocabulary, and phonetics. They don't understand the need for play and interaction with other kids. They're always saying to me, 'No homework today? What do you mean, no homework?' You can see what kinds of lives the children have from the way some become devastated when they lose a piece of a puzzle. We tell them that toys do break, and we will replace them. This is new to them."

Another teacher, a young Chinese woman named Tiffany, agreed that Chinese push their children too much. "The parents want the three-year-olds to learn their ABCs. I have one parent who always asks me, 'What did they learn today?' She wants them to learn a new word daily. We don't teach like that. We teach them the colors and the shapes, counting from one to twenty, and *then* the ABCs. When they first get here, the kids speak no English. They learn one new English word every three days. Not until the end of the school year are they up to one new word a day."

Parents' expectations are so high that in Chinatown, an above-average percentage of children do perform adequately or better. Some dazzle, and graduate from Ivy League colleges with Ph.D.'s. But those who fall behind, because of the pressure from their families for academic achievement, become frightened and frustrated. Teachers at Seward Park High School, the largest in Chinatown, where nearly half the students are Asians, mostly Chinese, say that the laggards are regularly lost to the gangs. "They attack the most disadvantaged, or those with family problems, or the ones who are not happy with their own progress," Jules Levine, the principal, told me. "They offer the kid money or girls, and promise that it all can be different. The kids are frustrated, and when somebody is nice to them, they are vulnerable. The gang members call themselves *dai low*, 'big brothers.' And the kids say, 'My *dai low* is so good to me!'" another teacher added.

David Chen of the Chinese-American Planning Council recalls one such teenager. "His father sponsored him to come here. He didn't bring his wife—he brought his number one son, and he expected the kid to excel. In fact, the kid was a truant. The father lived in a *gong si fong* with the kid. He used to come in at two A.M. and beat the kid after he lost at gambling, and burn him with cigarette butts. Abusive behavior like this is pretty typical of new immigrants frustrated by the language barrier, the poor housing conditions and job opportunities in Chinatown, and the failure of his expectations for himself *and* for the child. Chinese don't speak their feelings. The kid is everything they have. All their hope is on the kid. They feel love, but they don't say it. And, sometimes, they don't act it."

In schools, day care, and health clinics around Chinatown, I heard similar stories of parental pressure for academic excellence becoming child abuse. Parents pressure their children in other ways, as well. A good many expect teenagers to contribute to the family income; the majority of Chinese students in Seward Park's bilingual program work at minimum wage after school in factories, restaurants, or stores five hours a day. These students struggle to keep up in their classes. If they disappoint their parents, they may be physically abused. "In China, parents do discipline their kids," said Katherine Sid, the bilingual program's director. "The parents say, 'Why can't I hit my kids?' They don't think of it as abuse. And the kids don't complain—they're taught to hide their feelings."

As parents push their children to enter the mainstream, they hope that they retain Chinese personalities. But to compete on equal ground with their American counterparts, Chinese children need to embrace individuality. This inevitably brings them into conflict with their parents, who stress submission to authority, and "filial respect," the Confucian rule of obedience to the superior male—big brother, father, uncle, premier, or president—which even includes submitting to a lot of questions when bringing their dates home, for example, and not talking back to their parents. Teenagers who rebel against the conflicting expectations that they grow up Chinese but assimilate can be outcast by their peers and their parents as *juk sheng* ("hollow as a bamboo pole")—one who betrayed Chinese culture—or "bananas," yellow on the outside but white within. And, equally sadly, those who succeed at balancing these conflicting expectations may find themselves scorned as grinds or wonks by fellow students. These binds can lead to fierce identity problems.

Paul Lee, the actor and owner of Quong Yuen Shing, Chinatown's oldest store, fell out with his father, Peter, over these conflicting expectations. Embracing individualism had brought Paul Lee into conflict with his more traditional father throughout his life, but when Peter Lee discovered that he was terminally ill, the conflict exploded. Father and son stopped speaking to one another, deeply shocking the extended family. In Chinese culture, a quarreling family is a great shame.

Paul could not forgive his father for years of strained relations. According to Paul, Peter could not change his expectation that his son should never cross him, never speak against him, and always owe him filial obedience, as well as pay the many debts run up during his watch over the store.

The store became the battleground. Peter declared that Paul had stolen it from him and not compensated him adequately for it. Paul declared that there wasn't enough cash remaining after operations and repaying the debts to cash his father out at the price he wanted. His father could never acknowledge his errors, Paul Lee told me bitterly. "This is typically Chinese. We stink, you know, as fathers," Lee asserted. "What the hell will I be like? I've alerted all my friends that if I'm ever like my father, to call me on it. I really never saw him when I was growing up. In the morning, when I was going to school, he was asleep. At nights, when I was doing homework, he was at work. He was the boss—he didn't have to work long hours, never see the family. He was a workaholic. Vacation to his generation was slothful."

Like most of the second and third generation, Paul tries to unravel the legacy of prejudice from traditional Chinese culture— were Chinese passive, or did racism in America make them passive? Why did so few fight for naturalization? "Do you want to hear a perverse idea?" Paul Lee added. "I shouldn't really get into this. I've often wondered if Chinese girls marry white guys because their fathers were thought to be wimps—'passive' is the word used for Chinese men. Around other men, they strut their peacock feathers. But in public, they're meek."

During the feud, none of Paul's brothers or sisters offered to help him repay his father's debts. In the Chinese way, these are the burden of the number one son. Paul resented that his siblings criticized him for his rift with their father but did not come to his aid. "They changed the rules," he complained. "They're asking me to play by Chinese rules but they're American. The rest of the family says my father is my father, and he's old now, and anything that he's done has to be put aside and forgiven and he must be served loyally from here on. But the Chinese rules do not mandate that I must die on the cross for everybody. They say, 'Yes, you must if he orders it.' I'm head of my own clan," Paul protested. "I will not sacrifice my family to anyone else!

"This is so bad. This fight will last for twenty years after he goes. I'm an orphan now, I have no family. It's just crazy," he told me sadly. "This is common in Chinatown," he added. "I know of many fathers who have disinherited their sons and daughters because the kids do something they don't like."

Bi Lui Chen is more fortunate. The eleven-year-old daughter of garment workers was a bright child, but behind in school, when I met her in the garment factory where she waited for her mother after school every day. Bi Lui liked America. "The houses are so big and so beautiful and the furniture is so soft," she told me. Bi Lui, however, lived in fear—fear of disappointing her parents and her teachers, and a persistent fear of her surroundings. She had not been in Chinatown long before a thief broke into her bedroom and stole her "best doll from the fair. My doll is so beautiful," Bi Lui said. "I am so scared to sleep by myself, and with my doll, I am not scared. I am so young and when I go to sleep in the dark, I look up at the ceiling, and see black things and I am so scared. You know why? We have no locks on door on the street," she said sorrowfully. She was too frightened to stay at home alone or to visit a friend's house to play, Bi Lui told me. However, she freely contradicted her father, a sign of their warm and loving relations.

The effort Chen made to adapt to American culture gradually helped his daughter to feel at home. Chen shared some of the expectations common to all Chinese about children. He excused his own lack of drive, saying, "Once a person is over forty years old, you can't expect him to be doing something big. I expect a lot from my children. I think when they grow up, they will improve my wife's and my standard of living"—in other words, as mainstream Americans, the children would support their parents in a pleasant retirement—a vast change from Chen's boyhood on a farm in Canton. How Bi Lui entered the mainstream, Chen said, was up to her. "I can't decide for her and she doesn't need any permission. Her profession will be according to her talents," he stressed. After two years in Chinatown, Bi Lui was happy at school, more and more fluent in English, and most important, less anxious. Her father was pleased that she was playing less and studying more. He thought she would have a great future.

14

STRENGTHENING *QI*

One cold, rainy February afternoon, my translator and I shook off our umbrellas and entered the Chinese medicine clinic of Qi Ye Liang and his cousin Mei Fong Ng. I was feeling out of sorts and wanted to be examined by the doctors.

Chinatown has over two hundred and fifty Eastern and Western doctors—herbalists like Liang and Ng, acupuncturists, and specialists in Western medicine. Most residents can't afford Western doctors: with the only health insurance in the community provided by the International Ladies' Garment Workers' Union, and nearly all businesses offering no sick pay, people rely on self-medication. Even antibiotics, imported from the People's Republic and Hong Kong, are sold over the counter in Chinatown. If self-medication fails, residents turn to herb doctors. They are easy to find. Their windows are zoological grottos of deer horns, sea horses, bear's galls, and other dried inhabitants of air and water, all for medicinal use.

Liang and Ng's clinic is marked with a sign bearing hand-painted Chinese characters. It is a clean, soothing, spare place. A white cat named Lilly patrols the rear of the clinic, which is partitioned with white sheets into two small examining rooms. Green plants fill the windowsill, and a tank of gaudy orange fish bubbles quietly near Liang's desk. On the walls, embroidered pictures depict clouds and mountains, and storks roosting in magnolias. Behind a long glass counter, a cupboard with three hundred drawers contains the secrets of the Chinese pharmacopoeia. On top, in a row of glass jars, is more stock, most of it dried: jars of grubs for cleansing wounds; seahorses to strengthen the kidneys and pancreas; fritillary, the round, white fruit of an herb in the lily family; and sea dragons, long, bleached, stiletto-shaped fish. Hundreds of common Chinese pharmaceuticals, most of them based on traditional herb formulas, fill the shelves in the counter: angelica, good for menstruating women; Yin Chiao tablets, a cold remedy dating from the nineteenth-century Qing dynasty; Healthy Brain Pills for insomnia; ginseng root.

Liang, a happy man with long ears, tiny almond eyes, and pink cheeks, has a feminine air about him. His slender fingers are as graceful as a fan. Like everything else in the clinic, he is gentle and quiet. Before emigrating several years ago, Liang ran the internal medicine department of a community hospital in Canton; Ng was the head doctor in a hospital in Hok Shan in Guangdong Province. Ng looks like a pretty E.T. Her large, wide eyes are ringed with wrinkles, and her face is at once enormously kind and sad.

Speaking in Cantonese, Liang told us that in 400 B.C., the sage Shen Nung investigated and codified herbal medicines, and since then, Chinese medicine has become one of the treasures of China. "We don't need complicated technical operations and big machines," Liang said. "Western doctors take X-rays, blood samples, all sorts of invasive tests to make a diagnosis. We tell the symptoms right away, without tests. We're cheaper, too. An X-ray costs several hundred dollars. A Chinese prescription costs twenty to thirty dollars. Chinese like talking to Chinese doctors—we understand what people are saying. Also, our medicines are easy, dosage-wise. Most are taken once a day; Western medicine must be taken several times a day."

Ng interrupted to say, "A couple of doses a day—easy to forget. The only disadvantage in herbs is sometimes you must boil them because they cannot be processed into Western pills."

"Western medicine often uses systemic cures," Liang went on, "but Chinese medicine is tailored to the specific complaint. Usually our clients return and say, 'Oh, it healed so quickly!' Also, many illnesses cannot be cured with Western medicines—viruses, for instance."

Liang and Ng, like most Chinese herb doctors trained today, have studied Western-style medicine and use its techniques in diagnosis. Though they are not licensed to practice Western medicine, they

understand its theories of disease and prevention. In the early twenti-
eth century, advances in sanitation, antibiotics, and surgery in the
West greatly impressed China, and it began training its doctors in
Western practices. Herbal medicine was shunted aside, practiced only
in the provinces. But after the Communist Revolution, doctors were
scarce, and herbalists filled the gap. This led to a new appreciation of
their efficacy. Now, Liang and Ng explained, a doctor's usual course of
study in the People's Republic is either three years of Western
medicine and two or three of traditional Chinese remedies, or five
years of Western medicine supplemented by one year of Chinese
medicine. Some hospitals even alternate floors between Western-style
physicians and herbalists to give patients a choice of therapies.

In making a diagnosis, Liang and Ng told us, they rely on their
own intuition and experience much more than Western physicians,
because one axiom of Chinese medicine is that any part of the body
contains information about the whole. "First, we observe the entire
body structure—your eyes, your face, your gait, your hair, your com-
plexion, et cetera," Liang said. "We listen and smell—what is the
sound of your voice? Is it really strong and thick, or is it a thin voice?
We smell your perspiration, and whether you have bad breath. Then
we ask about your current complaint, and your family history, your
own medical history, your living habits, and your eating habits. We ask
a lot of questions. But for a minor complaint, like the flu, we skip a
family history. Then we take the pulse."

Liang jotted four Chinese characters on a pad. "So," he summed
up, pointing to the pad, "The four characters in our diagnosis are to
observe; to listen and smell; to knock, which means to ask the family
history; and to touch—this means to take the pulse and to feel any
aches or the affected area of the body, and to feel your temperature.
Some Chinese doctors just practice one of these. They only take the
pulse, for instance. That is not correct. It's dangerous—too limited."

A young girl in jeans, Weejuns, and a fashionable bob entered the
clinic, complaining of restlessness. Ng felt her pulse, steadied the
girl's head between her hands, and looked at her tongue. A minute or
two later, the girl left with the Chinese panacea—ginseng root. A
powerful and quick-acting tonic, ginseng cools down the blood. "In
our view of disease, any imbalance in the system causes illness," Ng
explained. "Imbalance can be between yin and yang, hot and cold,

excess and deficiency, or the five adverse climates and emotions"—a way of categorizing pathogenic conditions—"or in a person's *qi*"—the invisible life principle animating all living things. "We divide diseases into hot and cold types," Ng went on. "Cold ones we treat with ginseng. There are several varieties: cultivated, white American ginseng; wild American ginseng, which is a little more expensive, up to a hundred dollars an ounce depending on its age; and North and South Korean ginseng, the most popular. It can cost up to six hundred dollars an ounce. Asian ginseng tastes differently than American, and it is used to treat different problems. American ginseng cools down an overheated body. After you have drunk or smoked too much, or gone out dancing too late, for instance, you drink a cup of steamed ginseng. It's a thin, red, wry-tasting liquid—helps you recover your pep. In summer, everyone uses American ginseng. Other times of the year, we use ginseng from Asia, help fight off colds, and strengthen the system. Fortunately, ginseng can be taken every day—in capsules, jelly, or as a liquid boiled from roots." Some women also rely on ginseng, Ng added, to replenish the blood lost in childbirth.

Because people in Chinatown work sixty to seventy hours a week, many only come to a doctor when they are very sick. Flus, bronchitis, high blood pressure, and infertility are common problems, Liang told us, citing the story of one garment worker who came to Ng with a high fever. Ng "felt" the water in the woman's lungs with her hands and listened with a stethoscope for a wheeze in her chest, then advised the woman to go to a hospital and have her tubercular lungs drained. A week later, after a stay in the hospital, the woman began Chinese medicine treatments with Ng. She is in good health, now, Ng said, after nine months of medication. In such cases, where the preferred treatment requires Western medicine, Liang and Ng do not prescribe anything at the time of diagnosis and advise their patients to seek out a Western doctor. And, for psychological problems, Ng added, they can do nothing. Psychology is generally not recognized in the People's Republic. "You can't take a medicine to prevent your being unhappy," Ng said, contrary to other herbalists, who had told us that they could cure broken hearts.

The door opened again, and a young patient arrived for an appointment. Liang examined him in one of the private examination rooms, and then Ng boiled some Chinese medicine in the clinic's small kitchen. The man drank the brew and left. "He had bloodshot eyes," they said after he'd gone. "There's too much heat in his blood. It has to come out in the eyes. The medicine evaporates the heat, so the blood can cool, and stop entering the eye." Bloodshot eyes are not a symptom of a bigger illness, Liang added. "It's a very common complaint from eating too much fried food and from overwork and stress."

Ng was now ready to examine me. She stared at my face for several minutes, turning it this way and that. She looked deeply into my eyes. She asked me to stick out my tongue. "There's a separate book we study that just deals with the tongue," she told me, as she turned mine up and looked underneath it. "Do you have a sore throat? No?"

The taking of my pulse lasted several minutes, and it was unlike any other time I'd had my pulse taken. It was almost a massage. My wrist was palpated in three positions, each of which gave Ng information about the functioning of a different set of my internal organs. In this gentle, quiet place, where only the bubbling of the fish tank's filtration system could be heard, Ng's warm hand and dry, flat thumb on my wrist nearly put me to sleep.

Ng kept her hand on my wrist for perhaps five minutes. "Do you have problems sleeping? Do you feel bitter taste in your mouth when you wake up in the morning?" she asked quietly. I said no to both questions.

"Your pulse is consistent," Ng said. "However, your tongue is red and dry. You eat a lot of bread? Yes, that's why. Dry food. Drink more water and light fluids. You may also be talking a lot without drinking a lot of water."

Ng then felt my throat, massaging it a long time with her warm hand. "You have dry mouth," she concluded, and wrote out a prescription. My problem was not serious, Ng assured me. It was caused by an excess of heat, which was really a surface complaint, because my *qi* was sound.

Meanwhile, Liang was examining my translator. He pulled her eyelids down and studied the whites of her eyes. He looked inside her mouth briefly. "Every time you have a meal, you are a little dizzy afterwards," he asserted

"Yes!" she said, amazed.

Liang took her pulse, then pronounced her anemic and constipated.

The translator giggled, embarrassed. "How did he know?" she whispered to me.

"A doctor can tell constipation by the condition of a person's throat," Liang informed her.

As Ng opened shelf after shelf of the pharmacy, scooping out the dried herbs and weighing them on an old-fashioned bronze scale, an acrid smell like hay filled the clinic. On a piece of paper on the counter, Ng began to build my prescription. It had twelve ingredients: inch-and-a-half-long dried grasses; furry magnolia buds; miniature pointed seed pods, like whelk shells; chopped white root; hard, flat, bean-shaped slices of what appeared to be fungi; large pieces of twisted, smoky-smelling black root; several mats of dried, white chrysanthemums, their petals mashed and yellow as old slips; bits of a white root; bits of a brown root; white seeds, small as grains of sand; ten beautifully formed bundles of some kind of grass-like herb, bent and tied in the middle with a spongy stalk; and brown ruffled leaves.

"Boil this in four cups of cold water from the tap," Ng directed. "It'll evaporate to one cup, and look like tea. Drink it once tonight and once tomorrow. Your mouth much better."

On our way out, we tapped the display case by the door and asked about the four-inch-long dried deer legs alongside the flattened lizards. "One leg is about fifty dollars. This one in the glass tube is thirty dollars," Ng replied. "For male potency."

"More sperm or larger erections?"

"Both," Ng said, giggling.

I took the twist of paper with my medicine home and poured it on the kitchen table. My husband and I peered at the olive, brown, and black pile of acrid-smelling roots, twigs, and seed pods. It made a small pyramid four inches high. It did not look prepossessing. The magnolia buds were still attached to twigs.

"You really going to boil this?" my husband asked.

"Of course."

Half an hour later, he came into the kitchen and sniffed. "Smells exactly like pot," he said.

Drinking the liquid, black as bog water, was the worst part of the treatment.

The next day, my mouth was pink, not red. I felt better.

Western medicine has only begun to appreciate the thousands of

Chinese therapeutic plant medicines. Among Chinese, it's accepted that certain white fungi lower cholesterol in the blood, that chrysanthemum flower tea relieves headaches, that four or five cloves of garlic a day help prevent stomach and colon cancers, and that black mushrooms increase the body's immune system, for example. Researchers trying to build a pharmaceutical industry in Japan are analyzing hundreds of traditional Chinese medicines to discover their active ingredients. U.S. research is focusing on select plant remedies, like garlic, and astragalus for patients with HIV or AIDS, and many drug companies are beginning more comprehensive research. Doctors in this country understand the limits of herbal medicines: they are no substitute for surgery in most cases, nor can they be used to discover the pathology of a disease. But in certain instances, for example, post-radiation cancer therapy, they have proved useful in preventing hair loss and increasing stamina by activating the body's immune systems in ways Western researchers cannot yet explain.

A few weeks later, I took my remaining prescription back to the clinic and asked Ng to tell me what I had drunk. The inch-and-a-half-long grasses turned out to be leaves of the bamboo plant. I'd guessed right about the magnolia buds and the dried chrysanthemums. The miniature pointed seed pods Ng identified as from the farsymio tree. The white root was *radix adeophorae*, whose English name, translated from the Chinese, is "root of the beech silvertop." It is used to clear heat and expel phlegm from the lungs. What I'd taken to be flat slices of fungi was instead the dried fruit of a genus of bulbous herbs of the lily family, called fritillaria. The twisted, smoky-smelling black root was ningpo figwort, and the brown root was *radix sileris*. The white seeds were called lily turf, a plant common in the United States also. "The Latin name for these herbs tied into bundles is *medulla junci effusi*," Ng told me. The English name, translated from Chinese, is lampwick herb. The last ingredient, the ruffled leaves, were the foliage of the mulberry tree. "Each has its own particular property and uses," Ng explained, "but it's the synergistic effect of mixing them that produces the remedy."

Most of these herbs address coughs and dry lungs. In Chinese medicine, the gate of the lungs is the mouth and the throat. So, to nourish my lungs, Ng had mixed herbs that moistened the mouth and the throat. For curing my dry mouth, Ng charged me $12.

15

THE TRAVAILS OF LIN

When I next saw Mr. Lin, the peddler, a year had passed. He looked much the same, his face still open and lively, but this time, he sported a white baseball cap emblazoned with Bugs Bunny. It gave his handsome face a manic air, and made him laugh.

He told me with pleasure that his life had changed—he was now his own boss. The Korean vegetable seller, for whom he had worked, had switched to selling cheap clothing, and no longer needed him. So he was back where he started, selling toys and firecrackers illegally on the street. He'd knocked off working Sundays, so his monthly income was slightly less—$1,500 a month on average, instead of $1,800. But selling firecrackers was extremely lucrative. Over Chinese New Year, he hustled $1,800; over the week of July 4th, $2,800. Despite the drop in his income, Lin still saved eighty percent of his pay.

But there were drawbacks. Being illegal, Lin had to run from the police. He stayed only a few hours in a spot, shuttling back and forth all day over lower Manhattan. And the streets were rough. A Chinese peddler had beaten him up and so had a fireworks customer, who'd paid for his fireworks with counterfeit money. Lin had chased the man, and in the fight had lost several of his teeth. When the police arrived, Lin vamoosed. He had already been arrested twice for illegal peddling and selling firecrackers without a license. "I gave him false name, false address," Lin said, grinning. So far, Lin has outwitted the police, though they have searched his *gong si fong* for his firecrackers. They didn't find any because Lin hides them in a friend's store.

In the year since we'd met, Lin had almost doubled his savings. He now had $120,000 tucked away for a small business. He lent $37,000 of that nest egg to a nephew in Washington for investment in the nephew's relatives' Japanese restaurants. Lin likes the deal: The nephew's relatives pay him interest of ten percent a month, and he can withdraw his money at thirty days' notice. Lin keeps the rest of his savings in a commercial bank, because he expects to start paying taxes as soon as his green card, giving him permanent residency status, comes through. Not too long ago, Lin asked an accountant in China-town for advice on paying his taxes. The accountant told Lin to tell the Internal Revenue Service that he earned $800 a month—about half his actual earnings. If you do this, the accountant said, you will only have to pay a little bit—a thousand dollars in taxes, maybe. "Many Chinese people say that it's enough," Lin told me. Instead, Lin has decided to underreport his earnings by a quarter.

Prosperity has encouraged Lin to think of making another big change in his life—marriage. Lin was married once before, in the People's Republic, in the sixties. His son remained with his wife when she demanded a divorce. Now, he is scouting for a Chinese woman between thirty-eight and fifty years of age. "I think much better woman single—no children," he told me. "If she is only one person, can be very close with me. I also must love the person that I marry. Especially me. Because my sister, when she was very young—fifteen years old—she love some older Chinese. Because she's young, my father don't allow her to marry. So my sister's mind no good. If I don't like somebody, I don't contact them. Very few contacts women," he said, abashed. "Many people say, 'You spend some money, go fuckee-fuckee, only little money! I say, 'No, I don't want to do that!' Never!'

"I am not young," he went on. "Last chance to change my life. The woman must really want to set up a family. Family first. Then open shop together. I hope this year."

Friends have introduced Lin to several overseas Chinese women. He corresponded with one, a thirty-eight-year-old doctor in Argentina, who is an illegal alien, for eighteen months. He liked the way she looked in a photo she sent him, and Lin and she discussed marriage. She said she was very willing and he made preparations to visit her in Argentina. He promised that if they got along, they would marry in New York, and, once he had his green card and could sponsor her as his wife, they would open a shop together in Chinatown.

Then, the letters stopped. Weeks later, another arrived. It said that the chance of marriage was only fifty percent. "I wrote her and said I very, very disappointed," Lin told me. "Before, she say, 'Just come, okay. Everything very, very good. You everythings is very good.' 'I know that I old, you young. I afraid we can't because you like my daughter—why you like me?' Every time, I wrote her like this," Lin said. "I tell where I no good—I very dirty, I not pick up my house." Bitter that he was honest and admitted to faults, only to have the doctor change her mind without explanation, Lin wrote her off.

Instead, he concentrated on bringing his twenty-three-year-old son, whom he has not seen since he was a toddler, to Chinatown. He sent $4,000 as a bribe to immigration officials in the People's Republic for his son's exit visa. Lin had heard that the boy is honest but not clever. He planned to find him a job in a restaurant for six months. If he proved diligent, he intended to buy a business for them to run.

But Chinese immigration officials rejected his son's visa application. Lin urged his son to try again, without a bribe. Meanwhile, Lin longs for intimacy. "Husband, wife, very close. Son, sometimes not very," he told me, sorrowing.

Recently, a friend showed Lin the picture of a woman in Shanghai who advertised in a Chinatown newspaper for a husband. The woman has a sister who also wants to marry. But Lin does not want a "green card marriage," and discouraged his friend from matchmaking.

One afternoon, Lin and I had tea in Chinatown. He surprised me with some news: he'd fallen in love with a Shanghaiese woman. "Very young, very beautiful," he said. Lin had never used the word "love" before, so I listened closely.

He told me that the young woman had arrived in Chinatown a year ago with her lover. Both were married and could not live together in Shanghai, so they fled to America. The lover disliked the hard work in Chinatown and had returned home after several months. The woman had stayed on, earning her living as a cook in a restaurant. "She have on her apron a Chinese saying, 'I'm almost crazy.'" Lin laughed. "Very young, very beautiful," he repeated. "She not interested in marriage—tell me, 'Friends, only.'"

Lin doubts she will change her mind, but he cannot keep himself from hoping. He sees the woman for dinner often. They fight fairly often: the woman attacks Lin's anti-Communist views, and accuses Lin of being against his country. Once, she told Lin that she wanted to be like Jiang Qing, Mao Zedong's widow—sought after by men, and powerful. The comparison to Mao's widow disturbed Lin, and, he noted, she prefers rich, young men.

Recently, the woman asked Lin to loan her $45,000 for "tea money"—the Chinese expression for "key money," the illegal payments made to Chinatown landlords so that shopkeepers can set foot in a new store. Lin explained to me that his sweetheart lives in several places. "She have room—no need to pay money. She live at another place, too. I believe she sleep with her boss. And another man. Why the boss give her these rooms? Why? Must be," he said, not waiting for my response. "I tell her, 'You have two *so close* friends, you ask them for tea money! Don't ask me, because we only friends, not so close friends," he said, gesturing to indicate a sleeping couple with two fingers twined around each other. "Her boss also ask me for tea money! Sixty-eight thousand dollars!"

Lin looked disgusted and poured himself some tea. "They think I'm very stupid because I love her. They discuss how to take advantage of me," he muttered. His face darkened. "What should I do?" he asked.

"Be careful," I said.

"Yes, be careful," he said, and added that he had heard a rumor that his sweetheart's boss and his own landlady had cheated a partner of his savings ten years ago when they began peddling in Chinatown.

"Don't tell your Shanghaiese and that boss of hers how much money you have," I urged.

"They know me! I don't spend money. Every day, worker. They always ask me, 'How much money you have?'"

We sorrowed silently at Lin's bad luck in love. Everybody asked him for money, he complained: his brother wanted to borrow money to gamble; his nephew, for a new house; his Malaysian peddler friends, for a new shop; his former boss, the Korean, to expand his sidewalk stall; a friend, to import goods made by prison labor in the People's Republic. "I only work to oppose Communism. Otherwise, I don't need to work so hard," he said. "Maybe I leave this money to some government. Maybe I leave it to somebody."

"You have found the rich man's burden—sponging relations and friends," I said.

Lin laughed, cheered up at the reminder that he, who once was in prison in Mauchuria, eating corncobs, was a rich man now. Lin offered to show me his new *gong si fong,* and we left the tea shop and headed to the center of Chinatown. On the way, we passed a dumpling of a woman, hidden beneath a wool stocking cap, who was selling toys on the sidewalk. "My landlady," Lin whispered, pointing. "Her heart is very black—just money, money, money. Home in New Jersey. Daughter has restaurant. Husband has store. Very, very rich. She has three or four *gong si fong* she rent all over Chinatown."

Lin's new quarters in a one-bedroom apartment in a modern building were busy when we arrived at eight P.M. Most of his twelve roommates were home. One man stir-frying his dinner in the tiny kitchen looked extremely surprised to see a *low faan* greet him. In the main bedroom, a wiry man in cotton undershorts talked with a scar-faced Malaysian. A foot from their heads, another man lounged in a bunk bed, reading. Four bunk beds, ranged two by two on opposite walls of the former living room, accommodated eight people, including Lin.

Around the corridor to a tiled bath was the original bedroom, in which four people slept. The new *gong si fong* was cleaner than Lin's last, but fetid, and so tiny that tuberculosis could rage through it. "Bedroom before is seven feet by six. This room, eight by fifteen," Lin boasted. He didn't seem to mind that he shared the room with seven roomates, instead of one, as before, and paid $150 for it, a little more than his last accommodations.

Several days later, Lin and I again had tea. Unfortunately, he told me, I could not photograph his *gong si fong.* "When you visit my house, they were all against you," he reported. "'Why you bring *low faan* in our house?' they say. 'We living in a double bed, you want Chinese people lose face?' Two people say this—the man in the kitchen—he's peddler, was middle school teacher in China—and the Malaysian. He say you are a United States government official. 'She have a badge on her shirt with her name!' he say." Lin looked at me, incredulous. "You had coat! No badge! I tell him, 'You pay such attention to her, you must be mainland spy!'" That, Lin said happily, shut up his roommate.

He looked around the teahouse to see if anyone was eavesdropping, then leaned forward and whispered, "Some are Fujianese—my same province. Nearly every one pay thirty thousand. Smuggled here." He covered his mouth with his hand to further muffle his voice. "Most like Communist government. They come here, just want to make money. Say to me, 'We work here five years, seven years. For one year or two year—every dollar pay back debt. Then save, become rich, go back."

Lin looked at me to see if I was following. I nodded.

"They have organization. Keep silent, no talk anybody. Very unified, very organized," he said with emphasis. Many falsely swear that they arrived in America before 1981, he explained—the cutoff for permanent residency under the Immigration Reform and Control Act of 1986, which requires employers to verify that their workers are not illegal aliens. The act was intended to reduce the number of illegal immigrants in the United States, but it has spawned a widespread traffic in counterfeit green cards and people-smuggling.

His former roommate trafficked in both, Lin whispered. "He tell me, 'You want somebody run in America? You give me twenty thousand dollars, and I can get them here.' He has wife, he has green card, and son here to study. Daughter here also. He always go back and forth. In mainland China, he have big house—maybe four floors in countryside"—built with the profits of smuggling. "One evening he tell me he lost fifty or sixty thousand in Gamble City," Lin added, referring to Atlantic City. "He also play woman—do everything."

"Of ten Fujianese, nine come underground," Lin asserted. "No one legal, like me. My neighborhood—everyone is Fujianese. Mostly this kind of person not high education. Maybe farm worker. They say, 'Why you so foolish—you rich. Why not go back?'" Lin grimaced and swore that he would rather freeze to death in the streets than return to the People's Republic.

Lin looked over his shoulders once more before continuing. "Beijing encourages smuggling," he confided. "My neighbor bribed Party officers to come here. Government know. Government also has a group. Top leader open one eye and keep other eye closed," he said. "Of thirty thousand dollars cost to come here, he give ten thousand to Party person. Government make money! Also, Fujianese make money here, send back, so government has more money. Very useful!" Lin concluded, winking.

16

THE SNAKE

L in's observations about smuggling were right on target. Chinatown is the home of "the snake"—the Chinese smuggling pipelines in the United States. These are the most ingenious, sophisticated, and costly of those of any ethnic group trying to slip into this country. The snake is now a rival to heroin smuggling—just as lucrative, but much less risky. Penalties are slight; the chances of being caught, even slighter. And the market is enormous. Chinese are second only to Mexicans in the number who want to come here by hook or by crook.

Imagine a globe. Imagine the top half above the equator a cat's cradle of criss-crossed lines, the half below the equator unmarked.

This is the map of Chinese smuggling routes in the Washington office of Bruce Nicholl, the coordinator for organized crime investigations at the Immigration and Naturalization Service, who formerly ran the service's anti-Chinese smuggling efforts worldwide. "This bottom half of the globe is no longer empty," Nicholl, an affable London-trained Chinese scholar, told me when I visited him last year. "We had some people smuggled through Auckland in New Zealand recently."

Via the snake, tens of thousands of Chinese aliens reach Chinatown each year, after the longest journeys taken by any ethnic group to the United States. Most involve several "snakeheads," or smugglers, and several transit points. Lin's report of $30,000 as the going price is now the average: recent arrivals are paying as much as $50,000. Almost no one in the People's Republic, where salaries average $500 a year, can afford this, so relatives there or in the United States pay for them. Or the aliens pay some portion of their passage and live here virtually as indentured slaves until they repay the rest. According to the INS, no other culture forces illegal aliens into indenture. Pakistanis and Indians, for instance, pay almost as much to be smuggled here, but arrive free men.

Until recently, most of the pipelines were run by Fujianese for Fujianese. Chinatown's two largest employers, the garment factories and the restaurants, like the cheap labor that the snake supplies. Employers "order up," say, five cooks and two dishwashers, from an employment agency linked to the snakeheads. The agency guarantees to provide the labor from those people it knows are in the pipelines.

"Much of the coordination and organization of this happens in Hong Kong," Bruce Nicholl told me. "Hong Kong supplies the brains, the money, and coordination. The documentation is usually obtained in Bangkok. Transit points—where smugglers provide visas and safe houses—can be anywhere. We've seen them in Turkey, in Russia, in Bucharest, or more likely places, such as Fiji or Tonga. Aliens without documents tend to go through Latin America. The routes change yearly. Brazil is now becoming big. Argentina, too. We have unconfirmed reports that there are ten thousand Chinese in Venezuela waiting to be smuggled into the United States, five thousand in Panama, and several thousand in Bolivia. My guess is that probably, at any given time, thirty thousand Chinese are stashed away in safe houses around the world, waiting for entry.

"Typically, what happens is this: you are a worker in Fujian Province, you go to the head of the Communist party in your village, and he fixes you up with a smuggler. That person gets you a Chinese passport and an exit permit. At Hong Kong, you go to a safe house and someone else will get you the right kind of documentation for the rest of the trip. You can pass through up to ten arrangers, each responsible for one part of your journey. Usually, after Hong Kong, you go to Bangkok. A few years ago, some smugglers thought that their clients would get through easier if they spoke English, so they set up a two-month English course in Kathmandu, Nepal. But it didn't work well, and the school was abandoned.

"From Bangkok, it depends which smuggler you hook up with what route you take. It's not your free choice. It depends on how much you pay, and what level of service you're buying. If you avoid Latin America, your trip is much less difficult, and faster. So those with money hit Canada first, and apply for refugee status. Canada is very generous, just like us.

"If you have little money, you take the long route. You may go from Canton to Hong Kong to Moscow to Santa Cruz to Managua and by bus or foot across the Mexican border. That is fairly quick— sixty days. There are even longer routes. One is from the capital of Fujian Province by bus and mule train across Yunnan Province, over the Burmese border, and down into Chiang Mai in northern Thailand, where you catch the first flight to Bangkok. From there, you fly to the U.S. That's arduous! You might pick up a little heroin en route to help you pay for the trip. Or you go overland from Yunnan across Southwest Asia into Eastern Europe, and fly from Budapest, or Moscow. There are some people who pay as they go. They work in their transit cities to earn the money for their next leg. Those people take years to get here.

"A number are forced into crime along the way," Nicholl added. "Suppose you get rolled in a transit point, or your snakehead is rolled and loses the airline tickets. Or the smugglers get greedy and demand more money. You call your uncle in New York City who's already paid for you, or your buddies in Fujian, for more money. Or you agree to do something illegal like smuggle heroin, work in a gambling den, act as an enforcer for the snake in Chinatown, or go back to Hong Kong and lead a group of aliens through as a guide. We've seen cases of people sent home to smuggle others in because they couldn't pay off their debt. Women agree to become prostitutes.

"But let's say everything goes okay, and all you have when you arrive here is a big debt. Then, your life is laid out for you. You accept whatever work your snakehead finds, and you live in a *gong si fong* that he provides until you have paid off your debt. All your employer gives you is food and clothes. You don't go to the police because that would put your relatives in the U.S. and your family in China in jeopardy. We arrested some people with counterfeit passports recently, and while one of our officers was questioning them, a note in Chinese was passed around: 'If you tell them the truth, we will kill your family anywhere in the world.'"

In the winter of 1990–91, Nicholl noticed a change in the snake's cargo. A third of those arrested by the INS were members of organized crime groups who were smuggling their colleagues into the United States. "We know that the 14K triad in Hong Kong is involved, the Sun Yee On triad, the On Leong tong, and the Chinatown street gangs—the Flying Dragons, the Ghost Shadows, the Fuk Ching," Nicholl told me. "Also, two gangs in Queens—the Red Dragons and the Green Dragons. Last, but not least, we've seen United Bamboo, Taiwan's biggest gang. All of these groups want people here to operate their illegal activities. They want prostitutes, and also soldiers for their gang wars. We are certain that a number of the officers of the Fukien American Association in Chinatown are involved in smuggling as well as document selling. The people at the apex of smuggling in Hong Kong have very clean hands, let me tell you. We've never seen a Chinese businessman involved with the triads arrested."

Nicholl tossed me two passports. One smelled of mildew. It was from the People's Republic, and belonged to a young man with furry eyebrows who was born in Fujian Province in 1956. The other was Japanese, the bearer a man who also had prominent brows. The Japanese passport looked new: the photo, for instance, was sealed in plastic striped with anti-forgery lines.

"Which is real?" Nicholl challenged.

I studied the passports. The Chinese one had seen some use; there were several visa stamps in it. The bearer of the Japanese passport looked older than the man in the Chinese passport, but their brows were identical. "I have no idea," I finally said. "But the bearer is the same."

"The Japanese is the forgery," Nicholl replied. "Here's how it works: this Chinese guy handed his genuine passport to a criminal group. They made his Japanese passport." Nicholl flipped through it. "This is, from page to page, totally and completely counterfeit. It was to be sent to Japan and inserted with a group of one hundred and fifty Japanese tourists coming to the United States. The tour groups submit their passports in a box. Customs doesn't look at them individually, and usually it waives personal interviews. Once this man's passport is among the others—boom, he's in, because, generally speaking, Japanese tour groups don't cause anybody any trouble. Well, he didn't get in. We believe he's a member of the Fuk Ching gang—one of the thirty thousand Chinese waiting out there somewhere to get in here."

Though the snake now disgorges criminals into the United States, the penalties for smuggling are still slight: a first offense receives a maximum of six months' imprisonment; a second, not much more than that. One of Chinatown's notorious smugglers, Big Sister Ping, a middle-aged Fujianese businesswoman reported by *Time* magazine to have amassed a $40-million fortune in alien smuggling, was convicted of a first offense in 1991 and sentenced to four months' imprisonment. Her sentence was reduced by two months for cooperation leading to the arrest of another snakehead running aliens through Phoenix. Ping's husband, an officer of the Fukien American Association in Chinatown, was arrested a few years earlier, in 1989. He and three others were convicted of smuggling three Malaysians, a Chinese child, and a Vietnamese man across the Canadian border. The *Buffalo News* reported that this man and his associates charged $20,000 for the Hong Kong–New York passage—and threw into the package deal a job, an apartment in New York, and English lessons. When the raft carrying the Asians capsized in the Niagara River, four of the five drowned. For one count of smuggling, Ping's husband, Yick Tak "Billy" Cheung, was sentenced to nine months in prison. Both he and his wife were back running their Chinatown garment factory and Brooklyn variety store within months of serving time.

Contingencies such as death en route are covered by contracts. One I saw, which had been drawn up in Hong Kong, was a masterpiece of concision, fitting neatly on one page. It specified four points: first, within two days of the alien's arrival in the United States, his guarantor in Chinatown was to pay $12,000 to the smuggler. Within a week, the co-guarantor in Hong Kong was to pay the balance. But that co-guarantor was responsible for the entire fee in the event of default by the smuggler or the guarantor in Chinatown. Second, if the alien "disappeared" in the course of the journey, the Hong Kong co-guarantor owed the full sum regardless. Third, if the alien was caught, and bail required, the smugglers were responsible for putting up only $3,000; the Hong Kong guarantor paid the rest. Fourth, all this was null and void unless the journey began from Thailand within fifteen days of the contract's date.

Quite often, contracts are superseded. Kin Wah Fong, a Fujianese who wanted to join his wife in Chinatown, agreed to pay $25,000 to be smuggled into New York City in 1990. He arrived in

Chinatown in the fall of 1990 and immediately began washing dishes in his brother-in-law's restaurant in lower Manhattan. He repaid $5,500 of his debt up front, but when he could not immediately repay more, his Hong Kong smugglers had him kidnapped. Several men broke into the kitchen of the restaurant on New Year's Eve and abducted him. The brother-in-law's family received a call demanding a ransom of $50,000 ($20,000 to pay off Fong's debt and the rest for the kidnappers), to be delivered to 125 East Broadway—the address of the Fukien American Association. Instead, the family called the police.

The police traced the beeper number left by the kidnappers, and after a brief gun battle, found Fong, badly bruised from beatings with a hammer, handcuffed to a bed in a rented house in the Bronx. They also recovered $50,000 in cash, several semi-automatic handguns, and an AR-15 assault rifle. Of the twenty-four illegal Fujianese living in the building, thirteen were arrested, including two women believed to be enforcers for the snakeheads.

Three such cases occurred in a three-month period, all strikingly similar. All three came to light because terrified relatives broke the code of silence in Chinatown and reported the crimes. In another case, a factory worker who'd taken part in the demonstrations in Tiananmen Square, and who feared for his life, had paid $5,500 to be smuggled out of the People's Republic. He'd just landed at a relative's apartment in a run-down section of Chinatown when his smugglers demanded another $27,000. The man, who had not had the time to find a job, was broke.

He and another alien in the apartment were kidnapped, and "extensively tortured," I was told by Lieutenant Joseph Pollini of the Major Case Squad in the New York Police Department. "They were beaten and burned with cigarette lighters by a group of young enforcers ranging in age from fifteen to twenty-five years old, themselves illegal aliens," Pollini said. Six weeks earlier, the enforcers had been caught arriving in San Francisco with phony passports, and had been released on bond. They had skipped town and reappeared in New York. "The eight hadn't made payment for their passage, and now were employed by the smugglers," Pollini explained. Detective Doug Lee, a member of the police squad that rescued the aliens, recalled, "One of the victims almost died in the beating. He grabbed my hand and called me a savior. 'The New York City police are so good compared to China!' he told me. I couldn't believe it—those kidnappers looked so innocent—baby faces!"

The third case occurred on Christmas Day, 1990. "Six illegal Chinese came through customs at John F. Kennedy Airport and were greeted by INS," Lieutenant Pollini told me. "They presented their forged documents and passports, and were arrested. At that point, they claimed political asylum and said if they were sent back to China, they would be killed. Immigration believed them and asked for a relative here to vouch for them. They called a woman in the Elmhurst section of Queens and she vouched for them. There are individuals throughout the city that do this by pre-arrangement.

"Immigration let the six go. They took a taxi to a restaurant on Mott Street," Pollini went on, giving the address of an indifferent eatery called Bingo Seafood. Its owner, William Tsoi, was convicted in 1990 of alien smuggling in an INS sting that identified top New York arrangers of the snake. Tsoi had served a five-month sentence.

"At the restaurant, the six are met by a group of individuals who purport to want to aid them while they're here, and promise them jobs and food," Pollini continued. "They all go to an apartment in Chinatown. There, the story changes. The six are told they are not permitted to leave until their families each pay twenty thousand dollars. They remain at the apartment for ten days. They are handcuffed and repeatedly beaten, and given the minimal amounts of food and water to sustain life.

"On January 4th, there was evidently a gang shooting in Chinatown between the Fuk Ching gang that brought them to the apartment and a rival gang. The kidnappers felt the heat was on, and they transferred the six to 165 Sands Street in Brooklyn.

"That same night, a cousin of one of the victims came to us. He said that he had paid smugglers in China to bring in his cousin, but now someone else had kidnapped him. He was very fearful of the kidnappers. He didn't want them to think he was involved in any way."

When the police tracked down the abducted aliens, they were "lying in bed trying to look as though they were sleeping," Pollini said. "They had been told if they talked to the police, they'd be killed. We found another one stuffed into the closet under the sink. How he made himself so small, I have no idea. We expect to break up the entire operation. It's run by two cousins, one in Hong Kong and one in New York City. The Fuk Ching gang in Chinatown are their enforcers, but the smugglers are independent. Their only link is that everyone involved—from the aliens to the smugglers—is Fujianese."

The tens of thousands of smuggled aliens arriving annually in Chinatown are one of the forces that keeps Chinatown booming. Most disappear into the woodwork and do not become victims of organized crime. Still, their lives as indentured slaves are pitiful. After 1997, the snake will probably disgorge Hong Kongese disenchanted with Chinese rule, and perhaps also, Taiwanese who fear that Taiwan is next for annexation. Almost no one will speak out against the snake in Chinatown because it benefits nearly everyone. One businessman who did express objections told the *Village Voice* in 1991 that indenture was the cause of great misery in Chinatown. The man, a Fujianese garment shop owner, had, before he spoke out, left the Fukien American Association and formed his own district association for Fujianese. Shortly after he did so, four men broke into his office, pistol-whipped him, and reportedly warned him to not mess around in Chinatown. When I called to talk with him, someone had scared him again. He said he could talk to no one about smuggling and hung up.

17

OLD WIVES' TALES

In a community where veils are drawn over so many subjects, concubines are another forbidden topic. In China, until the Communist Revolution, rich men married as often as they could afford. They simply bought legal second and third wives, or concubines, sometimes housing all three in one large family compound. Tz'u-hsi, the Dowager Empress, had been a concubine before inheriting the Imperial Throne. Jiang Qing, Mao Zedong's widow, was the daughter of a concubine. In the 1950s, however, the Communists abolished the ancient institution of concubinage, and it was declared illegal in Hong Kong in 1971. Nonetheless, it survives there and in Chinatown, with poignant results.

"The Cantonese came over with concubines," newspaper editor Emile Bocian told me before he retired. "That's a secret social structure and you can't probe too deeply into it. Under old Chinese law, the first son inherits everything, but of which wife? What if, for instance, all three wives have sons? It's commonly known here who were concubines, or sing sing girls, who were sold as concubines. They're still around. They're in their seventies and eighties. They're highly respectable, part of the culture."

It's true, Mrs. Ming told me. Mrs. Ming was the only person I found willing to discuss the subject. Mrs. Ming (not her real name) is seventy-eight years old. A former teacher, she is a self-assured and handsome woman with black hair and penciled eyebrows. The day we met, she wore a loose and stylish jade-green pantsuit, an elegant gold bracelet of delicately wrought linked leaves, a jade bracelet, a gold necklace and gold watch, and large gold and diamond earrings. Not only is Mrs. Ming intelligent and sensitive, she is also to the point.

Her mother's marriage was dishonored by a concubine, she told me. Her mother was her father's first wife. In Hong Kong, he had a "little wife," a much younger concubine. Because he was already married in the eyes of the Immigration and Naturalization Service, he could not bring over his concubine as his second wife. Instead, he bought illegal papers for her. These declared that she was another man's sister, and with them, she gained entry to the United States. The concubine, Mrs. Ming said, inherited her father's considerable estate, although he had six children by his first wife and none by her.

Mrs. Ming told me another tale. "I know this story because, in this case, the first wife is my niece," she said. "In the thirties, there was a laborer here who could not bring over his wife because of the Exclusion Act that barred Chinese wives, so he went back to China to see her. His mother complained that his wife didn't know how to take good care of her, so she found her son a concubine. The man promised that he would bring to America whomever of his wives had a boy first.

"The first wife, my niece, had the boy," Mrs. Ming declared, triumphant. "She got the chance to come to Gam Saan! She was admitted as a war bride"—1945 legislation that granted visas to Chinese wives of American GIs. "Her husband cooked in a take-out place and she helped him at the counter. They lived together forty years here.

"Now, the second wife, who remained in China, also had a boy. She ran away because the husband never visited again. No one knew what happened to her. Her son was brought up by her mother-in-law.

"Before the husband passed away in 1980, he asked my niece to bring over his concubine's son. 'Don't leave him in China,' he said. She had to honor her husband. Maybe she thought this son would help care for her in her old age. He and his wife live with my niece now. But they don't get along."

In Chinese culture, Mrs. Ming explained, the children of concubines must be accepted and loved by a man's other wives, including the head wife, the first wife. "Whoever have a heart like this?" Mrs. Ming asked. "My niece tried to treat him as her own, but she's pretty old—seventy-five years old. She used to be a thread cutter in a garment shop.

"Her apartment has three rooms, very small. She has the bedroom. The son by the second wife has the living room. Been like that ten years, maybe.

"My niece doesn't talk about it, only when she's really mad. One time she went home and they'd changed her lock! She couldn't get in her own home! 'Why you change the lock?' she asked her daughter-in-law. 'Oh, I thought you weren't coming back,' she said."

"How long can this go on?" I asked.

"That's what the second son is thinking," Mrs. Ming said tartly. "She is seventy-five. He is in his forties. He's waiting for her to die so he can have the apartment. And she told Immigration that he was her own son! She didn't say *my husband's second wife's son*—he wouldn't have gotten in otherwise, except for her generosity! I told her, 'Why don't you kick them out? It's your apartment.' She did ask them to leave after they changed the lock, but they said, 'Where else can we find an apartment in Chinatown?' It's a fact that you can't get an apartment so cheap like this near Chinatown anymore. My niece pays under a hundred dollars. I have six rooms and I don't pay even five hundred dollars! And I have heat and hot water, too. Bathtub in bathroom! My niece's is in the kitchen—her place is rent-controlled.

"So her own son says, 'Forget it, Mother. Don't be miserable. Don't bother with him. Do what you want and let them do what they want.' My niece doesn't see that much of them. They don't eat together. When they come back from work, she is asleep already. They work late in the garment factories.

"Everyone in Chinatown mocks my niece. 'Oh, you're so stupid, how could you let your mother-in-law do that to you—find a little wife for your husband?'" Mrs. Ming paused. "She's easygoing. If not, she would have fought her mother-in-law long time ago. Mother-in-law was boss," Mrs. Ming said matter-of-factly. "Her husband nothing special, ordinary man. Pretty good. He take care of my niece?" Mrs. Ming laughed at the thought. "She take care of him! You think they kissed each other? No! You think they held hands! No! They didn't fight! Maybe, inside they love, but they didn't show it, you know. They weren't Americanized.

"In China, before the revolution, they marry the blind match. The mother did the picking. Man and woman didn't know each other. Whether they like each other or not, they stayed together. In countryside, no divorce."

A woman who ran away from an unhappy marriage was no better than a prostitute, Mrs. Ming explained. And women adulterers were drowned in pig cages. "To kill the pig in the old days, they weighed down his cage with bricks and drowned him. Same for women adulterers. *Man* not stuck," Mrs. Ming emphasized. "*Woman* stuck. Loyalty to the husband was the most important virtue of a wife. My niece was considered a good wife."

Chinatown conceals many stories like her niece's, Mrs. Ming told me. During the Bachelor Society, the culture that arose under anti-Chinese laws in effect from 1882 to 1943, few men were allowed to have Chinese wives. Only merchants, scholars, and diplomats were exempted from the anti-Chinese legislation and allowed to bring over their Chinese wives. "So, in the thirties, Chinatown had only one hundred Chinese women," Mrs. Ming explained. "Rich men bought sing sing girls or prostitutes. The lady was just the commodity. And if the man do not have a wife, she became his wife. And if he had a wife, she was his concubine." Bachelors made liaisons with non-Asians, mostly prostitutes or women who then became their common-law wives. These liaisons were tolerated in Chinatown despite the prohibition against marrying whites because they were not legitimate marriages.

"And what happened after 1943, when anti-Chinese legislation was repealed?" I asked Mrs. Ming. Chinese wives frequently arrived here to discover an American mistress or a Chinese concubine and a whole other family claiming their husbands, she said. "They have a family fight," Mrs. Ming noted matter-of-factly. "That's all." Inheritance in Chinatown is still complicated by the offspring of unions with concubines and common-law wives, since the children are recognized under state law as legitimate heirs of their fathers' estates.

These practices meant a very small community of children—and when they married, most had arranged marriages. "My father made

mine when I was eighteen," Mrs. Ming said. "My husband helped my
father in his business. He was about twenty-one when we were introduced. We went out together a few months before we married. The
difference between China and here was that if I didn't like him, I
didn't have to marry him."

The Second World War caused a revolution in marriage customs:
Uptown jobs became available, and women for the first time left the
ghetto and joined the work force. Many became too Americanized to
tolerate arranged marriages. But, today, with the community again
eighty percent foreign-born, blind matches are once again common.
"Matchmakers charge a hundred dollars to introduce couples," Mrs.
Ming said. "But girls who grew up here want to pick their own husbands. As long as they are the same color, the mothers don't ever stop
their daughters. As long as they are yellow, right? If the husbands are
white or black, a lot of mothers object. My own granddaughter wrote
me, 'Grandmother, I know you'd rather I marry a Chinese boy. But
what can I do? I can't find any as good as Father. My husband came
over, we all ate Chinese food.' By the way," Mrs. Ming added in a satisfied tone, "she is expecting."

Besides the former concubines, modern-day concubines live in
Chinatown as well. Most are from Hong Kong, which, when it out-
lawed concubinage in 1971, permitted those who entered into second
or third or fourth marriages prior to that year to retain their status as
legal wives. As a result, some new immigrants have one wife in Chinatown, one in Vancouver, and one in Hong Kong. "Hong Kongese
come here and they bring one wife and you don't know if this is the
first or second or third," Mrs. Ming confided, adding that it can make
for delicate problems meeting people for the first time. "I always
assume the woman is first wife. Anyhow, if she is second wife, she
won't admit it. She might tell only her closest friend. If I am that
friend, I may repeat it to someone else, but never in front of her. 'Ah,
she's second wife?' people would say. 'She don't treat first wife good.'
Talk behind her back, you know. Most first wives hate second wives.
Of course—they are competitors."

"Why would a woman consent to be a second wife these days?" I
asked.

"Why?" Mrs. Ming retorted, her bracelets shaking at my naïveté.

"Because you're ugly and poor. Because he have money, and you don't. You young and pretty? You won't marry him. But you stuck, too, if he take a third wife. So long as he continues to support you, you can say nothing."

"She could take her own lover, perhaps," I suggested.

"You're old then, who would take you? The ones who would, probably very poor. You might as well stay, get what you want, eat nice, live in a nice place, do what you want. One cousin of mine, he has his first wife here in Chinatown, and his second wife in Toronto. He don't want to make trouble, so he call the second wife 'a friend.' Up there, they think he's divorced," Mrs. Ming said, looking amused. "Here, nobody tell his wife. Everybody keeps the secret."

As we parted, Mrs. Ming advised me, "Oh, no, you won't find any little wives. They never admit to it. Even if I *know* that a woman is a second wife, she won't tell me. She lie."

After much searching, Connie Pang and I found Mrs. Lee. At eighty-nine, Mrs. Lee lives alone in a $30-a-month studio on one of Chinatown's main streets. Connie visited her several times and Mrs. Lee spoke warmly to Connie, as to a daughter. Mrs. Lee never mentioned being a second wife. Nor did Connie ever bring the subject up. We did not need confirmation because Mrs. Lee's daughter had confided her mother's secret to a friend, who introduced her to us.

Mrs. Lee told Connie that she had been nineteen years old when she married in China, and she had had a son a year later. Her husband, who married her during a visit from Gam Saan, didn't see her again until their son was twelve years old. After his second visit, they had another son who died in infancy. Her husband never visited her again. Though he sent money, he didn't invite her to Chinatown. His excuse, Mrs. Lee said, was that she would have to work. "But I would have liked to work and make money!" Mrs. Lee told Connie angrily.

When she was sixty-six years old, her husband finally asked her to emigrate. They "cooked separately," Mrs. Lee said, meaning that they had no intimacy. Her husband died a year and a half later at the age of eighty. Mrs. Lee lived alone after that: in nearly a half century of marriage, she had spent three years with her husband. Mrs. Lee's advice to Connie was bitter: All men in Chinatown are bad, she said. "Don't marry anyone until you have known them a long time, and don't depend on any man."

Connie arranged for me to meet Mrs. Lee. On the appointed day, I arrived at the senior citizens' center where Mrs. Lee plays mah-jongg and bingo with friends, all of whom avoid the subject of her marriage: Most knew her rival, her husband's first wife.

Mrs. Lee was on time. A small-boned, delicate woman, she wore a coat and hat, and had a careworn air. As she approached, I saw that she was exceedingly nervous and uncertain of herself. She shook my hand, turned around, and fled.

The director of the senior citizens' center told us he was surprised that she even ventured so far as to shake my hand. "Stories of second wives who were happy are just fairy tales," he said. "There was never any question of romance in Chinese marriages. They were always for a purpose—usually children. Second marriages were for the same purpose, or for prestige, if the second wife was beautiful. That's why in my parents' generation, there were so many abused and battered wives, because so many men kept concubines. Falling in love, as you have in the West, occurs in Chinese marriages after the marriage—if at all."

As Connie and I left the center, downcast that we had caused Mrs. Lee distress, Connie disputed the director's view of concubinage. Sometimes, she said, second or third marriages were a man's only chance at happiness. "Actually, my mom is a third wife," Connie said. "My father escaped to Hong Kong in 1949. His first two marriages in China were blind matches. The third one, in Hong Kong, was for love," she said, blushing.

More and more, Chinatown, like Connie's father, marries for love. But, as Mrs. Ming reported, the spouse is still not tolerated if he or she is of another race. Research by two Chinese scholars, Betty Lee Sung, a professor of Asian Studies at City College in New York, and Morrison Wong, a sociology professor at Texas Christian University, has found that Asian-American families demand that their children not marry "out." In her book *Chinese American Intermarriage,* Sung calculated that only sixteen percent of Chinese in New York City in 1972 and 1982 married outside their culture, even less than the thirty percent that Morrison Wong discovered nationwide. Of the fifty inter-married couples among Chinese-Americans in New York City whom Sung interviewed, very few were first-generation. Most were second-generation. In their thirties and forties, they were financially well-off, but still ostracized from their families. "Intermarriage is very stressful situation for many people," Sung told me. "After twenty, thirty, forty years of marriage, some couples are still not accepted. Slowly, inter-marriage is becoming more accepted. But, if you had your druthers, you'd rather not."

18

TRANSITION

The major difficulty all Chinese face in assimilating is shifting their traditional Confucian loyalties from family to state and nation. This difficulty often produces the circular logic expressed by jeweler Harold Ha, one of Chinatown's new millionaires: "Most people in Chinatown still struggle—not successful, doing really small business. They cannot afford to spend their time and their resources to help someone else—still making their own businesses." This logic, that Chinese cannot spare the time to help others because they are not yet wealthy enough, pervades Chinatown. It is the main reason that Chinatown, despite its extraordinarily rapid rate of capital formation, has no privately endowed hospitals, libraries, museums, or philanthropies. New immigrants, of course, have had no experience with democracy; its obligations—to serve the community, to volunteer time, to give a percentage of the profits of a business and a family's income to charity—strike many as a lot to ask. "We believe, 'Take care of your body, then take care of your family. When your family is in order, take care of your city. After that, deal with the world,'" David Chen of the Chinese-American Planning Council explained to me. "Chinese are not into raising endowments. Now, the giving is to their sons." However, Chinese culture defines the family so broadly that many Chinese are never done aiding their families, and therefore fail to contribute to the nation.

This problem in transferring loyalties has given Chinese a reputation for selfishness. Randle Edwards, the director of the Center for

Chinese Legal Studies at Columbia University, noted recently, "Some go further and say that they are not concerned about others, or their neighbors; that they are concerned only about their own family; that they are selfish and manipulative, and won't take risks to make a better society."

Heo-Peh Lee, a Taiwanese immigrant and a librarian turned newspaper executive and developer, is a study in the difficulties of assimilation. A diminutive, rotund powerhouse, Lee is one of the handful of new millionaires to have risen in Chinatown since the immigration laws changed. He runs Shie Jie Construction Company, a $20-million business, and is also a consultant to the *World Journal,* a Chinese-language daily, which is part of the largest Chinese newspaper empire in the world. It is owned by Lee's father-in-law, Wang Wu Tinu, a former member of the standing committee of the Guomindang in Taiwan. The *World Journal,* which reflects the views of the government of Taiwan, has great influence over the Chinese Consolidated Benevolent Association, Chinatown's informal government. This influence gives Heo-Peh Lee considerable power in Chinatown. It also makes him feared by some members of the new guard who have incurred the wrath of Taiwan.

"Chinese very hard to talk to," Lee told me when we met in his Queens office. "Either say they are so wonderful, be very boastful, or say nothing, and you think they are not important." Lee is clearly one of the former. "I came here as a highly educated person. I had both best from China and United States. I was a professor," Lee said.

Lee explained that he waited until the Chinese community swelled to make a change in careers from librarian to developer. "There's no water, there can't be fish," he noted. He built his first project at the foot of the old Brooklyn Naval Bridge, close to a low-income project inhabited mostly by black people. "I had full safety measures," Lee recalled. "Twenty-four-hour security, and a system of vans to shuttle people to and from the subway, so they didn't have to walk by the black project. That's how I sold all the condos in four months. At first, people had bad words for us. They called our building 'The Chinese Palace,' and kids threw rocks. Now, I am very glad to tell you, we have found peaceful co-existence."

From that $6-million development, Lee moved on to build a

headquarters in Queens for the *World Journal*. Now he has opened a hotel in Flushing. The $40-million development built for a franchiser of Sheraton Hotels is Lee's first venture into the mainstream: Chinese are expected to comprise only a third of the clientele.

"Six months ago, I wouldn't have talked to you," Lee told me. "We deliberately play low-key. The Chinese don't show off. If you do, we think sooner or later you pay. We stay low-key so we will have the least obstacles to success. We always said no to interviews, and when we were asked how large our business was, we always said, 'Not that large, oh, we're just doing small things.' But right now we are preparing for publicity. We want people to rent the hotel's atrium space and be our guests, so we talk to you.

"I think Chinese must consider ourselves American. How did I come to that idea? Three years ago, we bought a hotel in Plattekill, Upper Newburgh, New York. It was a Spanish resort. They served American food. Chinese don't like American food. After we bought it, we tore down everything—no more Spanish, everything Chinese. Now we have the consequences: not enough business. And we lost the Spanish business!

"So, I learn that our hotel must be regular, common Sheraton for Americans. You can target some of your marketing. Maybe in your decor, you include something the Chinese like, or avoid what they dislike. Black, for example. Chinese don't like black color. Chinese prefer red. Americans don't bother, they like both. But Chinese definitely prefer something red: it means happy, lucky, wealthy. Yellow means noble. Black means a very sad feeling. Chinese like fresh water, so we will build a waterfall in the foyer—represent liveliness, and money comes in like water, like a natural force. So that we don't antagonize anyone, we will have American and Chinese features in our lobbies."

The hotel will be the first built by a Chinese in Flushing, Lee marveled. "Flushing is international city. So talk about population— you have people from China, Taiwan, Hong Kong, people from Pakistan, Philippines, Afghanistan! There are Muslim temples in Flushing! Queens itself, if it were a city, would be ranked in the top ten in the country," Lee said proudly. "We believe that Long Islanders can drive to our hotel, avoid Manhattan, to meet their friends and have lunch. See, in New York, cost you fifteen dollars for parking! I believe that I can serve the people coming here from Asia in the future, if we Chinese handle our fate right. In plain language, that means what we can get. In good language, what we can contribute."

Twenty years after he arrived in the United States, Lee is learning how to contribute. The process began a while back when he grew frustrated that Chinese had no voice in city or national politics. He formed a political action committee, composed of conservative Taiwanese businessmen like himself, mostly Republicans. On the advice of a member of Chinatown's new guard, Virgo Lee, the head of a left-wing social welfare agency who was also an adviser to Jesse Jackson, Lee threw his group's support behind Jackson's Rainbow Coalition in the 1988 presidential primary. The move caused a sensation in Chinatown. "Because Chinese are really very biased," Lee explained. "To come out and support a black is not our thing. On the one hand, we say we are a minority. On the other hand, we Chinese have been many times the victims of blacks in crimes. Okay? We feel a lot of trouble has been caused by those people on us. Which is true! But the points Jackson was making, the things blacks have talked about for so long—they don't want privileges, they want their fair share—Chinese also are looking for." Lee's group raised $30,000 for Jesse Jackson's primary campaign. "That made us a very big group for him and, especially, it had a big impact on the Democratic party."

Virgo Lee, now a special adviser on Asian affairs to New York's Mayor David Dinkins, remembers the group's support well. "When I suggested a fund-raiser for Jackson, their business committee gave me stone looks," he recalled recently. "They met four times before deciding. See, China has no opposition parties, and they weren't clear what party affiliation means. I told them that the only way to understand American politics is to understand that Robert Dole hates George Bush, but that after the primary, Dole's people will contribute big money to George Bush. They had to learn that you can be a member of a party and hate its candidate, for instance. They had to learn that if you do an event for one candidate, you aren't tied for time immemorial to him. Their support was so controversial that Taipei said our community had gone nuts. The Taipei papers—the *World Journal* and the *China Times*—said what is our little Chinese community doing? Have they lost their bearings? Fund-raising for Jackson got Lee's group so much national press, and Chinese press, and Chinese television coverage, that they were thrilled. It put them in the mainstream."

The following year, as a result of the newspaper coverage of Lee's group, every candidate in the New York mayoral race appointed Chinese liaisons to Asian voters and asked people in Chinatown and in Lee's organization in Queens to raise money for them. This, Lee told me, greatly improved on 1980, when Mayor Edward Koch ignored Chinatown's protests against a proposed new jail, saying, "Why should I care about the Chinese? How many votes do they have?"

"In 1989, during the mayoral campaign, Mayor Koch changed his position, at least to me," Lee boasted. "He treated me like royalty. What did we do? We raised money for him in the primary. Since we raised the money, we became very friendly with him." However, Lee's group switched their support to David Dinkins in the general election, and raised $50,000 for his candidacy, about half of all the money contributed to the mayoral campaign from Chinatown. In a tight race, the effort was appreciated.

This effort was another step in the political evolution of Heo-Peh Lee, Virgo Lee told me. "Lee and his people underwent an education in city politics, and in the gradations in the Afro-American community. They learned, for instance, that not all blacks are bad people. Their support for Dinkins, so soon after their support for Jackson, caused another editorial debate in Chinatown. Many letters were written to the papers on both sides. The mayor's victory was a watershed because many, many people, especially in the Chinese community, doubted that a black could win. Now the Chinese feel that if a black person can win, *they* should have a position!"

"Mayor Dinkins appoint more Chinese than any of his predecessors," Heo-Peh Lee exulted. "Over six as commissioners. He's accessible to the Chinese. Give you an example. Yeah! Very simple example. When our group has inauguration of new officers, he spent whole evening with us at the swearing-in ceremony. That was the first time he came to Flushing," Lee said, nodding happily. "Second example. Three years ago, we asked the Democratic party leader in Queens to endorse a Chinese named Randy Ong for judge. The party leader gave us the same kind of feedback as Koch had over the jail—'How many Chinese votes are there?'

"Well, last year the party leader nominated Randy Ong," Lee said gleefully. "We are recognized now because raising that money for

Jesse Jackson made us known. Tell you what—a few months ago I had dinner at the Terrace on the Park"—a noted New York restaurant—"and I met the Queens Democratic party leader. I introduce him to the new president of our political action group, Mr. Cha, an attorney. He said, 'Oh, the second Randy Ong?' See?" Lee asked. "Because he was trying to show off to me! Compared to what he said last time, when we asked him to nominate Ong—'Well, Randy Ong, he can wait, how many Chinese votes are there?'" Lee laughed. "Now all we have to do is come up with some candidates."

Finding Chinese who have gone another stage in the transfer of loyalties, and are willing to stand out, campaign, and work for the welfare of the nation, is difficult, Lee observed. He himself is still getting the hang of the obligations of democracy. Recently, the Queens borough president nominated him for trustee of the Queens Botanical Gardens. "This is not my cup of tea," Lee said. "I barely know the difference between a rose and a turnip. But since I wanted to have a Chinese in the position, I found another candidate so I could withdraw." He sighed. "This Friday they drag me to the Red Cross. Want me on the board." He sighed again. "The problem is, there are so few of us Chinese recognized by outsiders, that they grab you. I am busy. How can I do Red Cross?" he asked, putting into a nutshell the dilemma of many Chinese. Lee looked tragic. He sighed some more. "In the old days, I feel I couldn't do these things. I become more civic-minded now."

19

EATING AS AN ART

When Chinatown isn't gambling, it is eating. Chinese delight in eating. In the immortal words of the noodle-maker of Green Street, "When [the Chinese] have a little money, they like to eat it all up." Great cooks have glory in Chinatown; even Confucius divorced his wife because she couldn't cook.

The open-air markets come alive early in the morning, and by nine A.M., wholesalers deliver live carp, catfish, large-mouth bass, and other freshwater fish from trucks outfitted with giant fish tanks. Throughout the day, fresh fruit and vegetables arrive from Chinese truck farms up and down the East Coast. Cantonese, the dominant cuisine in Chinatown, is the most delicate and subtle of many regional cuisines in China, and it values freshness above all. Fish must be wriggling in water before being cooked, vegetables harvested that morning, meat freshly killed.

Hong Kong–style cooking, essentially a more elegant version of Cantonese, is the first new style of cooking to excite Chinatown in a decade. Brought to the community with the torrent of people and capital exiting Hong Kong before 1997, it too emphasizes freshness, particularly of fish. With its proximity to the sea, Hong Kong serves a cornucopia of seafood. In Chinatown, residents told me over and over that the Triple Eight Palace, a fancy restaurant beneath the Manhattan Bridge, serves the best Hong Kong cooking. Its chef, Hoy Chuen Ping, a free and easy, saucy sort of a fellow, shops early in the morning at the Fulton Fish Market, and his restaurant is one of the few in

Chinatown to keep both fresh- and saltwater tanks for live fish.

Hoy was plucked three years ago from Hong Kong by Ming Chen, who owns several low-priced, popular Chinese restaurants around metropolitan New York. Chen had Hong Kong investors for the Triple Eight Palace, and he wanted a Hong Kong chef to turn it into an acclaimed restaurant. A Hong Kong food critic recommended Hoy. The son of a seaman, Hoy began his training at fifteen; at twenty-one, he was managing chef at Sun Kong, one of Hong Kong's larger restaurants, supervising sixty-eight cooks serving three or four thousand customers a night.

On a winter afternoon, Connie Pang and I arrived at Triple Eight's pink marbled reception area, which was decorated with a typically Hong Kongese display of spotlit Courvoisier bottles. Hoy, a tall, good-looking thirty-year-old, came out of the kitchen with Ming Chen and invited us to sit down at one of the tables. At this hour, we had the gigantic restaurant, with its blinking neon sculptures and fish tanks, to ourselves.

Speaking in Cantonese, Hoy said that his forty-eight-person kitchen served five hundred to eight hundred customers a night. "When a customer asks for fish, we select one from our freshwater or saltwater tanks, and kill it on the spot," he explained. "Everything must be *very* fresh. Maintaining a proper chemical balance in the saltwater tanks can be tricky, so most restaurants do not have this. Of course, we also have tanks for crabs, turtles, and lobster. Two or three cooks prepare the seafood, then we have the steaming section, and another for frying and baking. Four or five people just decorate the dishes. The main skill there is in using the cleaver to carve a carrot into a unicorn or a flower, or all sorts of other animals. We have seven chefs cooking, mainly with woks. Another twenty-four make dim sum, roast duck, and soy sauce chicken; these time-consuming dishes involve special techniques. In Chinese cuisine, cooks know not hundreds of dishes, but *tens* of thousands of dishes. We have a thousand on our menu and we change our menus every three months."

Ming Chen boasted that Hoy was one of the few Hong Kong chefs who excelled at both everyday meals and banquets. Banquet food is strictly traditional, Chen said: recipes for the special-occasion dishes like roast pig, abalone, shark fin and birds'-nest soup, crispy fried chicken, steamed gray sole (signifying good luck), and oysters (signifying good business), which are served at weddings, funerals, New Year's, and other holidays, are thousands of years old. The daily menu allows Hoy more creativity, Chen observed.

"I wear Chinese trousers and other accessories," Hoy said, explaining that he prepares dishes adapted from Vietnamese, Indonesian, Thai, Japanese, and Singapore-Malaysian cuisines using ancient Chinese cooking methods. "Thirty years ago, it might have been true that Canton had the most wonderful cuisine," Hoy told us. "Now, Hong Kong does. I will show you."

The dishes poured out of the kitchen for an hour and a half. They were led by French-style scallops in their shells, the richness of the scallops accented by a light bechamel sauce; a seafood puff, fried crispy outside, melting inside with milk and cheese, and an occasional crunch of celery and mushrooms; and a humongous oyster in a brown chili sauce. It contrasted piquantly with the vegetable soup, hearty as a stew.

The entrees took us on a tour of Asia. The Thai-style green mussel casserole, vibrant with fresh coriander, Chinese caraway, celery, preserved Chinese cabbage, and onion, had the snap of some chilis in the broth. A Hunan white rice dish was mixed with bits of duck sausage and scallions: the sausage had oozed fat and meat juices into the rice as it steamed, making the rice soft, oily, and spicy. An all-Japanese dish—salmon brushed lightly with a sweet orange sauce and garnished with a tangle of black seaweed—was succulent. Hoy's own creation, an Indian curried oxtail stew, overpowered me with its lustiness.

When Connie and I could not eat another water chestnut, we accepted Hoy's invitation to the next meeting of the Society Which Gathers Talented Chefs for Interchange. This, Hoy told us, was a new group he had started to encourage Manhattan's top Chinese chefs to swap recipes for new dishes. "This is casual gathering," he said. "Begins after we get off work, about eleven P.M."

Several weeks later, Connie and I arrived in Chinatown at midnight. I was startled to find the joint jumping. Our rendezvous, a restaurant formerly owned by the boss of the Tung On tong, was doing a fast trade in take-out meals for the occupants of stretch limousines waiting outside the door. Down the corner, a steady stream of single men disappeared into the Tsung Tsin Association. There were big gambling games going tonight.

Inside the restaurant, Hoy, seated among twenty-five men occupying two tables at the back, hailed us boisterously. The chefs welcomed us with applause, then joked that they would rather look at us than be serious and answer questions. We laughed and they laughed, and then they went back to their drinking, smoking, and thirteen-card and *pai gow.*

The chefs were also collecting a *hui,* a revolving pool of cash. Each man put $10 to $25 and a slip of paper with his name on it in a bowl. The bowl was passed to Hoy, who picked a slip and shouted out the winner's name. The man, grinning broadly, had won $300 to buy ingredients for new dishes—rather like a group of artists might pass the hat to raise money for one of their number to buy paints and canvas. The only stipulation was that the winner must give an accounting of his culinary discoveries to the society's financial officer.

One by one, more chefs arrived, and Hoy waved them in, yelling greetings, proud and noisy as a rooster. Younger than most of the others, he was bursting with vigor, though, like the rest, he was straight from eleven hours in a steaming kitchen. "This is a social function," he told us. "It's fun. We'll break at three or four A.M., and everyone will be at work at ten or eleven A.M. We all have a lot of stamina."

At our table, besides Hoy, were Kenny Chu, a dark-complexioned man with very fine features and a mustache; Mui Tung Leung, the executive director of the Chinese American Restaurant Association; Mr. Luing, a fair-skinned man from the Flushing branch of a popular Chinatown restaurant; Mr. Wang, the long-time chef at a budget Canal Street eatery; and Lee Wang, from Oriental Pearl, an important two-star restaurant. The youngest was a fellow in wire-rim glasses and a Calvin and Hobbes T-shirt who had come to cultivate customers among the chefs for his new wholesale seafood business. Among the group, all of whom were casually dressed in sweaters and chinos, only one spoke English.

They listened respectfully as Hoy announced that tonight marked the seventh meeting of the Society Which Gathers Talented Chefs for Interchange. This society is unique in Chinatown, Mui of the Restaurant Association told Connie and me. "Chinese keep their recipes secret," Mui said. "But most of the people here are in their thirties. Compared to older chefs, these young people won't care much if their skills are copied. The new thinking is that learning from each other is a way to improve."

I asked what new dishes the society had made, and suddenly we were on dangerous ground. Kenny Chu pulled on a beer and said that they had cooked many wild animals which are expensive and not usually available in restaurants. "We've eaten armadillo, alligator, palm of black bear, and rattlesnake. Sometimes we buy these, sometimes we get them from a friend who's been hunting. There's no formal market for crocodile and armadillo, for instance. You have to buy them on the black market." Armadillo, Chu told us, is fried in a big pot of oil, then made into a stew.

Hoy interrupted to say that none of these dishes was a failure. "So far, so good," he said.

"These wild animal dishes are quite common among the Chinese people," Luing added. "We believe that they are good for your health. For instance, if you eat rattlesnake, it replenishes the blood, improves the circulation, and makes you recover faster from fatigue and overworking."

Lee Wang, chef of the Oriental Pearl, said that rattlesnake is cooked with Chinese herbal medicines and made into soup. "This prevents your getting sick and gives you good health."

Such a frank discussion of a subject ordinarily forbidden—the consumption of wild animals, many of them illegal to hunt in the United States or to import from Asia—startled me, and so when Mui, who had been looking on uneasily, asked me to stop taking notes, I was not surprised. I knew that in Asia, black bears are hunted for their meat, claws, paws, and gallbladders. Chinese and Koreans revere the gallbladder as an aphrodisiac and a cure for many ills, including cancer. Widespread hunting in Asia has nearly decimated the species, and, recently, Chinese and Korean hunters have begun hunting in this country, where a patchwork of state laws have permitted a flourishing black market in bear parts. Virginia, for instance, prohibits bear hunting; West Virginia does not. New York permits bear hunting, provided it is in season. It also allows bear parts to be exported to Asia, where gallbladders bring up to $45,000 apiece. The Asian craving for black bear and other wild animals is causing an outcry from conservationists in this country anxious to stop the slaughter.

Mui's suggestion that I not write about the society's wild animal dishes cast a pall on the table. His words carried authority: The Restaurant Association is a powerful trade group representing Chinatown's third largest employer, and a chef who ran afoul of it was in hot water.

Lee Wang, the other chef of Hoy's stature at the table, evidently didn't scare easily. Ignoring Mui, I asked the group how much bear palms cost. "About one hundred and fifty dollars a paw," Lee said. Before he could tell me how many the group had consumed, Mui cut him off with a warning that bear parts are not allowed to be imported into the United States, and that any restaurant serving them could be shut down, as was a New Jersey establishment a few years ago. Mui insisted that, in fact, the chefs had been mistaken and the society had not eaten any palm of bear. "Armadillo can be available, but bear is difficult," he said. "The Animal Protection League will strongly object and we might be sued by the federal government. If you overemphasize this, customers will think that weird things are cooked in Chinatown, and business will fall off."

The table looked embarrassed. Hoy withdrew from the circle and chatted with friends at the next table. Some of the chefs there looked over curiously to see what the trouble was at our table. Mui spoke again. "Don't look down on us or treat us as inhumane barbarians in your book. We know that Americans won't eat bear, but it is a precious dish in Chinese culture, available only on special occasions. For centuries, it was available only to royalty."

After several minutes of silence, Lee Wang again broke the tension. "This group's main interest is in exchanging ideas about how to adapt our menus to suit American tastes," he observed. "For example, in ancient China, there was a dish called 'A Monk Jumped Over the Wall.' The monk was a vegetarian and didn't eat meat, but one day, on the other side of his convent wall, meat was being prepared. It smelled so good that the monk jumped the wall." Lee smiled. "Originally, this dish was made with bear in China. Here, we use substitutes—abalone or sea cucumber or shark fin. Shark fin is another ingredient once available only to royalty. It's supposed to be good for women's skin, by the way. Otherwise, we make 'A Monk Jumped Over the Wall' exactly as it is made in China. It's cooked in the *kao* method, an ages-old Chinese cooking method, which cooks food over a very gentle fire for eight hours."

Lee's speech formally closed the discussion of wild animal foods. Everyone began discussing the designated topic of the evening—how lobster was priced and where to get it cheap. At one-thirty A.M., dinner arrived. The dice and cards were put away, and the chefs got down to the serious business of eating.

A delicate, clear broth made from grouper and vegetables was first. Next, a Malaysian-style satay. The pyramid of raw red beef slices on a bed of baby spinach leaves was sprinkled with enoki mushrooms. The chefs stripped slices off the mound and dunked them into a bubbling, spicy, peanut-based sauce, which instantly cooked the beef. They nibbled appraisingly, then dipped the spinach leaves and mushrooms into the sauce, and nibbled some more.

It was a strange scene. Outside, the night was dark. Inside the restaurant, starkly lit by fluorescent lights, mobster types were coming and going, gamblers were dropping by for take-out, teenage gang members were heckling the staff (including one kid who mimicked firing a gun at the headwaiter and exited laughing), and twenty-five of Manhattan's top Chinese chefs wordlessly sampled dishes.

"This satay is very good," Hoy eventually commented. "I can't stop eating it." Lee Wang, seated at Hoy's side, remarked only that the restaurant had put a lot of thought into the satay's preparation. The restaurant's timid chef, hovering anxiously by Hoy, ventured that the key to the dish was the cut of the meat.

The next presentation, a clam, onion, and scallion omelet, was less successful. It was spongy with oil and oversalted. A whole fish, its head pointed at Hoy, the guest of honor, was moist and soft. My neighbor instructed me that this was the grouper from which the first course of broth had been made. "See," he said, "the body of the fish is intact. No flesh has fallen off the bone. That is the secret of this dish." It is difficult to do, he assured me. A frugal congee, a soup of soft-boiled rice often eaten for breakfast with ginger slices, and a last dish of curried noodles with vegetables, finished the meal. Each was sampled silently.

I could contain my curiosity no longer, and asked the table for their verdict on the satay. The awkward silence stretched into minutes. Finally, Hoy ventured his thoughts. The dish was not yet in his restaurant, he said judiciously, weighing his words. Now that he had tasted it, he had some ideas about how to introduce it. He wouldn't copy it, but instead modify it. He pointed out that this satay was served on a lazy Susan, but he might serve his in a metal pot to integrate the Malaysian culture into the dish. Or he might put the beef on ice, in the Japanese kobei style.

No one else said anything. Hoy had spoken for all. I was puzzled until my neighbor admonished me. "It is bad manners to criticize the dish of one's host," he said. "This is his restaurant: Here he is the commander and we are the subordinates."

Connie and I left the Society Which Gathers Talented Chefs for Interchange at two A.M., as the chefs began gambling and drinking again and growing rowdy. Outside, we were the only women in the streets, as we had been the only women in the restaurant. After midnight, Chinatown belongs to men—gamblers, revelers, chefs, and dishwashers going home.

20

REVOLUTIONARIES

When Chinatown is not working, gambling, or eating, it is foment-ing revolution in China. As in all exile communities, revolution-aries are behind every lamppost in Chinatown. The difference is, here, they have made revolutions.

Among the first was a former doctor, a wanted man named Sun Chung-san. He fled China in disguise, one step ahead of Manchu agents, in 1895. The other members of his triad had been beheaded for trying to overthrow the Qing dynasty. Moving in disguise from Japan to Europe, he survived several assassination attempts before arriving in Chinatown.

At the time, many of its residents were also revolutionaries: some were survivors of the Taiping Rebellion, which very nearly overthrew the Manchu rulers in China during the years 1845 to 1869; most, however, were monarchists who dreamed of restoring the imperial throne. They found the doctor's ideas of a republic in China comical, and he remained a shadowy, scorned presence, often without enough to eat. He persisted, however, preaching his idea in underground meetings in Chinatowns throughout the United States. In San Fran-cisco, he joined the Chih Kung tong, and, after winning over some of its members to his peculiar idea of a republic, raised money for the revolution from triad societies across the United States and Hawaii. After the Boxer Rebellion in 1900, and the Dowager Empress's death from natural causes, more Chinese rallied to the cause as corruption worsened in China. The doctor returned to Japan in 1905 and formed the Revolutionary Alliance, which established branches throughout China to organize resistance. On October 10, 1910, when Sun Chung-san was in Denver, revolution exploded in China. A telegram announced the downfall of the Qing dynasty and an end to two thousand years of authoritarian government, and offered Sun Yat-sen the presidency of the new republic.

Today, there are many exiles in Chinatown eager to finish the democratic revolution that Sun Yat-sen, the George Washington of China, began. They dream and conspire and rally to support their heroes, men who have the courage and dedication to defy Beijing. In 1989, they rallied to the revolutionary most celebrated in the West, twenty-one-year-old Wu'er Kaixi, the former chairman of the student leaders in Tiananmen Square. During the dreary months that followed the crackdown, when all Chinese were in mourning for their country, Kaixi made the rounds of Chinatowns in the United States, rallying support for democracy in China. To Chinese, he was the heart and soul of the uprising, the symbol of its youth, its naïveté, and its courage, as well as its frustrated hopes. Kaixi had become a celebrity for yelling at Premier Li Peng during a televised audience while pro-democracy crowds in Tiananmen Square called for Li's and Deng Xiaoping's resignations. He had escaped from China by mysterious means and was studying English fitfully at Harvard University, but spent most of his time raising funds for the Federation for a Democratic China. The new group, formed by recent immigrants and escaped pro-democracy leaders, was based in Paris, and Kaixi was its vice-president.

I'd first seen Kaixi at a memorial concert honoring the dead of Tiananmen Square at Lincoln Center in New York City. The audience of several thousand Chinese was Westernized, not Chinatown residents. Ladies wore suits and their hair was styled in French twists; their silent children wore their best clothes. Kaixi, the guest of honor, shuffled to the stage straight off a plane from Paris, on his way to Harvard. He asked the audience to excuse his rumpled khaki jacket and chinos.

Very slowly, a crescendo of applause built. Kaixi smiled a little, and joined in the applause. Hesitant and ill at ease, he gave an emotion-choked speech, after which he accepted a gift of a silver apple, a symbol of New York, not for himself, he said, but for his fellow students who had died in the uprising, or were imprisoned. Choking back tears, he recalled how happy it had made him to see so many Chinese striving for democracy in Beijing, but now, to be alive and able to "go outside to the free world, and think freely, and continue the movement" without them saddened him. The audience, deeply moved, stayed on its feet as the song "My Home Has Become a Killing Ground" resounded.

Before my meeting with Kaixi several months later, I asked students in a history class at Seward Park High School how many of them expected democracy in China in five years. No one raised a hand. Ten years? One boy raised his hand. Thirty years? All twenty students raised their hands. The class gave me a list of questions to ask Kaixi.

Kaixi came bounding into the restaurant where we met, casually dressed, boyish, and enthusiastic. I told him that I knew a skeptic in Chinatown who doubted that the government had killed perhaps a thousand people in the uprising because he'd never seen a photo of the People's Liberation Army firing on citizens. Kaixi replied that he had seen many people crushed by the tanks. "In the massacre that morning, over seven thousand died in Beijing," he said through an interpreter. "In the small Tiananmen Square, it's hard to say how many, perhaps five hundred. The most conservative estimate is five hundred." He was spared, Kaixi said, because he has heart trouble and fainted. "I was holding a dead body in my arms, and was taken away in an ambulance. Students carried me out of the square.

"There are more than twenty-one on the government's most wanted list of 'counter-revolutionaries' who led the uprising. In fact, I think over ninety are in hiding. In each school, we had one or two student leaders. Really, we weren't student leaders, we were student organizers. Very few got out of China—so far, only myself and one other," he said.

Then, Kaixi explained why the movement developed. "First of all, a feudal monarch has ruled China since the fifteenth century, and, for the last one hundred years, people have been fighting the oppression. So this move is actually a continuation of that long struggle. Also, the global trend toward democracy has affected China. And the last forty years of Communist rule have brought many miseries to the people. By the same token, Chinese people have lost confidence in the Party," he said. "So it was just a matter of time before this movement broke out.

"The more immediate cause is that ten years ago, when the Communist party found out it could not maintain its rule, it started this so-called economic reform. But it and the 'open-door' policy actually went hand-in-hand with the Four Principles—the Party line—and it proved an impossible course. That's why in the last decade or so there have been several pro-democracy movements in China—in 1976, 1978, and 1986. By 1989, the economy was fatally hit. This reactionary political system gave rise to a lot of phenomena like profiteering and corruption and brutality. So the movement was inevitable from the perspective of history.

"These are the basic causes. Now we talk about some side causes," Kaixi went on. "Because of the 'open-door' policy, democratic ideals really occupied a place in the minds of intellectuals. However, the forerunners of the democracy movement, Wei Jingsheng and Fan Li Ju"—China's two longest-held political prisoners, serving fifteen-year sentences for leading the 1979 democracy movement—"were severely punished. Still in jail. And another side cause is that there were many lucky days in 1989." Kaixi smiled. "For example, tenth anniversary of the arrest of Wei Jingsheng; also, exactly forty years ago that the Communist party took control; seventy years ago that the May 4th Movement started; and two hundred years ago that the French Revolution began."

A friend who accompanied Kaixi whispered something to him, and they both laughed. In slangy English, Kaixi said that his friend had reminded him of another important happening. "In 1989, Wu'er Kaixi was already twenty-one years old—old enough to make trouble." Kaixi laughed, delighted. He promised me that in the second wave of the movement, which he predicted would occur in the early nineties, he would go back to China. "I hope I will be on the most wanted list again." We all laughed at his appealing charm, his bravado.

I told Kaixi that the high school students in Chinatown wanted to know what Premier Li Peng said to him during their televised audience.

First, Kaixi quickly ran down the events leading to their confrontation. "From the 13th to the 19th of May, we carry out the hunger strike—during this period, the attitude of the government was inhumane, atrocious, and scandalous. On May 19th, the hunger strike entered the seventh day, and, according to international law, when a hunger strike enters the seventh day, the government should unconditionally enter into a dialogue with the strikers. So Li Peng decided to have a conference with two representatives of the hunger strikers. One was me. We met about fifty minutes. A lot of things he said didn't make much sense. He look very foolish sitting there. We can't really say that it was a back-and-forth argument. Li Peng was not in a position to lecture anybody. Li Peng has a very low intelligence. He studied in Moscow for seven years and was not able to graduate.

"This very cool, cruel attitude of the government toward us was exposed, and so we decided to end the hunger strike, and instead occupy Tiananmen Square. With the threat of military force, two kinds of opinions emerged among the students about whether to leave. The majority were in favor of staying, so we stayed. The government wouldn't accept our demands for freedom of speech and freedom to vote, and this most peaceful request for the government to enter into a dialogue lasted until June 4th. Deng Xiaoping, of course, ordered the troops into the square."

To a question about why he rose to the head of this uprising, the largest public protest since the founding of the People's Republic, Kaixi replied in English, "Why not?" And laughed and laughed.

"That's an American-style answer," I said.

He laughed again. "A year before I know I can do such a thing, but I haven't the chance to do that." He laughed and looked cocky.

"He is not Han Chinese," his friend said, blushing scarlet at Kaixi's boldness.

The translator, a former United Nations translator, interjected, "He's very charismatic, this guy. People love him for that."

"I really envy the American people because they enjoy so much freedom," Kaixi continued. "First of all, there is no public security bureau here to chase me! Overthrowing the government in China is not our goal," he said, becoming serious again. "Our goal is to establish a system that can dismantle a government that is not to the wishes of the people."

Wherever Kaixi appeared in the United States, money poured into the Federation for a Democratic China from people elated by his bravery, his youth, and his eloquence. Even those Southern Chinese who couldn't understand his Mandarin helped to raise $300,000 in 1989 to fund the Federation. Including money raised around the world, more than a million dollars flowed into the Paris group.

Shortly after our meeting, Kaixi dropped out of Harvard to launch the SS *Goddess of Liberty,* a French ship that sailed to Asia to beam pro-democracy messages into the People's Republic from international waters. Its radio equipment and much of its $1.5 million operating budget had been donated by rightist media companies in Taiwan. Concern mounted worldwide that China might capture the ship and imprison the dissidents aboard. "If I am not going to be there, who else will be?" Kaixi told friends before he left. No country in Asia would allow the ship to outfit itself for the broadcasting for fear of retaliation from China, and in the spring of 1990, it abandoned its mission.

That year, Kaixi did not run for reelection in the Federation. To many, it appeared he had become a victim of the West, seduced by fame and fortune. He dallied with writing his autobiography, and though he went back to Harvard, he barely attended classes, spending much of his time in midnight bull sessions with friends, and traveling around the United States lecturing. In 1991, he dropped out of Harvard again. Kaixi turned up later that year at Berkeley, once again fitfully studying English. He had effectively lost his standing as a leader of the pro-democracy movement.

By the fall of 1991, seven of Beijing's twenty-one most wanted dissidents had made their way out of the People's Republic through the underground. None revealed their routes, but the woman called "The Pasionara of Tiananmen," twenty-six-year-old Chai Ling, said she was sheltered for months by ordinary citizens and peasants in the provinces, as was her husband. To disguise herself, Chai Ling had surgeons make over her eyes and give her a separate eyelid, like Caucasians. The operation, common among the wealthy who wish to look more *cheung* or "super-cool"—that is, Western—helped Chai Ling escape detection until she arrived in the United States. Since then, like most of the other escaped Tiananmen Square organizers, she has become absorbed in her private concerns and has been virtually silent except for signing letters of protest and petitions to release jailed activists. Even astrophysicist Fang Lizhi, China's most prominent dissident, whose calls for multiparty democracy helped inspire all the democratic protests since 1976, has not been politically active since international outcry forced Beijing to let him and his wife leave the country following the crackdown.

Hundreds of activists remain in China, fugitives sheltered by sympathizers in the provinces, or at their jobs, protected by employers who lie to the government and cover up their part in the democracy movement. Dozens of underground organizations keep resistance alive, and it is with these groups that a modest, practical man in Queens has most communication.

Hu Ping is the most experienced activist in the United States. Others are more captivating, like Chai Ling, who was nominated last year for a Nobel prize, or more accomplished, like Wan Runnan, the president of the Federation for a Democratic China, who was an executive of China's most successful and controversial Western-style corporation. But few activists are more impressive. Hu, who is forty-five years old, endures. His name first reached the West in 1980. A graduate student in philosophy at Beijing University, he caused an uproar when he was elected as the university's delegate to the town council in Beijing, on a platform advocating free speech and democracy, in one of China's earliest experiments in direct elections. The elections were held in many towns, but the contest at Beijing University was the most open. It encouraged a generation of student activists, some of whom later led the Tiananmen Square uprising. After serving his term, Hu was unable to find a job for several years. However, he fared better than rivals in the election, who were under constant surveillance. In 1987, Hu was awarded a Chinese government scholarship and emigrated to the United States to study at Harvard University for a political science doctorate. A year later, because of his political activities as president of the Chinese Alliance for Democracy, the oldest Chinese dissident group in the United States, Hu's scholarship was withdrawn and his passport was recalled by the Chinese consulate in New York.

In his loneliness for China and his rigidity, Hu is indifferent to the seductions of the West. Compared to Sun Yat-sen's, his weapons to arouse change in China are modern ones: telephone, fax machine, and the mail. On the first anniversary of Tiananmen Square, Hu secretly faxed a call to Beijing for people to take group walks through Tiananmen Square. The demonstration was to be peaceful. "If I put it like a strike, that would arouse the government," Hu told me when I visited his home. "But if I call it a walk, the government can do nothing about it," he said, and smiled.

"The government became very concerned about it, so they decided that no one can enter Tiananmen Square on April 5th, the day of the protest, and they blocked off the square."

Hu was elated. "Actually, this is what we expected, and we achieved our goal in the sense that every person outside the People's Republic knew about this, because we got a lot of international coverage, and they saw how panicked the Chinese government is. They don't even allow the Chinese citizens to go for a walk! Also, the people at home received a lot of encouragement, because they see that a lot of the people have the same goal in their minds and deep in their hearts, and, also, they saw the government is very concerned about this, or they would not have issued such an order."

The small apartment Hu shares with his wife and son on a quiet street in Queens has no frills, not even pictures on the walls. The son's toys are the only extras. The ten-year-old is jolly and outgoing, and corrects his father's English. The home is one stop on the underground of Chinese escaping the People's Republic, and at the end of our lunch in a nearby restaurant, Hu carried home the leftovers to share with people passing through, looking for a meal or pocket money. "One day, China will be opened up and the people will want a lot of new ideas," Hu told me. "I'm working on giving them the new ideas now, so the change will be faster."

The new ideas reach China in an underground trade that Hu directs. Activists in the People's Republic smuggle accounts of political events to him. He and other members of the Chinese Alliance for Democracy write them up in *China Spring Monthly*, the Alliance's dissident journal. The journal, which is banned in the People's Republic, is then smuggled into China to inform Chinese of current events in their own country. For instance, the trials of the student leaders at Tiananmen Square, and of the workers who joined the rebellion, are not open to foreign reporters. The world hears only the verdicts, and these have been increasingly harsh. Two of Hu's rivals in the 1980 free elections are in prison for thirteen years, the stiffest punishment for political dissent since 1979, when Wei Jingsheng was sentenced to fifteen years. "Not only foreign reporters but Chinese would be very interested in knowing what is going on in these trials," Hu explained. "We get them that information. We run articles from the imprisoned leaders that are smuggled out of China. Letting the people know that they have heroes restores their confidence. If no one knows what has happened to the student leaders, they can't be heroes."

Recently, Hu went on, "we have become brave enough to call and speak directly to people in China to bolster their courage." Members of the Alliance have contacted the families of jailed activists and reformers in the government, some of whom are confined to their homes under house arrest. One whom Hu called was a former school-mate from Beijing, also a candidate in the 1980 free elections. The man had later joined the Communist party, but had resigned in protest at the Tiananmen Square massacre. "He has a telephone at home and we can just call him," Hu said. "Of course, the government listens in, but my friend is not afraid at all. Calls like these are a way to tell people how strong internal opposition is, even within the govern-ment." The Alliance also smuggles funds to newly released dissidents, families of jailed protesters, and underground democratic bodies— about $10,000 in 1990.

Much of Hu's time these days is spent writing for *China Spring Monthly*. A decade ago, it began with six pages, and it is now a fat, hundred-page journal with a circulation of ten thousand. Somehow, every month it manages to publish, supported by anonymous dona-tions. Its staff works out of a two-story house on a residential street in Queens. The large, rambling office is entered through a low porch piled with back issues. On the cold day in April when I visited, manag-ing editor Chen Jiaying and his staff had turned off the heat to save money, and we drank bitter tea to keep warm. Three years ago, they told me, our meeting would have been arranged very secretively. "But we have a lot of attention since then, and we have stopped worrying about the risk to ourselves," editor Sang Zhi-Yuan said.

The penalty for being caught with the banned magazine in the People's Republic varies, Chen and Sang told me. "Usually the Party doesn't make a great fuss. But it could block your way to leave China," Sang noted. The editors explained that the people who smuggle the magazine into China are usually strangers who call the Alliance out of the blue. Businessmen and other travelers to the mainland also help out. "We really don't know how many copies reach China every month, but we do know this—quite a few people have a chance to read it. They tell us when they get out, but no one has a constant supply," Sang said. "Some of the Tiananmen Square leaders told us when they got here that they'd read it—Wu'er Kaixi, for instance. It's been sold on the black market for ten dollars—about a third of the average monthly wage."

The Alliance also reprints key articles on one page, in reduced type, and mails them en masse to the mainland. These are "real valuable goods to the people," Hu explained. "And much easier to mail," Sang added. "You can put them in an envelope, and wrap it in a plain wrapper with a fake return address. The mailings are random. We have some targets in China, but we want them to be able to deny that they know anything about it. 'Unfortunately, my address was picked by some anti-revolutionary guys,' they can say, and deny any knowledge." Hu and Sang laughed. "We know that it's working because people who emigrate tell us that they have read it. These one-page digests are photocopied and circulated," Chen said. To keep hope alive, the Alliance during Tiananmen Square faxed clippings of press coverage from the West to a thousand fax numbers every day in China—an act that got them roundly denounced by the official press of the People's Republic.

"Private enterprise doesn't have faxes yet—it's mostly government officials, intellectuals, diplomats, and foreign offices that have them," Chen noted. "A blitz like that is a random thing. You don't know who's receiving it, or what their reaction will be."

"I believe what we have done will have a lot of influence on the future of China," Hu observed quietly. "Now the government is still not open enough. But one day, it will be, and our work will have a lot of influence then."

Last year, on the second anniversary of the uprising, when students at Beijing University marked the day by howling at the moon and breaking little bottles, symbols of Li Peng (whose name is a Chinese homonym for "small bottle"), the Chinese Alliance for Democracy voted to merge with the better-known, glitzier Federation for a Democratic China. "The Federation is a failure," Hu told me. "All its famous people like Wu'er Kaixi stopped their activism. Most are studying in university. The merger will save them." Chen Jiaying added, "The Federation spent all their money but we survived here ten years and we know how to make money and plan our future."

China's democracy movement is far behind Russia's, Hu Ping concedes. In the meantime, Hu and his supporters in Chinatown who fund the Alliance and smuggle money, messages, and articles in and out of China, dream and plan for the revolution. When it succeeds, they will go home. "Those people who organize activities here are those people who really want to go back," Hu told me. "What time and when, depends on the government."

21

A DAY OFF

On Sundays, half a million people descend on Chinatown. Most are Chinese, but tourists invade, too, and all nationalities and cultures drift down Mott Street. Sunlight sparkles off red heads and blond heads in the river of black-haired Chinese. Trendy young Chinese women with pipe-cleaner legs in cutoffs walk by with white guys; others, decked out in leggings and puffy skirts, are on the arms of Chinese men. Prosperous, beautifully dressed Chinese, in from Hong Kong or Europe, stroll through the streets, speaking English.

Above, leaning out of tenement windows, old men watch the drifting carnival. One lights a joss stick and, with a hairless, sagging arm, puts it on the fire escape to burn. Behind him, other old men in their undershirts move like ghosts in the dimness of a *gong si fong*.

On Sundays, no one toils except waiters and cooks and gambling house dealers. A burden lifts from this desperate community, strangled by miserable wages and organized crime. All over Chinatown, families stroll, shop, gather for the noonday dim sum. In the huge, noisy Triple Eight Palace, they *yum cha*—sip tea and gossip.

The OTB is mobbed, as it is every Sunday.

The Buddhist temples are also full. People pray to Kuan Yin, the goddess of mercy, for male children and for wealth.

Barbershops hum with business. Sundays are propitious days for haircuts.

Herbalists and acupuncturists are run off their feet. Their shops overflow with workers who have waited all week to spare time to see a doctor.

In the Kong soybean shop, Mrs. Kong cuts rice bean cake and taro pudding.

The waiter Leslie Lim is gone—back in Singapore—his place is taken by another Chinese from Malaysia smuggled through the snake.

Chinese from Fifth Avenue too proud to have much to do with this vital, squalid little piece of China, stroll through the streets and renew a sense of spiritual identity. Chinese from the outer boroughs and New Jersey and Connecticut make matches, celebrate birthdays at banquets, visit family associations. Students buy books from the People's Republic.

Hundreds push into the CCBA to see the Shanghai opera. Upstairs, in classrooms, children laboriously copy Chinese characters.

In the old Mee Heung Chow Main factory, four elders play mahjongg, wedged between boxes of noodles.

There is no sign of life in the On Leong building, at the portal of Chinatown. A curtain billows into the boardroom through a door that opens onto the balcony. Former national president Wing Yeung Chan is back in town, twenty pounds lighter since his Chicago trial, and nervously awaiting his retrial, people say. The word on the street is that Big Boss Eddie Chan may come back and cut a deal.

Today, peddlers have taken over. Dozens of them crowd the Bowery. Two men seated on low chairs on the sidewalk tell the fortunes of a couple squatting before them, by their facial bone structures. Nearby, another fellow sits by an open suitcase that is heaped high with pink, yellow, and white puffy hair bows, which he sells for 50 cents. He wears a pink bow on his head, laughing at himself.

Confucius has had a birthday. At his feet flowers bloom.

Along Canal, vendors with steel pushcarts display fish balls, intestines, chicken feet, peanut cakes, curried squid, deep-fried peppers and eggplants, and chewy fish skins stewed with turnips. All around Chinatown, vendors fry *chong yow bing*—thick, tasty scallion pancakes.

Mr. Lin, the Fujianese peddler, sells firecrackers at a corner. Children hawk blocks of frozen shrimp from Asia. The blocks drip on the sidewalk. Shoppers trample newspapers, mud, fishtails, betel nuts. The litter blows around their ankles.

On Pell Street, German tourists scramble out of a bus to videotape the vertical restaurant signs. Teenage gang members in Hong Kong suits pace outside Number 11 and watch indifferently. A car with New Jersey plates pulls up. "Oh, wow! Look! Chinese Dumpling House!" a girl inside shouts.

"You finally made it to Chinatown!" her date says, kissing her.

In the Wild West, up East Broadway, past the site of the latest gang murder, the overflow from Chinatown collects: repair stores for scrolls and jadework, warehouses, fledgling businesses such as beauty parlors with two chairs, take-outs with one table.

Several years ago, crowds watched news broadcasts from Taiwan and China near a Democracy Wall on Bayard Street, which was plastered with caricatures of China's gerontocracy, and they laid oranges and other food offerings at altars under signs saying MARTYRS OF TIANANMEN SQUARE, BRIGHTER THAN THE SUN AND MOON, SACRIFICE TO A RIGHTEOUS CAUSE. Today, the altars are gone, the outrage and the sense of purpose having seeped out in the drive to make money and escape from Chinatown. Today, a student trying to register voters complains, "It's a hard job. People don't know the candidates, and in Asia the tradition is that people don't get involved in politics."

The wonton man is out. A thin man with coarse black hair, he works on the sidewalk on an upended cardboard box, on which a ceramic plate is piled with ground pork. For utensils, he has two scrapers. In his left hand is a floured square of dough, the wonton. He scrapes twice off the pile of meat, puts the dab inside the square held in his cupped hand, and makes a fist, squeezing the dough until it resembles a belly button. Customers watch. He places the wonton on a cookie sheet on his counter—another cardboard box. When he has twenty wontons, he takes a customer's $20 bill. He asks for smaller change, but the customer has none. Looking around furtively, he slips the twenty down his sock and under his foot, and slips his foot back into his shoe. From somewhere else he extracts a wad of neatly folded singles.

"Wonton," he barks. "Very good."

His customer turns, covers one nostril, bends forward, and emits a jet of snot onto the sidewalk. Clears the other nostril, turns and accepts her change, $18 counted out slowly from the wonton man's floury hand.

Up the street, in a Thai grocery, the owner, a woman wearing wide green silk pants, stands on a plastic milk carton, bowing and praying to a Buddha on top of her freezer. Two open glass jars of coconut juice are up there, too, with bowls of offerings, two lighted candles, and a burning stick of incense. The Buddha looks like Jesus of Nazareth, a yellow sash across a white shift. The woman gasps, startled to find me staring. The only Western product in the grocery is Pringle's potato chips. There is dried octopus, with shriveled suckers, in plastic bags. There are black preserved eggs (raw eggs packed in alkali and mud for two to three months) from China. Duck eggs lie in sawdust, flies buzzing above. Sections of palm leaves for sale are shockingly green among the dried and packaged merchandise.

The mothers choosing cakes at bakeries to celebrate the Moon Festival ("Beauty Intoxicated to the Moon," "Fairy to the Moon") are a real power in Chinatown: many earn more than their husbands, who can no longer look on them just as baby machines. Remarkably, in this troubled community, there is little drug use, AIDS, homelessness, or teenage pregnancy. Here the major health problems are parasites; giardiasis, an intestinal ailment common in China, Cambodia, and Vietnam; hepatitis from poor sanitation; malnutrition; anemia; and high cholesterol from oily foods.

On Grand Street, the nougat vendor is out with her pushcart. In Little Italy, the feeling is different: people yell and argue in the streets, and fights break out. In Chinatown, no one yells or argues. It's too dangerous. Guns and cellular telephones are stashed all over Chinatown. Even gang members duck when a car backfires.

Uncle Seven is no longer his old self, some say. Maybe gone soft in the head, they whisper.

No one talks to me, a *low faan,* as I wander. I poke along Mulberry, notice an alley between two stores that is piled with boxes, and follow it into an inner courtyard backed by a decrepit low tenement— a rear tenement. Wedged between its taller neighbors, it was put up before the building code was changed at the turn of the century. In the courtyard, a man in an apron is bending over a metal tub, stirring bloody tripe with his hands. He doesn't live here, he says. He and twelve other bachelors share plywood sleeping cubicles in a *gong si fong.* The courtyard is piled with bags of cement, barrels of brick dust, discarded wooden shipping boxes stamped DRIED LOTUS ROOTS. It is a gritty, gray, forlorn place, a patch of old Chinatown more or less untouched since the 1880s.

The rear tenement, its windows broken or blackened with soot, its front door gone, looks uninhabited. Yet from a second-story window an ivy plant straggles. The stairway is nearly blocked with trash. Both ground-floor apartments are locked. I climb the stairs, expecting to find the second floor open to the sky and pigeons nesting. On the landing, a candle and two dusty balls of string, which on inspection turn out to be dried-up oranges, lie on the floor by a door. On the door is a red sign bright with gold calligraphy and happy dragons. The oranges and the sign grant blessings on everyone who enters this door.

I knock. A frail old man, like a withered moon, appears. He greets me quizzically. He has lived in Chinatown for sixty years, he says, and has never spoken to a white person.

INDEX